Musician and Teacher
An Orientation to Music Education

Musician and Teacher
An Orientation to Music Education

Patricia Shehan Campbell

with chapters contributed by
Steven M. Demorest and Steven J. Morrison

W. W. NORTON AND COMPANY
NEW YORK · LONDON

W. W. Norton & Company has been independent since its founding in 1923, when William Warder Norton and Mary D. Herter Norton first published lectures delivered at the People's Institute, the adult education division of New York City's Cooper Union. The Nortons soon expanded their program beyond the Institute, publishing books by celebrated academics from America and abroad. By mid-century, the two major pillars of Norton's publishing program—trade books and college texts—were firmly established. In the 1950s, the Norton family transferred control of the company to its employees, and today—with a staff of four hundred and a comparable number of trade, college, and professional titles published each year—W. W. Norton & Company stands as the largest and oldest publishing house owned wholly by its employees.

The text of this book is composed in Legacy Serif with the display set in Azkidenz Grotesk.
Book design and layout by Lissi Sigillo.
Composition by Matrix.
Manufacturing by the RR Donnelley—Harrisonburg.
Editor: Maribeth Anderson Payne.
Production manager: Benjamin Reynolds.
Project editor: Rebecca Homiski.
Editorial assistants: Graham Norwood and Imogen Leigh Howes.
Copyeditor: Patterson Lamb.

Library of Congress Cataloging-in-Publication Data

Campbell, Patricia Shehan.
    Musician and teacher : an orientation to music education / Patricia Shehan Campbell, with chapters contributed by Steven M. Demorest and Steven J. Morrison. — 1st ed.
        p. cm.
    Includes bibliographical references and index.

ISBN-10: 0-393-92756-3
ISBN-13: 978-0-393-92756-6

    1. School music—Instruction and study. 2. Music—Instruction and study. I. Demorest, Steven M. II. Morrison, Steven J., 1964- III. Title.
    MT1.C227 2008
    780.71—dc22

                    2007013482

W. W. Norton & Company, Inc., 500 Fifth Avenue, New York, N.Y. 10110
                    www.wwnorton.com
W. W. Norton & Company Ltd., Castle House, 75/76 Wells Street, London W1T 3QT

5 6 7 8 9 0

Brief Contents

Contents

List of Figures

Preface

Many musicians teach, and a considerable number of teachers make music. There are also those who follow a professional pathway into music education and who take great joy in living that complement of music making and music teaching that happens in their interactions with groups of young people in schools. They are the music teachers—singers, players, composers, improvisers, analytical listeners, and music scholars who are drawn to teaching the music they know and love. This book is aimed at those whose identity rests in both music and education and whose particular interests as trained musicians are directed toward the daily practice of teaching music to children and adolescents in public and private school settings. It is intended as an introduction to the field for university students who are either declared music education majors or who are considering professional certification as music teachers in elementary and secondary schools. It bridges the gap between the university experiences of students in private applied lessons, performing ensembles, and academic courses in music theory and history/culture and their teacher education courses, field experiences, and student teaching practica that lead them to teaching positions. It is meant as a bridge from life as a music student to the prospective life-career of a professional music teacher. It expands on the curiosity of university students of music for teaching young people, and is intended to serve as a conduit for ideas about life as a musician-turning-teacher.

The chapters ahead reveal foundational matters that shore up an understanding of the music education process in schools, framing philosophical issues cross-culturally and comparatively, so that prospective teachers might grasp a broader and more varied view of music in education across time and place. Music education is described in the United States and to a degree in Canada. An international perspective helps prepare future music educators for teaching in transcultural times where methods and materials are shaped to the needs of national and local school communities. A conscientious effort is made to balance the strong traditions of school music programs with the program transitions that are unfolding, just as society expands into technology and mediated popular culture. There are chapters and sections on theories of musical learning and development, motivation and classroom management, technology, and assessment as well as those that describe the essential elements of teaching music to children, in choral and instrumental settings and in nontraditional performance and course offerings. Chapters range from the philosophical justification of music to case studies of award-winning school music programs. Interspersed throughout are "break points" that offer observations and exercises. The "break points" prompt consideration of the relevance and potential applications of cultural and historic practices and processes to classrooms, studios, and rehearsal settings where music is learned and taught.

Readers will find here a balance of theoretical and practical information. Some will prefer to get right down to practice: knowing the vocal ranges of high school singers (Chapter 8), or the components of an Orff-Schulwerk experience (Chapter 7), or the ideal instrumentation of a middle school concert band (Chapter 9). Others will be initially driven to understand music in child development (Chapter 6) or the expectations of music education practices in the U.K., or Japan, or Brazil (Chapter 4). Questions may come sooner (or later) on managing and motivating student behaviors (Chapter 12) or grading students in performing ensembles (Chapter 13), with attention to the positions of John Dewey, Nelson Mandela, or Yo-Yo Ma on music's significance in education (Chapter 2). The book's chapters are ordered so as to address philosophical and theoretical issues in Chapters 1–6 and practical matters of curriculum and instruction in Chapters 7–16. However, the chapters can be easily reordered in accordance with particular interests and emphases.

Readers may find that Chapter 15, on field experiences in schools and classrooms, provides a realistic opening to the world of school music. It may be the chapter to which readers frequently return as they begin field experiences and even the ultimate internship as student teachers. Chapters 15 and 5 (Music in "Your Local") can be paired, as the latter involves case studies of three schools, their teachers, and their curricula. Another approach is the integration of theoretical and practice chapters. In this case, Chapters 7–10 (the core of music education practice for classrooms of children, choirs, instrumental ensembles, and "all the rest" of the musical possibilities) may be merged with Chapters 2, 3, 4, and 6, thus emphasizing the reasons for music in education, in various sociopolitical states, through an array of teaching techniques across phases of human development. Attention to diverse populations and learning styles can follow with Chapter 11, along with the practical matters that are the heart and soul of solid educational practice: classroom management, assessment, and technology (Chapters 12–14). The book-end chapters (1 and 16) offer advice to musicians who teach, and music teachers who continue to make music. While the sequencing may depend on readers' perspective and purpose, the principal point is that readers are thoughtful musicians and teachers who can grow to know the realities of teaching music while also discovering foundations of the profession.

This volume is philosophically grounded in the belief that music teachers teach "Music" with a capital "M." The mission of music education extends beyond teaching just band, orchestra, or choir. It assumes that music teachers are responsible for a broadly conceived curriculum that stretches beyond the enclaves of compartmentalized genres (particularly when the music teacher may turn out to be the single music specialist within a school). Thus, all music is fair game and can be featured within standard ensembles and classes, even as new instructional possibilities are developed to embrace styles as varied as guitar, steel drum ensemble, and West African drumming. This volume is grounded in the importance of developing teaching experience on a foundation of comprehensive musicianship that encompasses aural skills, notational literacy, vocal and instrumental performance experience, creative-expressive skills, and extensive knowledge of music's varied historical and cultural expressions. It adheres to this principle of comprehensive musicianship in the design and delivery of K–12 music education, so that children and youth may learn the maximal potential of music to develop their intellectual, emotional, social, and even spiritual potential. Music education enfolds history, theory, culture, and all of the commensurate listening, performing, and creative skills into its practice for purposes of making music more central to the comprehensive school aims of human development.

This orientation to music education is based on the scholarship and practical experience of effective music teaching. It is grounded in research, and yet it is meant to speak to students without the technical jargon of heavily cited research reports and reviews of literature. The volume covers a broad range of topics deemed essential to a thoroughgoing understanding of music education in its multiple dimensions: in local and foreign settings, with a strong philosophical base, and as practiced by musicians who are professionally prepared to teach in schools.

PSC
Seattle 2007

Acknowledgments

Books happen, but not without the inspirations and efforts of mentors, colleagues, friends, and family. Many thanks to the musicians who helped hone my skills, in particular the wisdom of pianist-teacher Jonas Svedas who set me on a musical pathway through the twice-weekly lessons he offered me at the Cleveland Music School Settlement and in his family home. Evangeline Merritt and Paul David Rorhbaugh opened up the way into vocal performance, and I am grateful to them for modeling well both the art of singing and how it could be taught. There are others along the way who served me many reminders of the importance of staying musical even while engaged in full-time teaching, and of teaching more effectively because of experiences in making music with them (and as guided by them): Ann Farber, Annabelle Joseph, Robert Page, Lisa Parker, Ramnad Raghavan, and Marta Sanchez. There are colleagues whom I have long admired and am forever grateful to for teaching musically, whose talent as teachers involved making music in the midst of a class—rather than talking about it—in order to make a point: Michael Bakan, John Feierabend, Charlie Keil, Barbara Lundquist, Marc Seales, and the late and dear Jean Sinor. There is also my husband, Charlie, who encourages the music-making in our home, and our son, Andrew, whose musical ear and inventive turns on his tenor saxophone help me to understand what students with good teachers can musically "do."

Words come to life through the photographs that grace the pages of this book. I am grateful to Jerry Gay, Pulitzer Prize–winning photographer; to Sean Ichiro Manes, my assistant during his graduate study here at the University of Washington; and to Ailisa Newhall, for their wonderful views of children, youth, and teachers in the acts of making music. Of course, thanks goes to those whose images are featured here, including Sarah Bartolome, Scott Brown, Anna Edwards, Brigetta Miller, Sarah Nelson, and Heath Thompson. Christopher Roberts opened his school to us on several occasions, and allowed us in and around the brilliant lessons that unfolded in his classroom.

I appreciate the professional expertise of W. W. Norton's editorial team, in particular Maribeth Anderson Payne, Music Editor, for her guiding light from the inception of the project and her careful attention to the editorial details that turn a raw manuscript into something pallateable and more worthy of readers' attention. With this book, we celebrate twenty years of a professional association and the treasured friendship that has grown from it. Many thanks to

Graham Norwood for offering suggestions and encouragement in the preparation of the manuscript and the art log.

Steven M. Demorest wishes to thank the many music teachers who introduced him to musical excellence, in particular Larry Mitchell, Gene McKinley, Frauke Haasemann, Joseph Flummerfelt, and Weston Noble. Thanks also to Leann Rozema at Shorecrest High School and the Laurelhurst after-school program for their cooperation. Peter Webster, Mary Kennedy, and Ann Clements helped tremendously by reading earlier drafts of some of his chapters. Finally, thanks to my musical trio of a family, Karen, Jessica, and Claire, for their love and support.

Steven J. Morrison extends his appreciation to Jerry Markoch at Athens Drive High School (NC), Dana Hire at Massillon High School (OH), Dave Johnson at Shorecrest High School (WA), and Michael James at Ballard High School (WA) for their time and effort on behalf of this project. An ongoing debt of gratitude is owed to Don Stahlberg, an inspiration as a teacher of band and a teacher of people. And, most of all, to Claire Waistell at Sylvester Middle School (WA)—there is no better partner, personal or professional.

This book happened because of musical and teaching encounters with so many good people. We would suggest that projects like this one result from an expression of the South African Zulu concept, *ubuntu*: "I am because you are." We offer this as a collective venture based on experience that is far greater than the sum of three authors. Rather, it emanates from the encounters with musicians and teachers we have known.

Musician and Teacher

An Orientation to Music Education

chapter 1

A Musician's Life in Teaching

Graduating high school student to his music teacher: You know, you really made a difference in my life.

Teacher: Glad I could help out.

Student: No, I really mean it. Even when everything seemed to be falling apart for me at home, I could come in to concert band, take a deep breath, and blow it all better.

Teacher: You blew very musically.

Student: You might not know what I mean, how your music sort of saved me.

Teacher: I do. Music once sailed me through some rough waters, too. Still does.

Seventh-grade student to her eighth-grade sister: Do you think she is really a musician? Or just a teacher? I mean, what does she play?

Eighth-grade sister: Well, she's always in the music room, and we do get to sing and play instruments in her class.

Seventh-grade student: Yeah, but does she play anything? Violin, or flute, or guitar, or what? I never heard her.

Eighth-grade sister: Maybe she can't, so she teaches instead.

Seventh-grade student: I'd just like to hear her sometime, that's all.

Music teacher A to music teacher B: Are you singing some holiday gigs this year?

Music teacher B: Naw. I'm exhausted.

Music teacher A: Are you serious? I thought that's why we were in this business, teaching by day to free up time for gigs.

Music teacher B: I guess I've gone over the edge, from performing to teaching. We can't do it all, can we?

Music teacher A: Hmmm. Teaching music from your ancient memory of what it once was like to perform it?

A Life's Calling

It is a noble calling to be professionally involved in music. Music is one of the beautiful things in life, and across the world people are drawn to listen and dance to it, to sing and to play it. Music is a human phenomenon, an artistic form that is both personally expressive and socially meaningful. The musical acts of performance, creative expression, and informed listening can be richly fulfilling to all who engage in them. By hard work and sheer determination, some of the truly fortunate land in situations where music is what they "do" all day (and maybe well into the night). They make music as performers, composers, improvisers, arrangers, and even sound and recording engineers, and as teachers they enable others to make music and to understand it for its full intent. These music professionals needn't work to support their musical interests; rather, their musical interests are the core of their professional work.

Frequently, music professionals play multiple roles in their work, for although musical involvement spans a wide spectrum of specialized forms and functions, there are many crossovers. Those who sing music may also improvise it, those who compose it may also arrange it, and those who play it may also be keenly involved in engineering its sound—or in the technical production of recordings of their own or others' music. A single professional musician may function in every imaginable musical way, including active engagement in the role of a teacher. In some communities, it may be true that a singer sings and a player plays, but in other settings a person who "does music" does it all. Depending upon the circumstances, the life of a musician can be specialized or blended, explicitly centered on one trade or technical task within the profession or mixed across all manner of musical activity. The chances of music professionals overlapping, extending, and crossing over from one realm of musical involvement to another are high because music is a many-splendored thing that encompasses multiple skills and engagements.

"Musicians who can, teach." Here is a phrase quite the 180-degree opposite of a stance taken by some who believe that if everything else fails, teaching is always there as "the fall-back career." This fall-back view is uninformed, of course, or ill-informed. It suggests a hierarchy of specializations, with teaching at the bottom and every other musical activity piled high above it. It assumes that while few may make it as professional performers (or composers, or arrangers, for example), everyone can be successful as a teacher of music. In truth, music education is a professional endeavor that requires particular traits and techniques, and not everyone has them or will be able to acquire them. The call to teach music is a selective one, and it takes careful listening and reflective

Montage of multiple roles of professional musician-teachers.

thinking—to say nothing of the rigor of study and practice—for a musically trained individual to determine whether he or she can meet the challenges of music education.

In one way or another, teaching (or to borrow a term from studies in anthropology and folklore, "transmission") is something that many musicians do. They learn their music and they pass it on: to their students, colleagues, family members, their very own children. They share favorite songs; their instrumental twists, turns, and techniques; their preferred recordings; and the music of a single artist or composer. Because music is a human need, it is also obvious to many that their role is to teach others the means for making it. Many musicians cannot help but to transmit music to others to know, to make, to enjoy—just as other musicians (or aspiring musicians) cannot help but to hear it, acquire it, and integrate it into their expressive lives. Musicians in many venues have had these transmission (or teaching) experiences.

Other musicians see teaching as a full-time activity. They are the ones who teach in their home studios, in conservatories and colleges, in community settings, and in schools. They enter music education for various reasons, chief among them an enthusiasm for developing in others the capacity to think and to express themselves in musical ways. Musicians who teach may have lived music all of their lives, coming from musical families of singers and players, beginning their own musical study at an early age. Or they may have been musically curious for many years before their entrance as late as adolescence into their first formal lessons and ensemble experiences. They "grow" their musical skills and knowledge over time, in grueling practice sessions and grinding rehearsals; in theory, history, and culture classes; and in the opportunities they can muster for making music. They recognize and relish the social interactivity of performing with others. They become aware of the good works of their music teachers, and their dedication, patience, personal warmth, and good humor, and they become inspired to follow in their teachers' footsteps. As rock-solid musicians themselves, they learn to guide others in discovering music and in acquiring the skills and knowledge for personal musical expression.

Not all musicians are meant to teach music. It takes a special blend of qualities both musical and personal. Those who teach children and youth, particularly in classes and groups within schools, need additional qualities—vital strategies of communication that many an experienced teacher will swear by. Even as a musician requires training and practice to become a proficient creator and re-creator of music, a music teacher requires the pedagogical training and practice that are wrapped solidly around the subject of music.

✣ BREAK POINT 1.1 The Call to Teach Music

> What is this "call" to teach music? In retrospect, what were the indications that drew you to "do music"? What draws you now to want to teach music? Enumerate some ways you may learn whether the music education profession is a "good fit" for you.

Tales of Five Musicians

People come to the decision to pursue music education studies at various stages: some as early as secondary school, some as late as a career change after experiencing the world of work. They declare their interest in music education because they have met with earlier musical successes in their individual study of an instrument or voice, in solo and chamber music recitals, in ensemble performances, in festivals, contests and competitions, and performance tours. They have a collection of earlier school certificates, the ribbons, medals, and trophies as symbols of their musical competence, and they are recognized by their teachers, friends, and families (and often their audiences) as beyond-the-ordinary in their musical accomplishments. They well remember their time as the "music nerds"—the music majors—of their schools, the "little Mozarts," the ace-players, and the ones who got the solos in their high school ensembles. They are drawn to a career in music because they have "a passion for music." Thus, they take the bold leap into university training in music where they spend four or five years studying performance, history, and theory. At some point, they must select their life's work. Music education is one of the options that deserves the thoughtful consideration of those who are musically accomplished and intrigued with prospects for sharing their knowledge and skills with others.

Following are brief tales of five musicians, all university students of music at decision points regarding their further training for a career path. They are on the brink of professionalizing musically, and music education is one possible route. There are multiple factors for their consideration in determining whether music teaching is "in the stars" for them, not the least of which are their past and current experiences, training, and interests, and their true motives for pursuing music education as a field of study, a degree program, a livelihood. Tune in to their hopes and dreams, their uncertainties, their likely "fit" as music teachers.

BOUND FOR GLORY

Rob is enrolled at a university with a reputation for its jazz studies and its saxophone studio, and is now in his second year as a sax major with a jazz concentration. He is juggling all the performance time he can get with his academic courses in music history and music theory; he is also managing to stay abreast of his "outside music" course requirements across campus in math and the sciences, the humanities, and the social sciences. He puts in long hours of practice (thank goodness, the School of Music's practice rooms are open until midnight!) and is gigging on weekends at one of the up-and-coming jazz clubs downtown. Rob has been raised on jazz since his middle school years when he came into a program whose teacher had sixth grade students in after-school rehearsals three days a week, playing improvisations in D-blues, G-blues, and E-blues scales. By high school, he was living and breathing jazz, playing in the elite studio jazz group during "zero-period" before school, in a lunch-hour combo, and in every festival his teacher could manage. Theirs was an award-winning ensemble, with several students like Rob who had become musically proficient through years of private lessons. Now Rob has set his sights on being a professional player, with every hope that he might graduate with a degree and the performance experience that will qualify him for a place in the New York jazz scene. At least, that is his long-term goal. Meanwhile, his parents, concerned about the practicalities of making it as a jazz musician, are pressing Rob to think realistically about what he might do with his life. Teach music, maybe?

"LOVES CHILDREN"

As long as she can remember Laura has wanted to teach children. It doesn't really matter *what* she will teach, but she feels that she was meant to work with children, to help them learn about the world, to lead them to the skills they can develop. For a while, she thought she might become an elementary classroom teacher, but Laura is a musician, and she is realizing that music may be a very important link in teaching children about themselves and their world. Laura has been studying piano since the age of seven, and music is a part of her identity. She was known as "the piano player" at her school, and was called upon to play the national anthem at assemblies, "Happy Birthday" for classmates, carols and seasonal songs, and accompaniments for her friends who studied musical instruments or sang. Now, after twelve years of study, she is preparing for her third recital in three years within the university's music department, a program of two Bach preludes and fugues, a waltz and a nocturne by Chopin, one Mozart sonata, and Bartok's Roumanian dances. She reads music easily, is employed as an accompanist for students in some of the voice and instrumental studios at her university, and runs a music class for children at the local church on Thursday evenings. In the last year, Laura has seen the streams of her life's interests in children and music come together in a confluence of sorts, and the more she learns about children in her education classes, the more she realizes that she is meant to teach them what she knows inside-out: music.

WITHOUT DOUBT

Few people seem as certain of their professional goals as Chad. He will be a band director just like his high school band director. He will have a marching band, a ninth grade band, a concert band, and a symphonic band (and he knows very well the differences among them, by repertoire and by the level of the musical competence that students bring to them). He will be one of five music teachers in the school that employs him, just as was the case in his own high school: two band teachers, a choral teacher, a teacher for the jazz ensembles and the keyboard and guitar classes, and an orchestra teacher who also covers the smaller string ensembles. He will have a drill team, "contract teachers" to offer small-group instrumental instruction at school, a summer band camp for transitional eighth- and ninth-grade students, and rigorous rehearsals for the marching band in the dog days of August that will inspire them to be the most exciting band on the field. Chad knows what he wants and what he needs to do to get it. He is one of three student assistants for his university's marching band director, sectional leader for trumpets in the symphonic band, and an ace conducting student. He is working as a private trumpet instructor at one of the local high schools, is paid to help chaperone students and conduct warm-ups for this high school's tours and festivals, and spends the summers as a band camp counselor and teacher. Now comes the formal training as a music education major, learning the historical and philosophical reasons for what is already happening in the schools, developing perspective, gaining depth and breadth on repertoire. Chad believes that the real training is "out there" in the schools but is curious as to what he might be able to "pick up" through the methods classes ahead of him.

SINGING FIRST

Rose sings. She has always sung and is planning to make a career of it. Her family sings, too: her mother and father in the church choir, her father in the tenor section of the symphony's chorale, and her two sisters in their high school choir, just as she had done. But Rose was also the favored soloist in that choir during her last two years of high school, the lead soprano in the triple trio, and the school's only student to qualify for the all-state choir. Now she's in the university's elite choir of music majors and graduate students, and sings frequently in her voice studio's master classes, in student recitals, and in scenes for the opera workshop. She plots and plans, dreams and daydreams, that she can make a good living as a singer. There may be touring ahead for her as a member of an opera company or as a recitalist or a soloist in symphonic-choral works like Haydn's "The Messiah" or Mozart's "Requiem." There may be community theater productions, church choir work, and even recordings. No doubt, there will be private teaching possibilities. But lately, Rose has begun to wonder about the possibilities for teaching young people to sing. High schoolers? Middle school, even? Does she really need a degree in music education? Could she teach and still sing? These and other questions are surfacing for Rose. She went back to see her old high school choir teacher last spring, and when she was invited to sing one of her songs for the students there, she felt that she could really communicate with them, and that she might enjoy helping them to find their own voices.

SHY GIRL

Sarah thinks she might like to teach but has always felt shy about getting in front of groups, using words, being demonstrative; she does not want to lay herself open to criticism about what she might say, or worry about whether people will listen, or wonder about how they will criticize her. She has preferred to play violin. Sarah has been singled out as "musically gifted" by her applied studio instructor, enough to be selected as the second violinist in the music department's "Scholarship Quartet." The quartet performs for university functions and has been invited frequently to play weddings, receptions for corporate gatherings in town, and in schools. Just last fall, at one school where the quartet performed, a teacher came up to compliment them and to invite them back. Intrigued, Sarah and the cello player accepted the invitation and brought their instruments to play for the third grade children in the teacher's class. One thing led to another, and the teacher and a supportive parent found the funds to pay Sarah to give violin lessons on Friday afternoons to every child in the class. While she had once been sure that such fundamental music would "bore her to the core," Sarah is finding new musical challenges in the colorful interactions she is having with the young ones. She is also finding that the children like the music, they like her, they're listening, and they're learning. Sarah is not certain whether she wants to teach masses of schoolchildren, but she is interested in discovering the possibilities. She continues to play in the quartet and as a member of the university's orchestra even as she believes that there may be a fork in the road ahead for her.

There are strong prospects, if varied routes, for these five musicians to be turning the corner toward music teaching as a life choice. With personal histories of music in their lives, curiosity and commitment, they are poised for a continued life in music with accents on teaching it so that others may share in the unique ways of musical expression. They have "potential" as music teachers, and if they carefully direct themselves, they may well find that this potential can be realized. They may even find themselves happily fulfilled as musicians helping other aspiring musicians.

❖ BREAK POINT 1.2 Telling Your Own Tale

What is your story of musical and teaching experiences, your known strengths and areas of need? Of the five cases noted above, with whom do you identify and why? Share stories with a colleague and notice the similarities you share.

The Makeup of a Music Teacher

What will it take to become successful as a teacher of music to children and youth? In a nutshell, both training and experience. Following entrance into a music education degree and/or a teacher certification program, students come to the threshold of their intensive period of preparation as music teachers. They enroll in pedagogical methods courses, seminars on professional issues, field experiences in schools, and a supervised student teaching internship. State requirements and university curricular plans vary: one music teacher may have had two methods courses, a seminar, and a ten-week internship, while another teacher, at a different university, may have had six methods courses, six seminars (three each offered separately in the music and education departments), and two semesters of thirty weeks in a supervised teaching practicum. The philosophical positions of state boards of education determine the number and nature of courses for all teachers; these may include, beyond the pedagogy courses, courses on special education, reading, multicultural education, technology, and state history. Likewise, university teaching faculty prescribe various courses and experiences for prospective teachers, based on their philosophical views of the missions and needs of schools, students, and teachers, and the expertise of the faculty. Wrapped altogether, these required courses and teaching internships comprise the training of prospective teachers of music for positions in K–12 schools. The real experience begins with the first day on the job which, coupled with strong training, shapes the successful teacher of music.

Music teachers become effective in the course of the music teaching experience, and as a result of it. A teaching certificate, granted by a state board of education at the conclusion of a program of preparation, is more a learner's permit than a capstone accomplishment. Despite the hard work entailed in earlier training, there is nothing like the reality of teaching for developing rehearsal techniques, the rhythm and pace of instructional delivery, modeling and presentational behavior, and the use of words and gestures to communicate musical skills and knowledge. Methods courses provide the rationale and context for teaching, ideas for the musical content of classes, the instructional materials and media, and the pedagogical techniques, but the art of teaching music can be fully learned only in by doing it.

With regard to musicians and teachers, the polar positions of nature and nurture, of being born or bred to the field, each have their advocates. There are those who see music teaching as a talent, part of a person's nature, and some have what it takes and some never will. Others believe strongly that good music teachers can be nurtured and that all can master the necessary musical and teaching skills through careful study and diligent practice. Some favor neither extreme but suggest that people possess natural propensities and innate drives

Montage of music teachers in their practice.

to want to make music, to share it with others, to guide others to the musical experience. These impulses and interests are "raw" and in need of development, however, of the sort that can only come through training that includes philosophical understandings and supervised and reflective practice.

❖ BREAK POINT 1.3 How Unique You Truly Are

Give some thought to the ways in which you stand out in a population. Consider the music you make so very well, beyond that of the "normal population," but also pay attention to your particular style and flair for interacting with people. There are marks of your identity that distinguish you, and which you will do well to recognize in yourself.

Like musicians (and fingerprints and snowflakes), no two music teachers are exactly alike. Each has his or her own style and flair, and if asked the secret to success, a system to swear by, each will respond differently. Still, some musical qualities and personal traits seem to be universal. Figures 1.1 and 1.2 offer features of successful music teachers that are worth striving for if musicians are serious in their intent to take on the teaching role. Some qualities are already obvious on entrance to college, other characteristics are honed in university-level courses, and a few are still coming to their full flowering in the practice of music making and music teaching.

Some personality markers of success can be seen and heard across many contexts. School music teachers tend to be more outgoing than private studio music teachers, performers, or composers. This extroversion may be natural, but it could also be the result of an increased consciousness among teachers of what is socially necessary in communicating with children and youth. School music teachers tend to be group-dependent—that is, they are aware of the feelings of their students and they are inclined to be responsive to the group's feelings, reactions, and behaviors. More than performing musicians, music teachers tend to be less anxious but more conscientious and adventuresome in their approaches to performance and learning to perform.

Productive music teachers with successful programs are known to demonstrate high intensity. Behaviors associated with such teachers include frequent eye contact, focused energy and honest enthusiasm, carefully structured programs that gain and maintain student attention on tasks and assignments, minimal teacher talk (so as to allow maximal student activity), and clear musical cues, gestures, and directions. These are not usually innate behaviors. They are taught and learned, and applied consistently by the most successful music teachers.

The Successful Music Teacher . . .

____ Is a competent performer on primary instrument (or voice)
    ____ is musically accurate
    ____ is technically competent
    ____ is musically expressive

____ Is a competent performer on secondary instrument
Which one(s)? _____

____ Can play by ear familiar songs, tunes, themes (on primary instrument)

____ Can sight-read with accuracy (on primary instrument)

____ Can utilize a solfege system to sing familiar and unfamiliar melodies

____ Can teach a song by rote, without reference to music notation

____ Can sing and lead song-singing with a clear, accurate, and expressive voice

____ Can lead warm-up exercises vocally, at the piano, and on various instruments

____ Can sight-sing melodies and rhythms with accuracy (vocally)

____ Can sight-read intermediate-level piano accompaniments

____ Can harmonize tonal melodies at the piano in any key

____ Can transpose tonal melodies at the piano from one key to another

____ Can improvise on piano, primary instrument, and other instruments

____ Can play SATB scores on the piano

____ Can reduce and play band and orchestral scores on the piano

____ Can arrange simple music for a battery of varied instruments

____ Can conduct band, choir, orchestral scores in any meter or style
    ____ with accuracy
    ____ with expression

____ Can detect and correct musical errors of students

____ Can communicate context and meaning of music relative to its time (history) and place (culture)

____ Can dance and respond through movement to music's qualities

Figure 1.1 • Checklist of musical qualities of a successful music teacher.

The Successful Music Teacher . . .

___ Is knowledgeable of the music under study

___ Can model the music by playing/singing it

___ Is aware of the skill level and knowledge base of students

___ Is responsive to the interest, feelings, and behaviors of students

___ Is sensitive to cultural differences and various learning styles of students

___ Treats all students fairly and refrains from "playing favorites"

___ Sets class rules and reinforces them

___ Can gain and maintain the attention of students through the lesson

___ Limits teacher talk to maximize student involvement

___ Speaks in a clear voice that is easily understood

___ Uses frequent eye contact in communicating with students

___ Addresses students by name

___ Offers meaningful gestures to emphasize spoken ideas

___ Shows enthusiasm in vocal inflection, gestures, and bodily posture

___ Communicates warmth and genuine interest through facial expressions and proximity to students

___ Shows a sense of humor

___ Selects music and teaches lessons to match student age and learning level

Figure 1.2 • Checklist of teaching qualities of a successful music teacher.

When music teachers reflect on and talk about the match between their university training and their teaching practice, they note that certain musical and teaching competences are critical to their work. They recognize both musical and "teacherly," or pedagogical, components that must be acquired in training and perfected through experience for music to be successfully taught. Music teachers are in general agreement on the need for aural skills (and particularly, error detection skills); applied performance ability; conducting skills; knowledge of music history/culture, technology, analysis and composition; and keyboard skills. They underscore the need for developing pedagogical techniques in assessment and evaluation, discipline, motivation, management, organization and planning, and communication techniques. Many of these competences apply to both elementary and secondary teachers. Some of these skills and knowledge areas are learned through life experiences and many years of applied lessons and ensemble performance, but many come through university programs and the supervised application of these competences in teaching.

Like music making, music teaching is a complex act. It requires a passionate commitment to music by young people to want to make a "go" of it. There are richly rewarding moments when teachers make a difference in the lives of children and youth as these students acquire musical skills and knowledge, but teaching is not without its challenges. A thorough musicianship is the starting point so that a repertoire of teaching and communication skills can be woven around the music, but there must be a concentrated dedication by prospective teachers to professional training and experience.

All Things Considered

Music is an amazing experience, and those who are in positions in which music is the centerpiece are indeed fortunate. If music is indeed their passion, they can be pleased to be living with it, playing with it, and working through it on a regular basis. Musical competence and the ability to communicate it are at the heart of music teaching. The professional realm of music education revolves around providing the most meaningful musical sounds that one can make happen for students. The means by which music can be passed along to others for its artistic and social values, and in ways that it can be reproduced and created anew by them, are critical components, of course. But first there is the music, and musical competence is the overriding initial qualification that must be present before further training is pursued.

There is a warmth and a humanness to the musical act, too, and as music making itself is a social activity, those who teach it are deeply immersed in all manner of communicative interaction. It is there in classrooms and rehearsal halls where children and youth gather to be guided by knowledgeable and skilled teachers, and it is played out every day in the give and take of what people say and do. There is a call-and-response dialogue present in the teacher's modeling and the students' reception, and in the students' creations and the teacher's feedback, and in all of the ripplings of interaction that roll like waves over all members of the classroom community of young musicians. Absolutely wedded to the musical competence of teachers is their sincere desire to want to be with people, to communicate with them, and to convey to them the core skills and understandings that may lead them to their own musical fulfillment.

❖ BREAK POINT 1.4 Let the Music Sound

> Pick a piece you have worked up in your studio lesson, on your principal instrument. Perform it for your music education student colleagues. Tell them about the piece: Who composed it? When? For what purpose/function? What might young students listen for were you to perform it for them in a school setting? What does this piece mean to you as a musician?

The journey from musician to music teacher requires self-knowledge, musical convictions, and knowledge of others. Teachers grow in self-knowledge through reflection on experiences and encounters, and in honest assessment of what they know and how they feel about ideas, events, and circumstances. They must constantly maintain and upgrade their comprehensive, all-round, musicianship. They also owe it to their students to know them for who they are, what they bring to the musical experience, and what they may learn from the musical education that music teachers can fashion and facilitate.

REFERENCES AND RESOURCES

Crafts, S. D., D. Cavicchi, and C. Keil. (1993). *My Music.* Hanover, NH: University Press of New England. Interviews with children, youth, adults, and elders on the diverse ways in which people enjoy, experience, and use music in their lives.

Kemp, A. (1996). *The Musical Temperament: Psychology and Personality of Musicians.* Oxford: Oxford University Press. An in-depth examination of the personalities of musicians, including analysis of such traits as introversion, independence, sensitivity, and anxiety.

MacDonald, R. A. R., D. J. Hargreaves, and D. Miell. (2002). *Musical Identities.* New York: Oxford Unversity Press. A thoroughgoing consideration of music as it influences the development of personal identity, with attention to identities based upon family, gender, and nation.

Stokes, M., ed. (1994). *Ethnicity, Identity, and Music: The Musical Construction of Place.* Oxford: Berg Publishers. An examination of music in the making of national and regional identities, with consideration of music in the descriptions of people and their places of origin and where they now live.

chapter 2

Great Minds on Music in Education

High school band director: Remember those methods classes in college—all that philosophy stuff?

Middle school band director: Oh yeah. Like it had anything to do with teaching music. It was a bunch of junk.

High school band director: Well, maybe there is something to Plato and all those guys. Yesterday, I found myself going through some class notes, and I wound up using a quote from ancient Greece in a memo to my principal.

Middle school band director: What about?

High school band director: Morality, and music keeping kids on the right path . . . morals and all. You know: Plato.

Middle school band director: Hmm. So you think there's something to those old guys?

High school band director: I guess so. More than I did in college, anyway.

Justifying Music

Administrators, teachers, and taxpayers who support music in the school curriculum may do so because of the powerful musical and music-educational experiences they recall from their youth. Yet in hard times of tight budgets, many administrators, teachers, and taxpayers may require convincing about the purpose and products of musical study before they decide to hire music teachers and cast their votes to save and even extend music programs. A music teacher's justification of music for the common good and for its artistic and social-emotional purposes is often key to its presence in the school program of studies. If a statement of music's contribution to the lives of young people is persuasive enough, it may secure music's place within the realm of common knowledge deemed necessary for all children and youth.

Throughout history and across cultures, people of prominence and of the workaday world have had much to say about the value of music for them and their society. For teachers, the ability to justify music—and to elicit the help of the great minds who have thoughtfully considered its importance—may save their jobs.

There are many minds, including those of notable historical figures and educators, who have carefully probed, spoken to, and acted on the essential role of music in society and its children. Knowing something of the philosophical perspectives that have been held about music historically can deepen the convictions that teachers have of music's role and function in education. Such insight can help them formulate a personal philosophy for music's mission in the schools. When pressed to explain why they do what they do, to write that memo to potential boosters of their program, the words of Plato or Martin Luther or Albert Einstein may come in handy.

"Musical teachers" and "teaching musicians" strengthen their daily practice as they thoroughly consider the ways in which music has been valued and used in many circumstances and settings from the time of the ancient Egyptians to the present. That "gut sense" of why music is important in education can be fortified and further substantiated by the ideas that have been crafted by musicians, educators, scholars, and statesmen. They speak for themselves but for others, too, as their words represent the deeply felt sentiments people hold about music's place in society and its schools. They supply support and substantiation for music education today.

Music That Means Something

Music teachers, like all other human beings, need music. Before they begin to depend on school music positions for their livelihood they find that they personally *must have music* in their lives. Ask David, a high school band director: "I've always been a music-nerd: played in the elementary and middle school bands, the high school marching, concert, and jazz bands. I was the bugler at Boy Scout camp, and played in a brass choir at church. I still play now in pit bands when artists come to town, and that's in addition to teaching all day. I do music because it's fun, a social outlet, decent money, and I'm good at it." Or Jackie: "I never thought of anything else for a job and a profession but teaching music. It's the thing that makes me feel the very best, making other people happy with my music and helping them to develop the skills they need to express themselves." Or Kathryn: "When I left music behind after high school to study chemistry? I couldn't. I came back, because I just had to have more music than

John Blacking, ethnomusicologist and educator.

just on the weekends. It's too deep to go into, but I guess I just crave it."

Music is meaningful as an artistic expression. The act of making music engages one's mind, body, and soul. John Blacking, who trained at Cambridge University, and rose to international leadership in the developing field of ethnomusicology in the 1960s, 70s, and 80s, established that music—even the children's songs of the Venda people of South Africa whom he studied—should be considered first as "pure" music for its sonic structures and only after that for its cultural and social meaning. He believed that music making was a profound artistic experience and that music listening could also be a powerful and all-encompassing event. Musicality is a human phenomenon, he declared, and all possess the capacity to listen to, respond to, and make music. That "music could become you," or that individuals could be drawn deeply into music, was a position Blacking frequently expressed; it is reminiscent of T. S. Eliot's poetic offering, that "you are the music while it lasts." For some, John Blacking's sense-making of music is more than a beautiful image: it is a guidepost for recognizing music's integral role in human life.

❖ BREAK POINT 2.1 Nurturing the Musical Experience

Contemplate the imagery and meaning of the two phrases "music could become you" and "you are the music while it lasts." What do these romantic expressions of the musical experience mean to you? Check sources for other expressions that speak to the musical experience. Discuss ways in which the teacher plays a part in facilitating and teaching for intimate personal and collective social encounters with music.

Music is a social phenomenon and a cultural tradition that can be shared and transmitted. Christopher Small, a sociologist who calls himself "a thinking musician" coined the term "musicking" to refer to the act by which people participate in a musical performance—as performers, as listeners, or as anyone who played a part in making the performance happen. The act of musicking refers to a set of relationships among performers, their families and their teachers, the technical help at the recital hall or club, the volunteers who usher and distribute programs, and most certainly the audience—all who make possible the sound of music even as they also receive its benefits. The social network of singers, players, dancers, conductors, and composers is the means through which musical traditions and innovations are nurtured at the symphony, in the jazz club, at churches and temples, on the mariachi stage, at the opera, in the schools, and within the garages and basements where makeshift bands and singing groups convene. Further, there is considerable agreement among teachers on Small's position that music stands for something that is socially driven: the young people who make it, the values they hold, the beliefs that they can express.

As children and adolescents find music meaningful in their lives, music teachers can do much to help them enhance their musical experience. When teachers know the music well, they become the model and the inspiration for those who aspire to perform and compose. They can offer training in the motor skills necessary to produce good tone, accurate pitch and rhythm, and musical flow. They can guide young people in the discovery of "the artistic self"—that part of themselves that can intelligently create and re-create music with emotive power. As they learn the musical capacity that comes from within them and is advanced through the educational strategies that music teachers can provide, students will understand not only music but in a deeper sense the manner in which it reflects the beauty of life itself.

The views following are from a sampling of prominent thinkers, including musicians and educators, kings and queens, scientists and statesmen who have shaped the substance of societies and civilizations in the West and throughout the world. Their words are meaningful for their times and form the basis for understanding music's place in our time as well.

❖ BREAK POINT 2.2 Musical Meaning in Transition

> List the key contributions of music to your own life. Reflect on how the meaning of music has changed for you, from your days as a young child, a middle school "music aspirant," to an advanced student of music, a performing musician, and a musician looking to become a teacher.

Ancient Minds on Music

A look into the past of some of the world's great civilizations shows that music was a valued feature of the full realization of the individual and the community. In Egypt, Greece, Rome, and Carthage, all centers of civilization in the Mediterranean region, in ancient China and in medieval Europe and Japan, music was viewed as having moral values, as a bridge to the sacred and the mystical, as a powerful diversion, and a force in developing social cohesion.

Egyptian monuments abound with depictions of singers, dancers, and players of harp, lyre, flute, and shawm. As early as the Old Kingdom (2650–2134 BCE), the era of the building of the pyramids, able musicians achieved considerable status. Singers were trained not only in how to use their voices but also in hand clapping and sistrum playing. Among the rulers, Cleopatra was depicted playing a crescent-shaped harp to a deity, and her father Ptolemy IX was said to be a fine shawm player. The pharaohs favored professional musicians for affairs of state and after-dinner entertainment. Music was valued, but since schooling was rare for children, they learned most songs, stories, folk rituals, and moral lessons and behaviors through observing and imitating their mothers and fathers.

Confucius of China (551–479 BCE) advised, "If you would know if a people be well governed (and), if its laws be good or bad, (then) examine the music it practices." He studied philosophy and music, and wrote the *Analects* in addition to editing the Chinese classics of *Shi Jing* (Book of Odes) and *Yi Jing* (Book of Changes). His main goal for himself and others was the cultivation of character, and he promoted the study of the Six Arts—ritual, music, archery, chariot-riding, calligraphy, and computation—to achieve this goal. He included the study of music and dance within the broader category of music, believing that these subjects would offer artistic training as well as give pleasure to people of all ages who studied them.

To the ancient Greeks, a public system of education could create the "right kind" of person, particularly when gymnastics were designed to discipline the body and music was in place to discipline the mind. Plato (427–347 BCE) believed that children who learned music became more civilized and grew into a harmonic balance between themselves and their world. Writing in the *Republic*, he asserted that "education in music is most sovereign" and that knowledge of music feeds the soul and brings beauty into the individual. He believed that teachers could use music to develop children's self-control and grace and to steer them from "evil-doings." He claimed that employing music in the education of youths would be the best remedy against their "falling into the need of the justice of the courtroom" for crimes they would otherwise commit. Attention to musical training, the study of poetry, and physical training would achieve the harmonious adjustment of the body and soul, and of energy, emotion, and reason.

A student of Plato, Aristotle (384–322 BCE) wrote of art as the realization in external form of a true idea, an expression and reinterpretation of what exists in life. In his time, music was one of the customary areas of education, along with letters (reading and writing), gymnastics, and drawing. Music kept the mind of the citizen occupied and was an appropriate use of leisure time. In his *Politica,* Book VIII, Aristotle discussed the use of "the songs of Olympus exercise," noting that music was a significant component of the early Olympics competitions. He claimed that these songs inspired enthusiasm as an emotion of the ethical part of the soul. Furthermore, Aristotle agreed with his teacher, Plato, that music was instrumental in developing the moral character of young people.

In the spread of the Roman Empire to northern Africa, Aurelius Augustinus, or St. Augustine (354–430 CE), was a figure of enormous influence. He was a bishop and a prolific writer in the early development of Christianity in Algeria, Tunisia, and into Europe. Struggling against the temptations of his earlier amoral life, he was attracted to music's beauty while at the same time he found music to be wildly distracting from the message of the biblical and devotional texts. He saw music as powerful, even irresistible, in its pull to the beauty of its sound. In his *Confessions,* Augustine claimed that all of his emotions could be echoed and made more alive in voice and song. He recognized the usefulness of music, too, in that people could be moved by the ideas carried by the text of a song rendered with a clear singing voice.

Boethius of Rome (480–524 CE) was a theorist who not only synthesized the musical practices of the Greeks and early Romans but also set a course on music in higher education for the Middle Ages and the Renaissance ahead. In his major musical treatise, *De Institutione Musica,* he proclaimed that "there is no greater path whereby instruction comes to the mind than through the ear." He supported the view of the ancient Greeks that music of the highest moral character—modest and simple, and masculine rather than violent or fickle—be composed and taught, as it would make its way to the soul. In another treatise, *Fundamentals of Music,* he acknowledged that music is a natural and necessary part of humanity and that the power of the intellect should be summoned to master the musical art. For all who sought it out, music could be intellectually stimulating as it was also the base of morality.

Across the Eurasian landmass to the northeastern islands of Japan, music was high on the recommended list of studies for young people. In the time of the Emperor Murakami's reign in the eighth-century Heian period, the emperor engaged a minister named Fujiwara No Morotada (718–769) who was raising his daughter as a young noblewoman of the court. His words survive him on the meaning of refinement: "First you should study penmanship. Next you must learn to play the seven-string zither better than anyone else. And also you must memorize all the poems in the twenty books of the *Kokin Shu*" (the anthology of ancient and modern poems). This was the time of Japan's gradual rise from Chinese influence to the development of its own literature and arts that would define the culture for many centuries to come. The role of music, along with the arts and letters, was central to the education of those Japanese youth who would lead the nation into its golden age.

Among the leading figures of medieval Europe, Charlemagne (742–814) reigned supreme as ruler of all of western Europe. He reversed the direction of the declining Christian monasteries by requiring the clergy to school the boys in the Psalms, chant, and notation as well as math and grammar. In this way, their religious training was enhanced by the music they learned, even as music enriched their devotional practice and academic studies. Charlemagne arranged for monks from Rome, the center of Catholicism, to come train his Frankish singers in the music and ritual of worship. This action not only revived church music but also set about restoring music and art across his empire.

Later Minds on Music

From the Middle Ages and into the second half of the millennium, music was significant to societies throughout the world. In the practice of religion, through an array of civic activities, and for entertainment and leisure, music was valued and thus taught to young people. In the courts, places of worship, and schools, they learned performance techniques and repertoire, and universities from Salamanca (Spain) to Oxford (England) offered studies in music theory. Music was heard in churches and temples, and in the parlors of kings, queens, presidents, and private citizens. Some of the leading religious and civic figures had much to say about music's importance in their time and place.

One of the greatest advocates for the musical education of children was Martin Luther (1483–1546), a former priest and leader of the religious reformation movement in Germany. He was exposed to music at an early age and saw it as a wonderful gift from God that should be used in devotional practice. He believed that the moral, temperamental, intellectual, and spiritual nature of people improved through performance. All teachers should be able to sing, so that schoolboys could be instructed in singing each day. He maintained that music kept the devil away and that it functioned as a discipline that makes people gentle, modest, and discreet. In a remark foreshadowing idiomatic speech today, Martin Luther observed, "In times of peace, music rules."

✣ BREAK POINT 2.3 Historical Musical "Takes"

> Far outside the realm of trained musicians, notable historic figures had much
> to say about music. Look into what esteemed statesmen (and women), sci-
> entists, artists, humanists, and philosophers-at-large had to say about music
> in society and the schooling of young people. Which ideals of some of these
> leading figures appeal to you? Do any surprise you?

Akbar the Great (1542–1605), one of the most revered rulers of Mughal India, brought about a renaissance of music and the arts in South Asia. He was knowledgeable despite his illiteracy, by nature a mystic who sought to attain the ineffable bliss of contact with the Divine, and he patronized musicians whom he held in highest esteem for their expressive artistic forms of devotion as well as for the entertainment they provided. He brought to his court musicians from Persia, Central Asia, present-day Afghanistan, and throughout India. Among them was the leading singer and rabab (bowed lute) player, Tansen, who continues to be viewed as the greatest master of the *dhrupad* classical song form even today. It was this key musician of Akbar's court who sang of the importance of learning music: "The instruction of the wise is to learn the rhythmic compositions of both the saints and the music of the folks. Various schools have interpreted the mysteries of music, meditating on the works of Brahma, Vishnu, and Shiva. Praise the teachers who unraveled these secrets."

The British philosopher John Locke (1632–1704) wrote *Some Thoughts Concerning Education*, in which he questioned the benefits of musical instruction in the schooling of all children and youth. He admitted that "a good hand upon some instruments is by many people mightily valued," but he worried that music was complicated and not likely to be learned well enough by the greater population. Instrumental music required a degree of innate talent, he maintained, so that some (but not all) young people could then accelerate in the development of skills and expression that would please and inspire those who listened. On the other hand, Locke waxed enthusiastically about dance for its benefits in giving graceful gestures, confidence, and freedom to the body. His work as a medical researcher, with some attention to anatomy, might have persuaded him of the beauty of the body in motion and of the human need to move—and to move expressively. Many would disagree with Locke's perspective, arguing that music is no more complicated than dance to learn and execute with skill and grace, and that all young people deserve the opportunity to become musically skilled at the highest level (or at the level they choose to attain). Still, as dance is the physical response that many listeners have to the music they hear, Locke's provocative position is within the realm of reason for music teachers to consider.

Just prior to the Napoloeonic period was the time of the philosopher Jean-Jacques Rousseau (1712–1778) whose ideas created disciples of brilliant eighteenth- and nineteenth-century thinkers: Immanuel Kant, Johann Goethe, Johann Pestalozzi, and Leo Tolstoy. A music copier and music teacher by trade, Rousseau's influence as the father of Romantic sensibility was extensive in politics, literature, and education. He was a moralist who believed in the goodness of nature and its corruption by civilization. In his classic work, *Emile,* he wrote of the importance of fostering in the child what is native and natural, and of drawing out of the child the human potential that is already there. He wrote that the purpose of education, particularly in pre-adolescence, is to cultivate the five senses; this then leads to the intellectual and emotional stability of the individual. Rousseau's impact on music education (and education at large) may be seen from several perspectives, chief among them the child-centered (rather than adult-dictated) curriculum and the propensity for active physical as well as intellectual activity.

King Chulalongkorn, also known as Rama V (1853–1910) of Siam (later Thailand), was responsible for modernizing Siam; avoiding colonial rule by England, France, and Holland; and unifying the kingdom. While his father, King Mongkut (Rama IV, the king of *The King and I*) introduced European-style education, it was Chulalongkorn who ruled during the height of the drive to bring compulsory education, including heritage songs and dances, to all Thai children. Music was taught to Chulalongkorn's many children, and the court ensemble of ranat (xylophones), kong wong (circles of brass gongs), pi (quadruple-reed shawm), and various drums and gongs was played for all official ceremonies and events for foreign visitors. The traditional court music is continued even today by His Majesty King Bhumibol Adulyadej, Rama IX (b. 1927), who trained as a jazz saxophonist. He has this to say about music: "To me, music is something fine and beautiful. It is a part of everyone, an essential part of us all. I think we should recognize the value of music in all its forms." Now his daughter, Princess Maha Chakri Sirindhorn (b. 1955), sets an example for young Thai people by her masterful performances on various stringed instruments and the ranat xylophone. The study of traditional Thai music is encouraged and has been supported as a valued educational effort throughout the reign of many kings.

Queen Victoria of England (1819–1901), also empress of India and much of the colonial world during the industrial revolution, was not known for her passion for music, singing, and Italian opera. Yet she perfected her voice over twenty years of lessons and consistent practice, and during her sixty-four-year reign sang many concerts at Buckingham Palace. She was also committed to education at large, and she and her husband, Albert, created a network of schools throughout Britain so that by 1891 elementary school was compulsory and free. While reading, writing, and math were central to the curriculum of elementary schools, a movement that developed toward the end of the nineteenth century, approved by the queen, brought traditional music into schools. English songs, singing games, and folk dances were woven into classroom activities so that an appreciation for English history and lore could be developed by young singers and dancers.

❖ BREAK POINT 2.4 The Daily Dose

Following is an exchange between two high school students concerning their need for music on a daily basis. Aside from the need to practice and rehearse music in order to learn it and become skillful, are there other reasons that daily music is a useful practice in schools? Discuss means by which a music teacher can spread music throughout the school community.

> **Tenth-grade student:** I'm doing music this year. I mean, it's me, a part of who I am.
>
> **Eleventh-grade student:** I know what you mean. I like the fact that choir will get me on the trip to D.C. in March, but really, I somehow need my daily singing.
>
> **Tenth-grade student:** Exactly. I could skip a few days of math, no problem. But music?
>
> **Eleventh-grade student:** Really. Gotta get the daily dose.

John Dewey (1859–1952) was a leading philosopher in the reform of twentieth-century American education. He recognized the integrity of all aspects of human experience, including the arts, and argued that aesthetic enjoyment should not be the privilege of the few but rather a vital component of education for the common good of all. In *Art as Experience*, he wrote, "Works of art that are not remote from common life, that are widely enjoyed in a community, are signs of a unified collective life." He viewed artistic expression, whether through music, painting, or dance, as a remaking of the material of experience that offers direction of greater order and unity for the community as a whole. Dewey's views are shared by educators of various nations—that the arts are essential in socializing the individual into the community, and in recognizing that the individual is part of a collective heritage both past and present.

In speaking about his renowned theory of relativity, Einstein said,

"It occurred to me by intuition, and music was the driving force behind that intuition. My discovery was the result of musical perception."

A classroom poster that highlights Albert Einstein's notable quote on the significance of music in human life.

Albert Einstein (1879–1955) was a renowned physicist who developed a new theory on the classic principle of relativity. He studied violin from the ages of six to thirteen and so developed an affinity for music from an early age. He wondered whether he might have been a musician had he not turned toward science as a vocation. As he reflected, "I often think in music. I live my daydreams in music. I see my life in terms of music. . . . I get most joy in life out of music." From his perspective, music did not influence his scientific work, but both music and science were nourished by the same sort of passion. Einstein concluded that they complement each other in the release they offer, a thoughtful position to take in seeking a balance in the fuller education of all young people.

Various American presidents have expressed their belief in the importance of the arts in society and its schools; some of them were amateur performers or saw to it that their own children were given musical training. John Adams (1735–1826) said: "I must study politics and war that my sons may have liberty to study mathematics and philosophy. My sons ought to study mathematics and philosophy, geography, natural history and naval architecture, navigation, commerce, and agriculture, in order to give their children a right to study painting, poetry, music, architecture." Over a century later, Franklin D. Roosevelt (1882–1945) proclaimed that "great music, great literature, great art, and the wonders of science are, and should be, open to all," recognizing music's place in public education. John Kennedy (1917–1963) declared that art is "an instrument of understanding of the futility of struggle between those who share man's faith," and that people will be remembered not for their wars but for their "contribution to the human spirit".

Nelson Mandela (b. 1918) president of South Africa from 1994 to 1999, has a keen interest in music. He declared that one of his greatest pleasures was to watch the sun set while listening to the music of Handel or Tchaikovsky. During the time of his imprisonment for his involvement in the anti-apartheid movement, he and his fellow cellmates would sing as a way to uplift their spirits over the repression and sadness of their situation. He saw the connection between music and the expression of sociopolitical concerns in the ubiquitous freedom songs and associated public marches heard in South African cities and townships, and he was drawn by diverse musical expressions, including European classical music and African choral music. Black South Africans have long recognized the musical power of spirituals and gospel songs of the African-American freedom movement, and Mandela was no exception.

> The life of the arts
> far from being an interruption,
> a distraction,
> in the life of a nation,
> is close to the center
> of a nation's purpose-
> and is a test of the quality
> of a nation's civilization.
>
> -John F. Kennedy

A teacher's posting of John Fitzgerald Kennedy's belief in the importance of the arts in society.

Musicians' Minds on Music

It is not surprising that musicians would have much to say about the place of music in the education of the young. Some have told of their own early musical training while others have advocated in the press, through correspondence, or in academic treatises and books the merits of a musical education. From the process of transmission and instruction at home or through informal means to the curricular structures at school that can support it, the means of musically educating children and youth has received the attention of performers, composers, and conductors.

One of the remarkable multifaceted musicians of medieval Europe was Hildegard von Bingen (1098–1179), a visionary poet and theological scholar. She was also founder of a vibrant convent for women; a medical practitioner who used plants, trees, and other natural materials to treat ailing members of her community; and a composer. She wrote liturgical plainchant, song melodies and texts, and antiphons—the substance of her Roman Catholic religious practice. Her writing about music described recapturing the original joy and beauty of paradise (that had been lost, as told in the biblical story, when Adam and Eve fell from grace). The quality of her own music offers a glimpse of her conception of the pure angelic sonorities of heaven, a vision that was important to the learning and lives of the women within her convent.

As the foremost representative of early American music, William Billings (1746–1800) was known for his work as an itinerant singing schoolmaster in New England as well as for his compositions. At his singing sessions in colonial villages and towns, he favored the fuguing tunes of greater rhythmic density over the older hymn tunes of steady rhythms and plain harmonies. In his singing school assemblies, the goal-centered singing master introduced repertoire and honed sightreading skills, and thus he required the attention of his singers, their full participation, punctuality and prompt adherence to his requests, and their submission to him for his musical judgment. His advice, that "all scholars should submit to the judgment of the master, respecting the part they are to sing," is still, in a modified form, a goal for modern teachers.

Wolfgang Amadeus Mozart (1756–1791) was *die wunderkind*, the boy wonder, whose gifts as pianist, violinist, and composer were widely celebrated throughout Europe before he was ten years old. His listening acuity, technical performance competence, and brilliance (and speed) of invented musical ideas were astonishing to all who knew him or heard him. He seems always to have had music close to him, as he remarked: "When I am, as it were, completely myself, entirely alone, and of good cheer—say traveling in a carriage, or walking after a good meal, or during the night when I cannot sleep—it is on such occasions that my ideas flow best, and most abundantly. Whence and how they come, I know not, nor can I force them." Such may be the nature of not only musical geniuses but others as well for whom music is there, constantly in mind, calming, energizing, influencing. In his adult life, Mozart worked as a court musician and teacher, offering instrumental music instruction, coaching musicians, accompanying singers, and churning out a repertoire of over 600 works—including operas, symphonies, concertos, sonatas, and string quartets.

In the United States, Lowell Mason (1792–1872) was a working musician—singing teacher, composer, arranger, conductor—who was drawn to the possibilities of making music a regular curricular component within public elementary schools. He persuaded the Boston schools to test the inclusion of music within the curriculum, offering vocal training and music-reading lessons twice weekly. He presented public concerts of works by Mozart and Haydn (and an array of original and arranged compositions) to demonstrate the considerable musical ability of children, and delighted school officials, parents, and community members with his pragmatic method of learning-by-doing, and his focused listening and rote repetition of vocal music that moved children toward music literacy. Not only were children's musical voices a joy to hear, but the arguments for music's moral, physical, and intellectual merits were irresistible. Mason's "sound-before-sight" approach was influenced by the Swiss educator Heinrich Pestalozzi (1746–1827); this method used listening and singing experiences as the central means by which knowledge of notation and theory eventually developed. By 1838, the Boston public schools led the nation in officially establishing music as a subject for study, and one city followed another in taking Mason's pedagogical approach into the realm of the official school subjects for children's study. By the late nineteenth century, music was a standard offering within the curriculum of American elementary schools—even as music was also a growing presence in secondary school programs.

Zoltán Kodály (1882–1967), composer, conductor, linguist, and collector-preserver of Hungarian traditional music, spent the greater part of his life advocating and inspiring the development of a solid national system of music education for children and youth. He believed that "no other subject can serve the child's welfare—physical and spiritual—as well as music," and wrote and spoke continuously on behalf of children, that they be given every opportunity to know their musical heritage. He believed that they should learn music of the best quality, and that all listening and performance experiences should be directed toward the development of children's inner hearing such that they would hear the music in their heads just by looking at the notes on paper. Kodály articulated reasons for music in schools, noting its part in developing a sense of the Hungarian national history and heritage.

The Reverend Thomas Dorsey (1899–1993) wrote 400 compositions, most of them blues-based hymns called gospel songs, including the famous "Take My Hand, Precious Lord." He left school in Georgia at the age of eleven to take a job at a local vaudeville theater; there he played as a "whispering piano player" at the after-hours parties when the music was played quietly enough to avoid drawing police attention. As a Baptist minister in Chicago, he became known as "the father of gospel music" when he converted from blues and secular show music to the sacred song. In reflecting on the essence of gospel music, he proclaimed that "there is no such thing as black music, white music, red, blue music. . . . the gospel music . . . is good news, and that's what the world needs: the music and the gospel." Dorsey advocated early involvement in learning the music of the church, and many followed his view by establishing in their churches choirs of children who could sing gospel.

Shinichi Suzuki (1898–1998) lived his life in music, first as a violinist and then as a dedicated teacher of violin and the musicianship that grows behind it. His Talent Education method was developed from his understanding that young children could develop musical ability in much the same way they learn language: orally, with consistent listening, parental involvement, and positive reinforcement. He articulated the goal of his pedagogy: "I just want to make good citizens. If a child hears good music from the day of his birth, and learns to play it himself, he develops sensitivity, discipline and endurance. He gets a beautiful heart." Suzuki set music education practice on its ear, especially strings education, through his stipulation of principles that included starting children early in their musical training, initiating the development of playing skills through aural and kinesthetic means—without notation—providing group practice as well as one-on-one lessons, and inviting parents to learn and practice alongside their children.

The American composer Aaron Copland (1900–1990), whose works such as "Billy the Kid," "Rodeo," and "Appalachian Spring" are standard repertoire for many of the world's symphony orchestras, learned to play piano from his older sister while growing up in New York City. He traveled to Paris as the first American student of famed teacher Nadia Boulanger and oriented many of his works toward American folklore, jazz rhythms, and music heard on the radio. He wrote What to Listen For in Music, claiming that "Music expresses, at different moments, serenity or exuberance, regret or triumph, fury or delight. . . . It may even express a state of meaning for which there exists no adequate word in any language." Copland urged intelligent and unprejudiced listening to all styles and schools of music, so that the listener could have a profound understanding of the musical art. His ideas on listening are foundational in many music education programs.

Great American jazz musicians had much to say about the value of music in human life, and about their genre in particular. Composer-conductor-arranger Duke Ellington (1899–1974) spoke of music as expressing the inexpressible: "You've got to find some way of saying it without saying it, and that's where music comes in." For talkative teachers and students, this advice is particularly relevant. John Coltrane (1926–1967), jazz saxophonist, claimed that music could align the performer with nature, and perhaps the supernatural as well: "All a musician can do is to get closer to the sources of nature, and so feel that he is in communion with the natural laws." These natural laws are embedded in the psycho-acoustics of music and the music-making experience, an understanding to which effective teachers are able to guide their students. Jazz trumpeter Miles Davis (1926–1991) spoke to the essence of improvisation, and by implication offered advice on life as a constant process of experimentation: "Do not fear mistakes. There are none." Where improvisation is of growing interest as a skill to be developed by all musicians (and not just jazzers), this advice fosters an approach to playing that allows ideas to grow from "right" and "wrong" notes— all of which can be tasteful in themselves and for where they lead.

Wynton Marsalis (b. 1961), trumpet player, artistic director of Jazz at Lincoln Center, and one of the most acclaimed musicians of his generation, began his classical training on trumpet at age twelve. Having made over forty jazz and classical recordings, he is not only a performer but also a respected teacher and spokesperson for music education. He has marveled at how he came to understand himself, his strengths and weaknesses as a person, through his performance, and compares music to a big playground with many avenues and items to learn. He stands at the forefront of jazz education in America, and speaks of "the vibration" between band directors and their students, praising these teachers who affirm music through their knowledge, skills, and enthusiasm, and who make an indelible impact on their students.

Cellist Yo-Yo Ma (b. 1955) was born to Chinese parents living in Paris; he began cello studies at the young age of four with his father, later studying with Leonard Rose at the Juilliard School of Music in New York. He is committed to educational programs that bring music to young audiences but that also allow them to perform music in master classes and discovery programs for musicians and nonmusicians. With his amazing musical artistry, he explores music as a means of communication and, in his "Silk Road Project," as a vehicle for the migration of ideas across the historic trade route stretching from the heart of China to Rome. He has expressed this interest as such: "I want to investigate different cultures, to see how their identities and values affect their music." His interest in young people's musical and cultural enrichment is legendary.

❖ BREAK POINT 2.5 A Letter of Invitation

> Write a letter of student recruitment to parents. In discussing the importance of music to the holistic development of children, use the perspectives of at least three notable historical or contemporary figures.

Minding Music Education

Within the field of music education, there are music teacher-scholars who argue powerfully for why music should be taught and learned in schools. Bennett Reimer, Keith Swanwick, David J. Elliott, and Estelle Jorgensen are among those who have articulated the many ways that music education benefits young people, and who have described aspects of the pedagogical process that are effective for use with children and adolescents. As musicians and music teachers in schools and communities, and later as members of university faculty in music education, these individuals have crafted their views based upon experiences in and thoughtful observations of music education.

Books of wisdom for music educators.

BENNETT REIMER

Aesthetic education developed as an important force which made its way into the mainstream of North American educational practice in the 1960s and 1970s, and continued to be influential there and elsewhere in the decades that followed. The term "aesthetic" was typically used in discussions of music to refer to both the artistic/creative aspects such as performing and composing and the listening aspects. In reference to music education, the term encompassed artistic, creative, listening, critical, historical, and theoretical realms. It resounded well within the educational community among those who sought the depth of artistic experience to justify music as a substantive subject for curricular inclusion, and who looked also to the intellectual facets of musical study to anchor it.

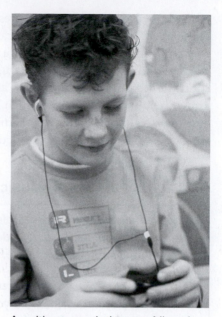

An ultimate goal: the art of listening well.

As a leading voice of this perspective, Bennett Reimer stated in 1970 that a primary aim of music education as aesthetic education is for children and youth to grow through an instructional program in grasping "the beautiful" and the depth of feeling that is experienced in life that can also be expressed artistically in music. He believed that the purpose and meaning of music education was in large part determined by the purpose and meaning of music, and so he constructed a philosophy for music teachers that would pay tribute to the sonic properties of music that make it meaningful to those who perform it and listen to it analytically. His view was sometimes explained as emphasizing listening as a passive response to music, perhaps because he was so influential in the development of listening in practice. However, Reimer's view was always broader than that, with listening as an end in itself as well as a means for other substantive experiences.

Music's import then and now, through more than a quarter of a century of thoughtful contemplation by Reimer and other proponents of aesthetic education, is seen as an expressive form and a reflection of life itself in its structures, its tensions and releases. This conceptual understanding of music becomes more fully understood through experience and study. In the movement of music education as aesthetic education, the task of teachers was viewed as drawing young people into experiencing music as absolute expressionism, that is, to lead them to the knowledge of music as expressive of deep human emotion and meaning. As Reimer conceives of music education as aesthetic education, it is changeable over time and place, and can adapt to movements and issues such as those of cultural pluralism, multicultural music education, and musical intelligences. He continues to hone his philosophy, and suggests that musically educated people know the unique manner in which music calls upon their minds, their bodies, and their feelings. He further maintains that music education offers students the opportunity to share in their culture's values and needs.

❖ BREAK POINT 2.6 Music Is Me

A conversation between two professional jazz musicians follows, getting to the heart of a complex musical identity, and when it first develops. Discuss how the music fits who you are, and in what ways it is reflected in what you do.

Trumpet player: So when did you get the music bug?

Drummer: They told me I was beating time in my crib. You?

Trumpet player: Fourth grade, when they passed out horns for us to try out. Turns out, I'd been waiting for it all my life. It fit me. Now it's who I am: the way I think, act, work out, play.

KEITH SWANWICK

For well over four decades, the works and words of British music educator Keith Swanwick have been highly influential in the advancement of music within the primary and secondary schools of the United Kingdom. Swanwick has been instrumental in Britain—and far beyond it—in articulating music's critical role in human development and thus its place within the institutions that society has established for the education of children and youth in valued skills, domains of knowledge, and cultural symbols. In his vast assortment of books, from *Popular Music and the Teacher* (1968) and *A Basis for Music Education* (1979) to the much-cited *Music, Mind and Education* (1988) and fuller evolution of his philosophical stance in *Musical Knowledge* (1994) and *Teaching Music Musically* (1999), Swanwick has asserted that music is a way of knowing and a complex symbol system that can only be fully understood through the educational experiences offered in school.

As a practicing musician (of trombone, piano, and organ) and conductor (of choirs and orchestras), Swanwick has probed the nature of the musical experience and the maturational changes across children's development that necessitate various pedagogical techniques for allowing natural musical intuition to grow into greater musical insights. From the very young sensory-oriented child to the adolescent well along in developing abstract thought, the activities of composing, performing, and analytical listening are constructed and clarified for the ways that they each bring unique personal and social enrichment that cannot be enjoyed through any other means. The materials of music—its elemental features—are worthy of dissection (listening), re-creation (performance), and creation (composition), with attention to the last of these as a deeply meaningful way of knowing the building blocks of music. Swanwick summed up his philosophical perspective on music education by claiming that as "music has the potential to take us beyond ourselves, our own small space in time and our local tribe," teachers can frame their curricular experiences in ways that are compatible with extending knowledge and enlarging students' capacity for knowing music more fully.

DAVID J. ELLIOTT

The word "music" has been variously used to refer to a song or an intact instrumental piece, or a set of songs or pieces, or a whole repertoire or style. Music is the product of performance, composition, and improvisation, and the physical objects of scores, sheets of notation, recordings, and the collective set of instruments that make the sound. Its reputation is as a noun, and yet it may function as a verb that points to the process of making music. While Christopher Small first coined "musicking" as the social network involved in the making of a musical performance, Canadian-born David J. Elliott established the verb "musicing" to refer to the process of musical performance. The words and their meanings are close but not precisely the same, as Elliott is concerned about the process of the music makers themselves while Small's interest is in the social relationships among all those who make a performance possible (including the audience, the ticket-takers, and the technical help). For Elliott, music is neither the collection of objects nor the social phenomenon of the music performance. Nor is music the product at the end of the process. Rather, Elliott uses music, musicing, and *musicers* in underscoring the intentional activity of making the music.

Calling it a praxial philosophy of music education, Elliott centers on the importance of musical doing, the musical product that results, and the context of the doing as features for understanding "MUSIC" as a diverse human practice. He defines context as the full array of ideas, associations, and circumstances that frame an understanding of the music, and his perspective is that all of these dimensions inform an understanding of MUSIC and are the basis of a music education philosophy. The hope for strong and effective music education lies in musical teachers, and thus the praxial philosophy targets the improvement of the musicianship of prospective and practicing teachers and the continuing quest by them to understand music in all of its component parts. Despite the accent on performance, there is in Elliott's philosophy a comprehensive sweep of multiple approaches to knowing music as listeners, too, and as conductors, composers, arrangers, and improvisers.

ESTELLE JORGENSEN

More than they themselves may realize, music teachers are thoughtful professionals with the capacity for making informed decisions about the content of their instructional practice. Estelle Jorgensen poses questions for their own probing and reflection, and is confident in teachers' ability to figure out the means for effective instructional practice within their own settings. Teachers determine their own destiny rather than being completely dependent upon others in an administrative hierarchy as to what to teach and how to teach it. They observe and listen, and in time and through experience, they decide when it is appropriate for them to "take the bull by the horns." In her books, *In Search of Music Education* and *Transforming Music Education*, Jorgensen recognizes music teachers as highly capable of thinking and doing.

Jorgensen, a native Australian, recommends a dialectical view of music education as an effective framework for examining the field for its strengths and weaknesses, and for the challenges it presents to working teachers personally and professionally. Her dialectical approach involves paired concepts consisting of perspectives at the far ends of individual continua, in the belief that teachers can think through the dilemma that each pair constitutes and find their own positions on them. These dialectics address both musical and educational issues as they overlap one another in the process of making sense of music through an educational plan. Jorgensen's dialectical view of music education is presented in Figure 2.1, along with questions relating to them that are worthy of contemplation by teachers.

While these dialectics offer polar opposites on issues concerning music education, there is yet the potential for teachers to take the middle ground, to meld their views that may at first appear to be mutually exclusive, to find themselves flexible in their stance and selecting their position based on the circumstances of their work. For example, there may be times when a teacher determines that her curricular program (or even a particular lesson) may be more about receiving music, about listening with careful analysis of its components, than about making music as performers, composers, and improvisers. There may be times when a teacher understands that the wise decision is to develop from the students' knowledge of other musical expressions far from their experience rather than continue to build upon skills and knowledge they have already acquired. Teachers may find that a balanced curriculum might require a little of this and a little of that, such as studying both Western art music and the

Musical form ⟸⟹ **Musical context**

How much is music education about music's formal properties versus the cultural context in which the music is made?

Should teachers teach music for music's sake or music as cultural expression?

Great traditions ⟸⟹ **Little traditions**

Do teachers teach the internationally recognized Western art music in its notational form or the localized music of oral cultures?

Transmission ⟸⟹ **Transformation**

Should music with long artistic lineages comprise the curriculum, learned intact from artist-teachers, or should the music of the masses, including oral traditions and popular forms, be learned through the oral or literate means with which they are associated?

Continuity ⟸⟹ **Interaction**

Is a music teacher's aim to build instruction from students' previous experiences or to relate the curricula to situations they do not know but should?

Making music ⟸⟹ **Receiving music**

Should music education be about active music making through performance and creative composition and improvisation or listening and responding to the music?

Understanding ⟸⟹ **Pleasure**

Do teachers teach students to grasp the meaning of music or to know the sensory and emotional components of music?

Philosophy ⟸⟹ **Practice**

Is music education practice governed by theoretical notions or does practice shape theory?

Figure 2.1 • Jorgensen's dialectical view of music education.

music of local cultures (such as African-American gospel, Mexican mariachi, Jewish klezmer, or Puerto Rican salsa). There is more than one pathway to an effective musical education for young people, and the flexibility of teachers to move here and there may be critical.

At first glance, the domain of music education activity may at first appear to be exclusively K–12 schools. Jorgensen's perspective offers a more expansive view of the profession, one that encompasses music teaching and learning in schools and also other formal and informal venues. Her interest stretches from the teaching that happens in private lessons and community bands and choirs to the life-long process of enculturation by which people acquire their musical identity through the social influences in their environment. She looks at the ways music emerges for us: through family, religion, politics, commerce, and the music profession itself.

The Precious Presence of Music in Life

Music shows itself time and again as vital in society and in the progress of young people's education and development. It is part of the human condition to make music, to listen and make sense of music, and to respond to music in ways that range from laughter to tears. Many of the world's great musical minds, and a surprising cadre of notable figures outside the realm of the music profession, have claimed music's multiple benefits to themselves and others. They have advocated music for its moral, intellectual, emotional, social, sensual, spiritual, and physical factors. They have articulated music's meaningful place in the everyday life of all people and have found that the musical training and experience of young people enhance them in holistic ways. With the help of "teaching musicians" and "musical teachers," music can become an even more precious presence in the lives of children and youth.

Musicians on the brink of teaching careers do well to consider these perspectives as they forge a personal philosophy. All the dedicated music teaching in the world and the joyous music making by schooled children and youth are not quite enough for some school boards, principals, teachers, and taxpayers who are standing by, awaiting testimonials, persuasive logic, and clear-headed explanations for why music must be included in the curriculum. They who know about the outside-school music clubs, the community music activities, and the privatized (and often costly) lessons for some children need also to understand the critical import of providing music instruction in schools for all children. Young people of all circumstances might otherwise never know the wide-ranging benefits of music that a music teacher can help them learn.

The key to a personal philosophy may lie within the words on music offered by many great minds.

REFERENCES AND RESOURCES

Blacking, J. (1973). *How Musical Is Man?* Seattle: University of Washington Press. A classic work that articulates the role of music in society and culture; Blacking takes lessons from his fieldwork among the Venda of South Africa to launch his position that music is a universal human phenomenon.

Elliott, D. J. (1995). *Music Matters.* New York: Oxford University Press. A conceptualization of music education that examines its nature and value in performance and in listening experiences.

Jorgensen, E. (1997). *In Search of Music Education.* Urbana: University of Illinois Press. A philosophical vision and critical analysis of music in educational practice, with attention to a dialectical view of contemporary issues relative to repertoire and instructional process.

Jorgensen, E. (2003). *Transforming Music Education.* Bloomington: Indiana University Press. Following up on her earlier volume, Jorgensen seeks to resolve tensions of the repertoire and process of music education in classroom practice, negotiating compromise and creating alternatives for teachers and students in a wide variety of contemporary contexts.

Reimer, B. (2003). *A Philosophy of Music Education.* Upper Saddle River, NJ: Prentice Hall. A philosophical examination of precepts and principles of music in educational practice, with attention to music as meaningful expression of life experiences; this is the third (and updated) edition of the 1970 original.

Small, C. (1998). *Musicking: The Meanings of Performing and Listening.* Hanover, NH: University of New England Press. An examination of the social circumstances and networks affecting the performance, learning, and teaching of music in society.

Swanwick, K. (1988). *Music, Mind and Education.* New York: Routledge. Drawing on both musicology and psychology, this book offers a cross between philosophy and pedagogical theory to teachers who wish to explore the music curriculum for its attention to child and adolescent development and ways to integrate composing, performing, and analytical listening into lessons and programs.

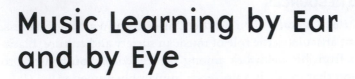

chapter 3

Music Learning by Ear and by Eye

Eighth-grade saxophone student: I keep getting turned around on this "A Train" piece. If I'm reading it right, it says one thing here in the notes, but it's just not the same on the CD.

Band teacher: That's because it's jazz. What's written is just a map, a main idea for where you-the-musician can go with it.

Sax student: So I don't have to read the notes? Awright! Any other music like that?

Teacher: Actually, even when you make your music tasty, you have to follow the rules. The notes are there to guide you. But most of the world's music isn't notated. Take African and Indian music, for example.

Sax student: I will. I gotta look into this: music without notes.

Teacher: You use what you've got—your eyes *and your ears*—to make music. As I always say, "Listen up," and you'll make your best progress.

Transmitting the Aural Art

Wherever in the world music is made, it is experienced aurally; it is learned wholly or partly by ear. Those who transmit or directly teach music to learners in various contexts are constantly modeling it, conveying orally and by demonstration what is then received aurally by learners. Skilled musicians, and nearly everyone else who has ever had a song to sing, engage daily in oral transmission, passing on the music they know. They transmit music by rote (and sometimes by note), and their students learn by ear (and sometimes by eye) melodies and rhythms of traditional, "folk," and popular music, and even much of the art music of the world's cultures. The sound of the music is sometimes captured in notation so that it can be preserved over time, particularly when it is complex. Still, as music is the supreme form of humanly made aural expression, a pan-human trait is to emphasize its sound rather than its printed form. Thus music transmission typically consists of performance by the musician, reception by the learner, and emulation of the model.

Just how music is learned and how it is directly taught by a designated teacher or casually acquired through a process of cultural osmosis depend on the underlying social structures of a society. What works in the Moscow Conservatory may not work in a high school in Manhattan or Memphis—not exactly, and yet there is overlap. Young boy choristers of King's College, England, learn their evensong repertoire through a choral sequence that is markedly different from the way young Zulu singers learn their South African township songs but there are shared principles in the practices. When music is transmitted and taught, and when it is acquired and learned, it is done so in ways that express the cultural priorities of teachers, learners, and the culture in which they live. These values of individuals and their cultures operate with certain cross-cultural "universals" of human learning, leading to evidence that young aspirant musicians learn by ear—or by eye, in families—or through a community system, through a demonstration-imitation process, or via sheet music and scores.

Music is sound, first and foremost, sound that is driven by the human need for expression. It is organized sound, personally and culturally meaningful sound, to those who create and re-create it, and to those who listen to it with understanding and can respond to it intellectually, emotionally, and physically. Music is a cultural symbol, a reflector of human values, interests, and needs, and like most cultural symbols, it is a learned behavior. As music is the primary aural form of artistic expression known to the world, it is no wonder that listening is central to music's transmission. There are other time-honored techniques that are fully integrated in the teaching and learning process, and yet the oral and aural strategies of giving and receiving "the sound of music" are prominent in countless contexts in which music transmission occurs.

Formal, Nonformal, and Natural Learning

Music can be learned in many ways, from the most formal means found in classrooms and studios to the least formal, seemingly happenstance and unintentional processes far beyond institutions. In fact, learning has three levels of teaching/transmission: (a) formal, occurring through a teacher's intervention in highly structured settings such as school; (b) nonformal and only partly guided, occurring outside institutionalized settings through the prompting of occasional and nonconsecutive directives, frequently by expert musicians to novices; and (c) enculturative, occurring naturally, nonconsciously, and without direct instruction of any sort. These levels involve both the giving and receiving of music, but their transfer and reception strategies vary.

The first realm of learning, formal, is most closely related to what happens in schools and in university settings. It is thoroughly linked to teachers, including their selection and presentation of music for learning and their rehearsal of students in explicit knowledge and skills to be learned. The second, nonformal, process may be a father's occasional coaching of his daughter in the bar chords on a guitar, or a neighbor's infrequent modeling for a youngster of repertoire and techniques at the piano. In the third realm, enculturative learning, the psychic structure of a societal group is passed from one generation to the next through a cultural immersion process, so that a child can develop an implicit understanding of the values of a musical piece or full repertoire by his or her membership and participation in that society. Language and communications, including self-identity, gender role, kinesthetics (body language), and daily rhythms, are *learned but not taught*; they are acquired in ways that are automatic and outside children's own conscious awareness. These cultural patterns have always been part of a people's lifestyle, and they permeate their thought, expression, and behavior. Enculturative learning happens, and it is often in place as a child enters school— even as it also continues "in spite of" schooling.

There are further differentiations in the three levels, too: apprenticeships and live-in private study with a teacher (as in the case of Indian gharanas of singers and sitarists), growth-oriented experiences occurring outside institutions that are arranged within a community (such as parent-organized play groups for preschoolers), and socialization, the process by which families share beliefs and values in learner- (rather than teacher-) constructed experiences (as in the case of children whose families sing a before-meal song of thanksgiving with words and melody that suit children's experiences. Yet regardless of the degree of formality, teachers and learners employ common strategies to enhance the transmission of musical ideas from sources to recipients. These strategies facilitate the flow of information along the oral-aural channel, including (a) the various symbolic notational systems that preserve music graphically, (b) the verbal and gestural means of conveying the music to be learned, (c) the technique of vocalization by way of sung melodic phrases (and chanted rhythmic patterns), and (d) solmization techniques—the *do-re-mi*s of solfege, numbers, letters, or any other devices used to deliver phrases and full pieces by expert musicians to novices.

Some music uses no notation whatsoever (as in the case of music in North India). Other musical cultures feature notation that is to be played precisely as written (the common practice of Western European art music), while still others utilize notes as frameworks for improvisatory expression (as in the case of jazz). Regarding the use of verbal and gestural techniques, some conductors fill their rehearsals with descriptive words to explain how they want the music to sound, while others allow their movements to convey much of what might otherwise be said. (There are ensembles in the world where the conductors are hardly differentiated from the performers, as with the gamelans of Indonesia where only the sound of the drum the leader plays at the center of the ensemble signals changes of tempo, dynamics, and sections.) Some teachers will use a solmization system of naming pitches in teaching a choral piece, while others prefer to talk analytically of a piece, play a recording of it, or just read it through.

✤ BREAK POINT 3.1 A Continuum of Learning

Give examples from your experience of the music you have learned through strictly formal, informal, and or enculturative means. How did the music suit the transmission and learning style? Who were the teachers/transmitters of these styles? Did you retain it well enough such that you can still play it or sing it? What strategies did you use to learn this music?

There is plenty of variance across the teaching and learning processes, and yet there is probably more to unite than to distinguish how music is typically transmitted—wherever it is transmitted. What could Gregorian chant, Native American song, and jazz possibly have in common, from an educational stance? The levels of formality of music's transmission and the strategies of those who transmit and teach it are aptly illustrated in a selection of historical and cultural contexts from various times and places.

Medieval Europe: Inside the Scholae Cantorum

Pope Gregory "the Great" (540–604) was notable as composer of a collection of chants known as Gregorian Chant. He established the Schola Cantorum in Rome in the sixth century as the place where his ecclesiastical chant could be taught and learned. In the developing years of Roman Catholicism this Roman school began a model of music education that was to spread to cathedrals and monasteries across medieval Europe. While the clergy had earlier performed the chants as well as other aspects of the liturgical service, the sung portions of the liturgy became brilliant with the advance of trained singers under Gregory's rule. The school's choirboys learned psalms and hymns and other standard musical components of the Ordinary and Proper of the Catholic mass. An official teacher, called the *prior scholar cantorum* or simply *cantor*, presented the music orally, singing to the young singers with expectations for their imitation. He would begin with semi-phrases and then gradually link and lengthen them until whole pieces were taught.

At Scholae Cantorum throughout Europe, the reading and writing of neumes and notes were taught as they were gradually developed. The early notations were as little as accent markings over the text to indicate a rise or fall in pitch or a syllable that should be emphasized. Later, texts were set at different heights in a box-like chart of rows and columns, and gradually a set of lines and spaces evolved. These visual graphics depicting the music were inspired by the need for a memory aid for the young singers, along with the desire to communicate liturgical music across the many miles of the Holy Roman Empire from its source in Rome to the modern-day nations of England, France, and Germany. Handwritten scores were delivered by messengers to numerous singing schools, and the singers learned the chants to sing in services in cathedrals and monasteries.

Choirmasters in Europe's medieval cathedrals needed an efficient way to train their young singers that would replace the time-consuming rote method of listening and imitation. Some of the graphic designs of early notation were fascinating to them as visual mazes but confusing in how they depicted the principal components of pitch and rhythm. Enter Guido d'Arezzo, an eleventh-century Benedictine monk, who created a system of solmization for his young choristers that has had staying power through the centuries. He selected a well-known

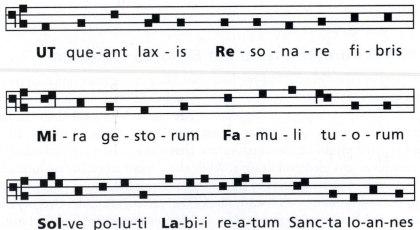

Figure 3.1 • "Ut Queant Laxis," hymn to St. John.

Figure 3.2 • **The Guidonian Hand: learning by ear, eye, and "feel."**

hymn to St. John, "Ut Queant Laxis," which could be used as the basis for learning Gregorian chant (Figure 3.1). He claimed that since the first syllable of the first six phrases of the chant began on a successively higher degree of the major scale from c to a (or *ut* for "Ut Queant Laxis"—which has been changed to *do—re* for "Resonare fibris," *mi* for "Mira gestorum," *fa* for "Famuli tuorum," *sol* for "Solve poluti," *la* for "Labii reatum Sancta Ioannes"), the syllables from the hymn could be associated with notes in any melody with one of these six pitches. Thus evolved a solmization system, called *solfege* or *solfeggio*, that is still used today in Europe and European-influenced cultures. A second lasting legacy of Guido's work was his use of parts of the hand as a tactile reference to pitches of a song or scale: pitches and their sung syllables were assigned to the various joints and tips of each finger. Singers were thus able to remember the rise and fall of the melodies they sang by touching their fingers (Figure 3.2).

Choir rehearsals in the Scholae Cantorum were typically scheduled for several days each week, although sections (sopranos or altos, for example) might meet on alternate days. The cantor often demonstrated the music by singing and using hand signals to represent the melodic pitches. Until the fifteenth century, there was no more than one "group sourcebook"—a single large-sized collection of notations set on a lectern for singers to share from a distance, or even just the one notated score brought to them by the messenger on horseback from a distant place such as the papacy in Rome. Thus, listening to the cantor's voice was critical to the choirboys in learning the music. As music became increasingly complex, notation was developed that could flesh out the multiple lines of polyphonic song. Yet organum, discants, and motets were commonly learned for their basic shape and then improvised on, keeping the music fresh, innovative, and with an element of surprise.

⁙ BREAK POINT 3.2 Solfege Survival

> Consider the practice of sight-singing and song learning in vocal and choral settings. What components of the scholae cantorum are still in practice today? How have some solfege techniques continued for so many centuries? Have they undergone any modifications?

Japan: Time-honored Music Learning

In the imperial palace of Japan as early as the seventh century, an ensemble of instruments known as *gagaku* (translated as "elegant" or "refined" music) was assembled to perform for the emperor and his family, guests, and international dignitaries. Percussion, string, and wind instruments of mostly Chinese origin but with influences from Korea and India were adapted to suit Japanese taste. The gagaku included drums (*da-daiko*), zithers (wagon, and an ancestor of the *koto*), a lute (*biwa*), double-reed oboe (*hichiriki*), mouth organ (*sho*), and several transverse flutes (for example, the *ryuteki*). Japanese monks, returning from studies in China, brought back the instruments and music, and over several centuries the repertoire was transformed and even composed anew to meet Japanese ideals of beautiful sound and ritual. By the tenth century, the gagaku sound and performance style were solidified and have survived to this day. Contemporary gagaku court musicians proudly trace their teacher-to-pupil lineage back many generations and strive for a purely preserved performance tradition that is learned aurally from the masters. While the gagaku sound has no doubt changed, it retains the essence of its ancient aesthetic roots.

Many of the instruments of the gagaku have carved distinctive niches of their own, along with their continuing use in the ensemble. Such is certainly the case with the biwa, koto, shakuhachi, and *shamisen* (plucked lute). These niches are perpetuated by a system of teaching and learning guilds, which are created and led by an expert musician who then draws students to him (or her) to learn

particular techniques and performance styles that distinguish them from musicians in other guilds. The student gives the utmost respect to the teacher: he or
she belongs to the guild, does not perform with those from other guilds, does not
ask excessive—if any—questions (as this is considered impolite), and awaits the
teacher's decision on whether and when it is appropriate to perform in public.
The guilds are a formal learning system that is traditional and continuing still.

The traditional style of teaching Japanese musical instruments is characterized by ritualistic structures such as the sequence of bows and verbal expressions at the start and close of every lesson. Notation is optional (see Figure 3.3).

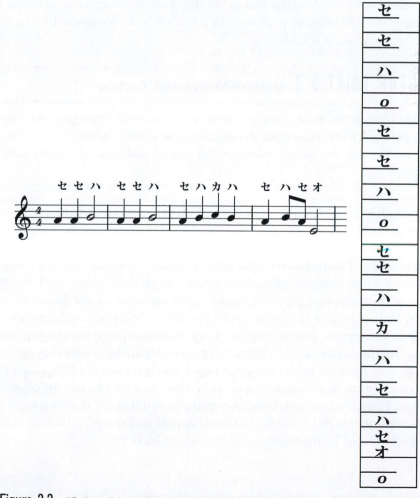

Figure 3.3 • "Sakura" in vertical Japanese notation, with Western staff
notation and cipher symbols for the thirteen-string koto.

Verbal explanations in koto and shakuhachi lessons are rare, as teaching and learning is considered intuitive and focused on the musical sound rather than on talking about it. Demonstration and the physical interaction of teacher and student in the clarification of finger and arm positions are common strategies. Rote teaching is standard practice, as teachers will not only play the instrument with expectations for students' imitation but may also sing the melody utilizing a solfege technique. A cipher system of number-notation is available, but it is typically intended for use outside the lesson to remind the student of the melodic and rhythmic material that was presented during the lesson. Reading and writing is unusual in the lesson, as the student is expected to focus on absorbing the subtleties of performance etiquette and expression by listening closely to the musical sound.

✦ BREAK POINT 3.3 Verbal–Nonverbal Tactics

Make a list of the most effective verbal and nonverbal strategies used by teachers you know. How does the situation—the musical genre, the teacher, the performers, the venue—influence the use of particular strategies over others?

Although Japanese lessons on traditional instruments are individual, they are seldom private, for it is expected that students will come early and watch, listen, and learn from observations of other students. This observational approach also stimulates a competitive spirit among students—which has the effect of motivating those students who observe well. An essential element of the performance of traditional Japanese music is the aesthetic of the beautiful performer, and so posture and position are frequently addressed and consistently modeled. The specific positions of the body in relation to the instrument and even the manner of fixing one's gaze on the audience are behaviors that are carefully stressed from the initial lessons forward. Instrumental study in Japan typically commences in childhood, and while there is a steady stream of young people in piano and violin lessons, a significant number are drawn also to the traditional instruments both for the sonic appeal and the performance rituals that are embraced by the teacher and the culture at large.

West Africa: Family and Nonformal Learning

Music plays an all-encompassing role in the lives of people of West African societies. The Akan, Asanti, and Ewe of Ghana, the Yoruba of Nigeria, the Kpelle of

Liberia, and the Wolofs of Senegal are among the groups who naturally enculturate their children into social worlds in which music plays a high-profile role in their daily lives. Children sing, dance, and play from their earliest childhoods. Strapped to their mothers' backs, children learn from infancy the rhythms and tunes of their culture. They continue as infants and toddlers in a cultural practice of listening and feeling the rhythmic movement and sound vibrations of their mothers at work, walking, talking, chopping, stirring, stamping, singing. They come under the watchful eye of older siblings and neighbor children, who teach them songs, stories, and games through which they may learn useful life skills and initial understandings of their cultural roles.

The combination of informed listening with mimesis, or learning through imitation, is a powerful one in the transmission process. This is the way young people learn stories and riddles, songs and dances, often interspersing spoken and sung interludes in their stories, interjecting their spontaneous exclamations, and dancing as it suits the story and the song. Children learn singing games at play with their peers in this manner, as they also learn their church hymns, the rhythms of the drumming ensembles, and the grooves of popular music such as *juju* and *Mande-pop*. The call-and-response melodies and rhythms of ensembles of xylophones, drums, flutes, horns, harps, and lutes surround them in their

Playing by ear on the xylophones of Africa.

growing years, so that calling and responding comes easily to them as they sing and play familiar and spontaneously created songs. Children learn the timing and turn-taking of the call and the response, even so far as to understand the importance of an equal balance in some genres between the length of the call phrase and the response phrase.

For those young people who are taken in by the sound of an instrument and who wish to learn it well, there are pathways to follow that involve informal and enculturative processes. Drummers in West African societies, from the Akan to the Yoruba, tend to learn drumming early, with the critical period of developing their drumming talent falling between the ages of two and ten years. Children are immersed in the sounds of drums and drummers from infancy. With drums in the home and yard, babies may grab them to steady themselves when learning to walk, or might be offered a turn on the drum to appease and reward them. Young players watch and then imitate the adult drummers, sometimes playing on empty cans and plastic containers when they are just three and four years old. Since they are brought to adult gatherings that feature music, children hear characteristic rhythms and complicated phrases and may chant them and dance to them. They then apply the music to their toy drums the next morning, sometimes alone or together in small groups. If a child growing up in a West African society is observed to be particularly talented, he is taken under the wing of a male relative and trained until he is sufficiently skilled to contribute his minor part in a public festival.

❖ BREAK POINT 3.4 Family Music

> Family life is important for instilling the musical repertoire, skills, and values in young people. Reflect on your own family music experiences and how parents, siblings, grandparents, a favorite uncle, or a family friend helped to get you where you are. What can teachers do to connect to the musical interests of their students' families, so as to make music at school relevant and a development of music at home?

Ireland: Heritage Music at Home and in Competition

The sung ballads of Ireland and the Irish jigs, hornpipes, and reels played on flutes and fiddles have long been learned by ear. Like many European folk traditions, the music transmission and learning process in Ireland is largely a social one. Rank beginners and accomplished musicians alike have continued a traditional give-and-take process through the group session and in personalized lessons with an expert musician. Experienced elders act as musical role models, offering young and less-experienced singers and players the musical repertoire and the stylistic nuances and techniques of performance.

In the family music making in traditional Ireland, children grow up with members who have for decades fiddled, played flute, pipes, harp, or concertina, or sung sean-nos style. Children attend celebrations of weddings, christenings, holidays, and family reunions at which music and dance are prominent. They may also attend wakes, when the memory of the deceased is honored in the family home and tribute is paid through song and sessions lasting long into the

Harp and fiddle for Irish heritage music.

night and over several days. Like the air they breathe, music surrounds the children of professional and amateur musicians in Ireland, and the melodies become a part of their natural sonic fabric. In the changing scene of a contemporary Ireland, adults and children, including those with no family history in musical practice, are finding music to be an important component of their Irish identity.

Just as it is natural for them to listen, children living in an environment where Irish traditional music is actively performed also "pick up" instruments to play. Pennywhistles are sometimes played by children as an entry-point to instrumental music. Some pick up the fiddle, or transfer tunes from pennywhistle to the Irish flute or concertina. Years of listening to the elders have taught them repertoire and a sense of style so that their performance can advance more rapidly than if they had not absorbed the music. Children may graduate into lessons with more expert players and of course continue to learn as they play in ensembles.

⬥ BREAK POINT 3.5 Picking It Up

What music have you picked up by simply living in the environment, listening, and learning? Can you sing or play any of this music now? Or do you simply enjoy it because of the circumstances in which you heard it sung or played? Who "taught" you this music? Are you aware of any strategies you used to learn and remember this music? Discuss how young people continue the natural process of picking up music today, and how that relates to the music they learn at school.

One of the strongest contemporary supports for continuing traditional music outside school and for training Irish children and youth in their cultural music is the organization known as Comhaltas Ceoltoiri Eireann (or just Comhaltas). Established in 1951, the organization promotes Irish traditional music, dance, and language nationally and abroad by motivating the young to learn these traditions. The competitions include all major traditional instruments, "lilting" (singing vocables to the dance tunes), and Irish and English singing; they are divided into age levels for children under twelve years, youth from twelve to fifteen, from fifteen to eighteen, and over eighteen. The Comhaltas branches are responsible for organizing the community schools, arranging sessions, teaching the music, and preparing the young musicians for competitions. Training in the schools tends to be a mixture of oral and literate means of teaching the repertoire in sequential and structured group lessons, where notation, verbal and gestural techniques, and vocalization of tunes are the standard practice. The songs and tunes are selected by Comhaltas, so both the musical content and its means of transmission are in the hands of the organization to preserve or modify.

First Nations: Music as Indigenous Knowledge

Among the people of the First Nations, or Native Americans, of North America (including Canada and the United States), music is a communal event as well as a deeply personal phenomenon. Its transmission may be a matter of one's age, gender, and rank within a community, or it may be a result of a personal journey that leads to spiritual inspiration. Music is deeply embedded in the ritual and social customs of the clan or tribe, in coming-of-age ceremonies, and in coming-to-terms with the supernatural, the ancestral spirits, and the spirits of nature and of living creatures. Some songs are group-owned and intended for all to know; others are considered personal property, to be sung only by those whose songs they are or by permission given for their use. For many people of the First Nations, song is the equivalent of the Bible in the moral lessons it holds, and those without knowledge of song are considered "poor," uneducated, or lacking an important piece of who they are.

Music is a part of the personal and social identities of children growing up in Native American communities. Music is a way of recounting history, predicting the future, passing on local wisdom, reflecting on meaningful places and contexts, and clarifying one's role within a nation and a clan. Modern indigenous music and dance has emerged even as older layers are continued, so that a group of unaccompanied singers and dancers can still hold its own even as wired rock and country music bands perform their own blend of contemporary and indigenous expressions. Intertribal celebrations are raising new issues of ownership, borrowing, and sharing, as songs cross groups and become fused with different cultural expressions. Meanwhile, young people are often caught in

Indigenous knowledge is embedded in song, just as it is also communicated in artistic objects like this wood carving of a killer whale, salmon, eagle, and sea monster created by a member of Kwakwa'wa'kwa Nation (British Columbia).

the middle of the contemporary cultural revitalization that is occurring, trying to make sense of older layers of culture, including music, in their changing world.

Families are responsible for teaching songs and dances to family members to perpetuate the traditions. The Spokane and Coeur d'Alene tribes of the interior of the American Northwest assert the primary place of song in their development as children. They remember it as the sound they awakened to, and to which they would go to sleep, when mothers, fathers, grandparents, and other family members sang alone and together. From birth to death, songs mark points through the day and through their lives, from the morning song, the song for the birth of a child, of becoming a man or woman, of being in love, for marriage, for sickness and death. There are welcoming songs, songs for learning dances, for being a warrior, and for battle itself. Such song genres and these ways of their transmission are continuing among the Lakota Sioux of the Dakotas, the Navajo of the southwestern United States, and the Tlingit of the Alaskan panhandle.

The traditional music continues despite an attempt in the nineteenth century to "civilize" the children of First Nations communities. Indigenous people in Canada and the United States were banned from practicing their Native rituals, holding religious celebrations, and having extended family gatherings; children and youth were sent to boarding schools where traditional practices, including heritage songs and dances, were replaced by the curricular content of mainstream schools. By the 1890s, these schools were mandatory for all Native children; here they were subjected to studies that were alien to their tribal life, and they were clothed in uniforms. Their hair was cut short; they were housed in barracks-style halls and fed foods that were foreign to them. Many schools were run like military academies, and wind and brass bands similar to those found in the military were established. These actions were intended to assimilate Native American children into the mainstream of the majority society and to focus attention away from the culture they would have known at home. Yet in summer, when school was out and the children were back at home, the traditions, including the music, were again part of their lives. They serenaded one another, sang and danced with their families, and (depending on the particular tribe) found drums to beat, rattles to shake, and flutes to play. People of the First Nations survived the boarding schools, and gradually the government-sponsored schools closed and children were returned to their families to be educated in their local schools, where the curriculum today includes Native American cultural studies and celebrations of music and dance along with standard public school fare.

❖ BREAK POINT 3.6 Music as Culture

> Discuss the ways that cultural understanding can develop through musical experience and study. What might students learn through music? How can teachers facilitate learning of the broader concepts of a culture or a historical event through music lessons and classes?

Jazz: Taught and Not Taught

Mention jazz and thoughts of improvisation immediately come to mind, for the two are often regarded as synonymous. The genius of jazz is in its spontaneity, and yet the century or so of its evolution boasts a heritage, a common set of performance techniques, a canon of standards, and a transmission system of strategies that cross both formal and informal avenues of its learning. Jazz is

Jazz students in rehearsal.

generally regarded as an aural process, and yet the "tunes," "heads," or melodies are written. Ideas for jazz improvisation are derived from these notated melodies, so that improvisatory music in fact arises from these sketches or skeletal frames. Transcriptions are available of the improvisations of jazz masters, too, from Louis Armstrong to Arturo Sandoval, and these are read, studied, and played. Yet aural inspiration typically takes precedence over the written note, giving jazz its characteristic quality of free expression. One thing is certain: ideas for jazz improvisation do not come out of thin air, for beyond the seeming "magic" is a learning experience that is steeped in the nuts and bolts of the music.

The pathway to jazz performance may involve formal or informal transmission and learning, or both. Old-time jazz was truly "ear music," evolving from oral traditions, and yet by the time of Fletcher Henderson and Duke Ellington, jazz musicians were often musically literate. Some of the top training programs in jazz today are associated with universities and conservatories, where the complexities of jazz are learned through established courses in jazz performance, theory, and history. The strategies employed in both the traditional transmission practices and in the highly structured programs of contemporary institutions run the course of the oral/aural and literate spectrum; they entail the use by expert musicians and teachers of words and gestures, the vocalization of instrumental melodies, and a solmization of scat syllables that have developed into a language all their own. Jazz musicians "then and now" are in agreement that ear-training and observation are critical requirements of skill acquisition, and that technical and artistic skills take plenty of time and some sort of training, whether through formal lessons or informal sessions, along with a commitment to practice.

For young instrumentalists who would rather play than sing, vocalization is a time-honored technique. Louis Armstrong learned to play the trumpet by ear, but not before he was already singing. He strongly adhered to the adage, "If you can't sing it, you can't play it." The voice is prominent in jam sessions, in rehearsals, and in any circumstances where jazz musicians gather to share their music and work toward an ensemble sound. Syllables like "ba-do-ba-do-dah" and "dwee-dat" are attached to the riffs to be learned, as in "Let's make it sound like this" followed by the singing of the scat syllables. Players put down their horns to make a point by singing the phrase, and the voice then breaks through the sound of brass and wind instruments to emphatically state what the musical sound should be. This combination of vocalization with solmization is consistent not only in jam sessions but also in the director-player discourse of jazz ensembles in secondary schools and universities. While the director will throw out to students some verbal feedback as to their sound quality and ideas, he or she will sing phrases to identify them and to demonstrate what they might sound like.

❖ BREAK POINT 3.7 Singing, Playing, Moving

Discuss how singing what students might be expected to play on instruments can aid the development of student musicianship. As an extension, are there benefits to moving (clapping, tapping, etc.) what will eventually be sung (or played)? Is this an approach that is exclusive to jazz, or can it be applied to learning other musical styles?

Jazz improvisations tend to bear the marks of other jazz musicians, as the musician is always listening: to recordings, to the director, to students with whom he plays. While young jazzers new to the style may play precisely what they can read, have heard, or have worked out as their own, for professional jazz musicians, there is a constant modification and adaptation of a previously learned stock of melodic and rhythmic ideas in the moment of the jazz performance itself. The goal is for the performer to "blow himself out," thereby ridding himself of ideas close to the surface of his memory so that the real expression can begin. It is at that moment, after years of serious study, that the truly personal statements of jazz are communicated.

Cross-cultural Pathways to Music Learning

As music is a human phenomenon, it is also a learned behavior. People are to an extent similarly "wired," and some of the ways they perceive and grow to know music are evident across cultures. Teachers are concerned primarily with the similarities of the music learning process, regardless of its content and the context of its learning, and it is worthwhile to look across cultures to the ways musicians are enculturated, trained, and educated. Figure 3.4 provides a sketch for thinking about the features operating in the six cultures and genres described in this chapter. Many of these have broad application.

	Cantorum	Japan	Africa	Ireland	America	Jazz
Formal Teaching-Learning	✤	✤				✤
Informal Teaching-Learning			✤	✤		✤
Enculturation			✤	✤	✤	
Aural Techniques (Orality)	✤	✤	✤	✤	✤	✤
Note-Reading (Literacy)	✤					✤
Improvisation (All/Part)			✤	✤		✤
Solmization (Sung Pitch System) (Sung Rhythm System)	✤	✤ ✤	✤			✤
Vocalization (Players Singing)		✤	✤	✤		✤
Teacher Demonstration	✤	✤	✤	✤	✤	✤
Student Imitation	✤	✤	✤	✤	✤	✤
Verbal/Nonverbal Emphasis	V	N	N	N	N	V/N

Figure 3.4 • **Shared features of music transmission and learning.**

Adults have much to offer young people in musical knowledge and skills, yet children and adolescents deserve the support and freedom to evolve beyond the direct influence of well-intentioned adults. With an open and receptive approach to music transmission—how it is taught, modeled, and enculturated—teaching and learning may well be enhanced by taking the best of the transmission techniques from all cultures and applying them.

REFERENCES AND RESOURCES

Agawu, K. (1995). *African Rhythm: A Northern Ewe Perspective*. New York: Cambridge University Press. A construction of the soundscape of the Ewe of Ghana, with attention to the interplay of rhythm in life, language, song, drumming, dancing, storytelling, and folk narration.

Berliner, P. E. (1994). *Thinking in Jazz: The Infinite Art of Improvisation*. Chicago: University of Chicago Press. Examination of the process by which jazz instrumentalists learn their performance art through listening to and emulation of the masters.

Campbell, P. S. (1991). *Lessons from the World*. New York: Schirmer Books. A cross-cultural guide to music learning and teaching in varied historical and cultural contexts, with classroom applications of principal features of the oral-aural process to the development of creative musical expression.

Hast, D., and S. Scott. (2005). *Music in Ireland*. New York: Oxford University Press. An introduction to Irish traditional music, including song, instrumental music, and dance, and how the music is transmitted and brought into the global marketplace.

Malm, W. P. (1959). *Japanese Music and Musical Instruments*. Rutland, VT: Charles E. Tuttle. A path-breaking and colorful "coffee-table" book of Japanese instrumental and theater music forms (including noh, kabuki, and bunraku), with considerable attention to the role of notation and orality in the transmission systems of lessons and ensemble rehearsals.

McCarthy, M. (1999). *Passing It On: The Transmission of Music in Oral Culture*. Cork: Cork University Press. A historical chronicle of formal, nonformal, and informal transmission of Irish heritage music in Ireland, with emphasis on music in schools and far beyond them.

Smyth, W., and E. Ryan. (1999). *Spirit of the First People*. Seattle: University of Washington Press. A book and CD that document Native American sacred traditions of song and dance, based on personal narratives of tribal elders who recount the circumstances of their acquisition of the music.

Stone, R. (2004). *Music in West Africa*. New York: Oxford University Press. A case study of performance of the Kpelle people of Liberia, West Africa, with consideration of the creative means by which musicians develop ways to fit small parts together and layer them into full-fledged musical events.

Wade, B. C. (2005). *Music in Japan*. New York: Oxford University Press. A study of Japanese traditional music, its interface with Western art music, and the rise of Japan's popular music industry, including glimpses of traditional training and transmission.

Waterman, C. A. (1990). *Juju: A Social History and Ethnography of an African Popular Music*. Chicago: University of Chicago Press. Detailed account of the social significance of juju music of Nigeria, with discussion of contexts, social organization, aesthetics, and symbolism of the genre.

chapter 4

Systems and Standards of Music Education

Teacher A: When I was on that international tour with my choir last summer, I sat in on some of the rehearsals of the host school. Ouch!

Teacher B: I hear you. I can't believe how far behind they are in schools outside the United States. Their senior choir was doing the level of music we did with my ninth-grade group.

Teacher A: Yeah. I checked in on the band class, and it's pretty basic repertoire they're doing. I mean, we are light years ahead of them.

Teacher C: I guess you didn't sit in on their composition class?

Teacher A: They teach composition?

Teacher C: They have four levels of comp class, and the top students are taking national and international prizes. Their works would rival some of what the pros do.

Teacher B: So we're talking priorities. And ours are not theirs?

Teacher A: Thankfully, our programs are about performance excellence.

Teacher C: At the risk of letting everything else slide?

Logical and Localized Systems

It is a human tendency—and a transnational trait among teachers—to make comparisons. Musicians and teachers live in a global village where comparisons across cultures and nations are a natural outgrowth of their international connections. As they travel and trade ideas about music, teaching, learning, and living, they do make comparisons. It may sometimes appear to them that the system with which they are most familiar is *the universal way*—the only way—for musically educating children and youth, when in fact the curricular aims, materials, and methods have been developed to fit the social and cultural contexts within which they work. The societal philosophy and principles of a nation, region (state or province), and local community direct the course of educational design and delivery, and the efforts within a classroom, school, and school district reflect explicit and implicit values of the society to which the schools belong. What works for "us" may not work for "them." Of course, an obvious question is this: Just what *does* work for us within the realm of music teaching and learning in school programs for children and youth? And what components of other approaches to music teaching and learning, in other nations, could be successfully applied to enliven, enrich, and extend the musical education of students in our own system?

In comparisons of international school music scenes, further questions demand attention. At home and abroad, what similar and differentiated goals are there in elementary and secondary schools, in instrumental and vocal/choral settings, in various large and small communities, and in urban, suburban, and rural settings? What emphasis is given to performing, listening, movement/dance, and creative expression? What national standards are maintained and upheld, for the various age and grade levels—or is music a very local and decentralized concern? What expectations do communities have of their music teachers, and how are these teachers prepared to take on the responsibility of musically educating students enrolled in school programs? Where does popular music, music of indigenous peoples, and music of the world's cultures fit? Teachers must know their own systems and standards, but they can also be enlightened, refreshed, and inspired by knowing approaches and practices to music making and teaching beyond their own perspective. Knowledge of other

A classroom bulletin board: singing, listening, dancing, creating, playing instruments around the world.

national systems can guide the crafting of best practices for nurturing the musical development of young people. Through examination of the school music practices and policies of a variety of nations, from China to South Africa and then home again, teachers can learn more about avenues and options for adaptation and use in the familiar system of music education. Break points follow descriptions of national systems and are intended to call up components of the most familiar system (the home system) for comparison with the less familiar system (the distant system).

✣ BREAK POINT 4.1 Familiar Territory

Within your familiar "music education territory," what do you know about the national policy for music in elementary and secondary schools? Are there national standards, or laws in effect, that regulate the place of music and the arts in the curriculum? Are there even tests intended to uphold those standards? Discuss the strengths of the national policy of music in schools, and project the possibilities for ways to strengthen music's curricular position.

This chapter examines the music education systems of eleven nations. The countries vary in population and size, economic development and activity, government ideology, and philosophical systems. They are scattered across the globe, with three in Europe (France, Hungary, and the United Kingdom), two in Asia (China, Japan) and in South America (Argentina, Brazil), one in Africa (South Africa), two in North America (Canada and the United States), and one in the Pacific region (Australia). Some have long considered music as critical to in-school education, while others applaud and nurture the informal processes of music learning that exist outside schools (sometimes to the point of wondering whether music needs to be taught in the school curriculum, since it is already so widespread). The preservation of traditional music may be central to some national systems of education whereas Western classical music is the prominent feature in others. An emphasis may be given to one or several of four domains: performance, listening, creativity, and musical knowledge (history/theory/culture). The meaning of music to a nation and its culture(s) may well influence its curricular emphasis as well as the pedagogical approaches to teach it, so that some countries may value specifically musical aims (performance and aural skills, for example), while others may see the value of music as part of a child's personal development, or as a reflection of the sociocultural principles by which the nation stands.

These international sketches describe different but equally logical means of musically educating young people. In making comparisons, teachers can see what is constant across national systems, why there is variance, what works well (and what does not operate at all) under the wide music education umbrella, and what principles and techniques might have application at home.

Argentina

Music education in the southern South American nation of Argentina began with "Law 1420." Passed by the national parliament in 1884, this law decreed that music—particularly singing—was to be a mandatory subject in the primary (elementary) schools, and thus classroom teachers would themselves be trained in singing so they could teach children. Music education in Argentina was already established during the seventeenth and eighteenth centuries in the Jesuit missions, where Indians and *mestizos* performed in choirs and small orchestras, and religious services and processions mixed Indian and European expressions. The Catholic services in the cathedrals and churches were also centers for artistic and cultural life, where young people learned to perform Gregorian chant and polyphonic song. Following the expulsion of the Jesuits, when an independent *Republica Argentina* was declared, opera flourished with spectacular performances at the Teatro Colon in Buenos Aires. When the Conservatory of Music of Buenos Aires was founded in 1893, music education in Argentina was well established for those who aspired to be professional performers as well as for those who were taught music in schools as part of their collective knowledge.

The National Ministry of Education regulates the music education system throughout the twenty-three states of Argentina. National, provincial, and municipal taxes provide a free education for young people in primary and secondary schools, and for those who progress to the conservatories. Financial support for equipment and resources has been difficult to come by, however, since the 1950s, although a national law (24.195) offers support for not only the implementation of new requirements but also the means to achieve them. The ministry issued aims for music education several decades ago that are still maintained today: to develop the skills, capabilities, and habits of students to participate as singers, performers, readers, listeners, and creators of music. There is also interest in developing students' capacities to discern the relationship between music, literature, and the arts, and in increasing students' knowledge of Argentinian music and musicians.

Teachers have considerable freedom in planning the curriculum for their students in every subject. Today there is no required musical study, nor is music treated as an elective course in most secondary schools of Argentina. In the primary schools, singing remains a prominent goal, with all children singing together with their classroom teachers. Music specialist teachers at some schools form select choirs, provide ear-training and sight-reading exercises, and may teach skills in instrumental performance as well. Recorders and guitars are used in class instruction, both for musicianship exercises (such as developing music literacy skills) and for preparing children to perform for their parents. Children learn music appreciation through recordings, radio and TV broadcasts, and live concerts. Eurhythmics, the practice of learning music by responding through bodily movement to concepts such as rhythm, melody, and form, has been important in the primary grades since at least the 1950s. The pedagogical approaches of Carl Orff, Murray Schafer, Maurice Martenot, Edgar Willems, and Zoltán Kodály have also inspired the teaching of music specialist teachers. Preschool and kindergarten music is seen as vital to young children's development, and instruction typically features singing, movement, and listening experiences.

There is growing interest among teachers in exposing children to the music of contemporary composers, particularly those living in Argentina, and the folk songs and instrumental music traditions of Argentinians, including the indigenous peoples, the Spanish, Italian, and Jewish communities, and other immigrant groups who have contributed to the multicultural society of the nation. Creativity is another developing area of classroom practice, with small-group and individual compositions facilitated by teachers. Leading Argentinian music educators have contributed much to teacher education in music in conservatories and universities, including Rudolfo Zubrisky and Ana Lucia Frega, both of whom were influential leaders in the International Society for Music Education.

❖ BREAK POINT 4.2 In Study of Composers

> If you, your teaching colleagues, or local standards determined that the study of contemporary national composers was an important goal of music education, how would you proceed? Discuss prominent composers and particular works as well as how teaching and learning would proceed.

Australia

Australia has a strong history of music and arts teaching across its nine education authorities or districts. There is national unity on the importance of fostering the self-expression of children and youth through music education experiences that are holistic and grounded in creativity. In 1994, the Australian

Curriculum corporation published *A Statement on the Arts for Australian Schools* and *The Arts—A Curriculum Profile for Australian Schools*. Particular thrusts of these statements were that music could contribute to the children's aesthetic development through sequential instruction in performance activities, musicological analysis, and aural skill development.

Within their curricular policies and directives, music teachers in Australia are free to choose repertoire for performance and study, pedagogical methods and techniques, and types of assessment. Music is required through school years seven or eight, and it is assumed that all schools will make music available to children across the thirteen years of schooling. The arts (music, dance, drama, visual arts, and media) are collectively a Key Learning Area within the curriculum. In the primary grades (equivalent to the K–6 grades of elementary school in North America), a general music education is integrated in the curriculum so that music is often combined with lessons in language arts, social studies, and physical education. Secondary school music study is more directly focused on ensemble performance, creative composition, aural/listening skills, and musical analysis. A strong band movement is in place in secondary schools, and various instrumental solo and ensemble competitions are held at the state and national levels. Orchestras are rarely found in secondary schools, but choirs are common both in school and in the community.

At the primary level, music instruction has evolved through three stages since the 1950s, from music appreciation, to performance-based learning via Orff and Kodály instructional approaches, to student composition. The current view on composition focuses on musical understanding rather than a final product. Music specialist teachers direct student composers toward musical understanding by manipulation of musical elements and structures, particularly at the secondary level. In composition activities, students may imitate a model, provide new accompaniments to familiar pieces, or work preexisting material into new expressions.

❖ BREAK POINT 4.3 Process and Product

Devise a project that enables students of a particular level (elementary, middle, or high school) to explore a musical concept through creative composition. Choose musical features or elements to which all students must adhere (for example, 3/4 meter, Dorian scale, AB form, 16 measures). Parameters like these can guide students in a compositional experience that mixes specific structures with freedom of expression.

An awareness of the multiculturalism of Australia's population has led to the inclusion of a broader repertoire as a source of illustrating musical concepts. Music syllabi in several states differentiate between world music cultures and "Australian music from diverse cultural backgrounds"—for example, Greek or Vietnamese music—that have been brought to Australia, taken root, and undergone transformation. Students have practical experiences in these musics—from singing and dancing the music to instrumental performance—and learn cultural analysis of such music as the Balinese gamelan. (After all, Bali is just north of Australia.) The study of Aboriginal and Torres Strait Islander music is important to Australian music education, and developments are in progress for understanding the connections between the music and the musicians who express and own it. Developments in teacher education are expected to increase access to materials and community resources, including singers, dancers, and artists, so that this music can be brought more fully into the curriculum.

Generalist, all-subject classroom teachers are often charged with teaching music in Australia's primary grades, although private schools may employ specialist music teachers. Secondary schools have specialist music teachers almost exclusively, as the musical study is more rigorous and demands a teacher's comprehensive and extensive musicianship. Music specialist teachers are trained in programs leading to a four-year undergraduate degree or postgraduate teaching certification.

Brazil

In the Federative Republic of Brazil, a nation that covers almost half the land area of South America, music has been a prominent fixture in society throughout its documented history. It is a valued school subject, and yet the availability of rich informal and outside-school musical activities prompts some policy makers to question the necessity of keeping music in the curriculum. With these opposing views, there is not a united position on music in schools, and there is an absence of continuity across time. As elsewhere in South America, the Jesuits educated indigenous peoples and millions of African slaves in the Portuguese language, the moral code of Roman Catholicism, and skills in the performance of European music. Opera houses appeared in Brazil as early as the seventeenth century, and community choirs and orchestras flourished, especially for performances in churches. With the proclamation of the Republic in 1822, music education was no longer in the hands of the Jesuits even though European music and music education practices became enmeshed in the country. The Music Conservatory of Rio de Janeiro was established in 1847 as Brazil's earliest attempt to establish music as a profession.

Nearly a century later, in 1932, composer Hector Villa-Lobos implemented a singing movement in Sao Paolo through teacher-training programs and mass concerts for children, and the quest for music education spread throughout Brazil. This movement, sponsored by the Superintendency of Musical Artistic Education, stipulated that music be required in the school curriculum and that it involve the study of (and experience with) Brazilian artists and composers. With the departure of Villa-Lobos from this government-sponsored council in the 1950s, music fell away from the curriculum. The methods of Dalcroze, Orff, Kodály, and Willems were brought into specialized schools about this time. John Dewey's liberal view of child-centered education and Brazilian Paulo Freire's stance on the "pedagogy of the oppressed" were influential in the design and delivery of music in those schools that could hire specialist teachers. Freire's work was important to the Brazilian belief in a cultural democracy, especially in the 1970s and 1980s, where the individual experiences of students were woven into strategies to help them understand real-life problems. Thus, their knowledge of popular music (*bossa nova, baiao, Tropicalia*) was honored in schools and many youth organizations.

Music does not often hold its own as a curricular subject in Brazilian schools today, although it is very much in evidence in the festive celebrations and special events of school calendars and agendas. New educational guidelines were introduced by law in 1996 and included the recommendation that music be taught within school programs, and there is a consensus that, at the very least, music is important in schools for nonmusical purposes. Where school music does occur, it is more likely in the primary schools where weekly thirty- to forty-five-minute lessons are offered in singing, rhythmic activities, and experimenting with vocal and instrumental sounds. Musical study at the secondary level is seldom an option. The presence of music in the community—*samba* (and samba schools), *capoeira* (a choreographic style of martial art that is accompanied by the one-string *berimbau*), *carnival* music, and music for worship and ritual—is currently the most effective means of engaging Brazilian children and youth.

❖ BREAK POINT 4.4 Youth Music

Investigate the music that draws young people in your community. Build a case for its presence in the school music curriculum, or argue against it. In either case, seek out the incidence of popular music in the lives of adolescents and provide support for your argument for the presence or absence of youth music in the school program.

Music teachers are trained in either a general arts or music education course or in a course that mixes performance, composition, and conducting. The general arts course is geared more extensively to education and pedagogy, but with less depth of musical knowledge and skill development; the latter emphasizes musical training but with little pedagogical instruction in working with young people in introductory and general music classes. The Music Specialists Committee of Brazil's Ministry of Education has produced documents for raising the quality of university music courses, with the aim of influencing the preparation of music teachers that might in turn lead to the musical education of children and youth in schools.

China

From ancient times and into the twentieth century, the Chinese viewed music as a means of knowing morality, beauty, and goodness. The Confucian ideal of virtuous living was believed to be attained through learning music, which could cultivate honesty, love, and filial piety. Enormous political and social changes came to China through the ruling Communist Party in the mid-twentieth century; the value of music in an educational system geared toward socialist principles is stated in the State Education Commission report of 1994: "to nourish pupils' love of country, work, science, socialism and unity," "to cultivate pupils' wisdom and aesthetic sense, so as to grow with physical and mental health," "to develop their reading ability in music," and "to nourish pupils' national pride and self-confidence through the teaching of representative Chinese folklore." In the first part of the twentieth century, emphasis was on the study of Western music theory and group singing (of songs from Europe, North America, Japan, and China). After 1949, the revolutionary communist government's links with Soviet Russia brought about an elitist approach that offered music lessons to the talented in specially designed institutes of music. However, no music instruction was provided to the masses in their general education. The Cultural Revolution of 1966–69 closed all schools and sent musicians out of institutes, conservatories, orchestras, and schools into reeducation farms and factory jobs.

With the re-opening of schools and then the rise of a foreign policy of peaceful co-existence in the 1980s, the Chinese were introduced to music methods and music education literature from other nations and cultures. Kodály, Orff, and Dalcroze approaches were modeled by invited music educators, and their techniques were worked into music instruction in the primary grades. A *Proposal for Improving School Music Education* was signed in 1985 by leading musicians, composers, and music educators in China and received a positive reaction from government officials who financed teaching materials and musical instruments, especially keyboards.

Singing by rote is still the most frequent school music activity, although children are also learning to read both Western staff notation and *jianpu*, a cipher notation system based on the movable doh. Music is prescribed in the secondary school curriculum, too, but because of the time that is devoted to academic subjects (as well as a shortage of music teachers), few secondary schools are able to offer a music course. There is considerable disparity among schools as to the presence of music, the availability of equipment (including musical instruments, computers, and music books) and well-trained music teachers on staff. Shanghai and Canton schools have excellent school music programs; rural schools often have little to no music education opportunities.

❖ BREAK POINT 4.5 Notational Systems

Western staff notation is just one of the systems by which music is preserved for posterity. In parts of Asia where notation is utilized, a cipher system is widely understood for associating numbers with pitches and horizontal space (and dots or dashes) with rhythms. Read the following familiar melodies in the Chinese jianpu system. Try noting familiar tunes in this system.

"Frere Jacques"
1 2 3 1 1 2 3 1 3 4 5 - 3 4 5 - <u>5654</u> 3 1 <u>5654</u> 3 1 1 5 1 - 1 5 1 -

"Ode to Joy"
3 3 4 5 5 4 3 2 1 1 2 3 3 . <u>2 2</u> . 3 3 4 5 5 4 3 2 1 1 2 3 2 . <u>1 1</u> .

At international music competitions, Chinese musicians have often emerged at the top of the ranks. Some of them find their way to Western conservatories and later to positions in Western orchestras and on faculties of conservatories and universities in China and abroad. The Central Conservatorium of Music in Beijing and the Shanghai Conservatory of Music are among the most competitive places for Chinese musicians to study. They are associated with key primary and secondary schools where musically talented young people receive comprehensive and intensive training on piano, violin, and various Western orchestral instruments. Beginning as early as five years old, children are auditioned on standard repertoire by Mozart, Beethoven, and Chopin into these conservatory-sponsored programs; if accepted, they may have music training throughout their school years and into postsecondary school conservatory education—and on to a career of competitions and performances.

Music is proclaimed by national policy as compulsory to the education of young people in China, yet it is still given less importance than math, languages, and the sciences. Even teachers trained in music look to opportunities to teach other subjects, given the greater social stature that this brings to them. Still, guidelines on music curriculum are in the process of study and revision, and there is a serious movement among professionals in music and in education to offer children experiences in musical creativity and child-centered learning that include opportunities for them to engage in musical explorations and experimentations. Some believe that a philosophical change may be in the wind that would provide music education for all and not just the talented few.

France

From Paris to the Pyrenees in the far south of France, education in the arts is directed by the French ministries of National Education, Culture and Communication, and Sports as part of the general education of children and youth. The three ministries cooperate closely with local school board authorities, and with the National Inspectorate and the Regional Directorates of Cultural Affairs, to ensure that the "life rhythm" of children and their childlike ways of learning are respected in the development of all activities within their school day. The French perspective on education is to teach the next generation the important values that have produced French culture, and the study of philosophy and rational thought plays deeply into this view. Rooted in a history of Cartesian ideals where an intellectual ideas-based curriculum is valued, the arts are seen as mostly outside the scientific parameters of logic and reason and more within the realm of expressive experiences in "beauty." The general French public questions the usefulness of education in the arts as anything more than recreational in nature. Still, the ministries signed a protocol on arts education in 1993 that reaffirmed the fundamental role of the arts in education, and this has renewed attention to bringing the study of music, the arts, and culture into children's daily educational plan.

For children from ages five to eleven, music and the visual arts are compulsory (if "minor") subjects in France to be experienced and studied from six to eight hours per week. French children frequently learn to play an instrument in their music classes—recorders and keyboards but also orchestral instruments. They learn to listen analytically to music of different historical periods, to memorize and identify musical compositions of progressive difficulty, and to develop the terminology to describe the music they hear. Classroom teachers are more often than not charged with teaching music as well as all academic subjects, but some primary school programs enhance these class sessions with artists who provide performances and workshops and may even be hired to organize and direct choirs and instrumental ensembles. These enhancements are typically funded by local authorities or private donations rather than the national ministries.

❖ BREAK POINT 4.6 Name That Tune

One long-standing instructional practice is memorization of the themes of symphonic and chamber works, learned by listening repeatedly to them, singing them, and playing them on available instruments. Assemble a set of themes, then organize students in teams or individually in spelling-bee fashion to "name that tune" by title and composer on hearing the listening selection. An alternative approach is to give title and composer, and have students play or sing the themes. Expand the repertoire beyond Western European art music to include vocal and choral works, and selections from jazz, popular, and world traditions.

Music is still required study for French youth ages twelve to fifteen, where the "colleges" (schools) commit one hour per week to a listening analysis curriculum. For students from the ages of fifteen to eighteen, there are five artistic disciplines from which to choose as a "required elective": music, visual arts, theater, cinema, and art history. They can enroll in one of these courses as a compulsory subject in the literature-arts section for four hours per week or take it as an optional subject for three hours per week. Assessment is more rigorous for students who study music as a compulsory subject, and this subject prepares some for specialized music study in the university. Cultural classes are offered by some schools to lead young people to experiences with artists or culture-bearers from a heritage sector, often at the site of the community and its living culture (for example, a *dan bao* or *dan tranh* player in a Vietnamese neighborhood in Paris or a rustic village band of *hurdy-gurdy* and *vielles* outside of Dijon). For French students at all levels, there are also cooperative arrangements between schools and national orchestras, theaters, and museums that allow them to visit, observe, and interact with professionals in their particular artistic forum.

Hungary

Mention Hungary to a music teacher and the name of Zoltán Kodály immediately leaps to mind, as does the "the Kodály method" of music literacy. Yet Hungarians call their pathway "the Hungarian method," which they maintain to be the composite tools and techniques that develop in children a comprehensive musicianship—that quality that begins with the singing of Hungarian folk songs, leads through ear training, and culminates in a musical independence producing people who can sing, frequently play an instrument, and continue to deepen their relationship with music because they understand its structure. The Hungarians will also remind you that (a) Kodály was the inspiration and spokesperson for a rigorous system of music education, but that his students and colleagues forged the pedagogical method; (b) not all Hungarian school settings are able to provide the sequential system of music instruction, as local contexts bring varied philosophies on curricular time and emphasis; and (c) with the end of the communist era (and the passing of Kodály as chief advocate of music) came decided changes in the nation's priorities, diminishing somewhat the importance of music as a curricular subject. Still, Hungary's reputation remains as having one of the most musically educated populations in the world,

Do-re-mi houses for classroom display: playful use of solfege in Kodály-inspired teaching.

and it continues as a mecca for music teachers to visit in search of schools where music is valued and purposefully taught.

"Kindergarten," prescribed for children ages three to six years, is the beginning of the musical education of Hungarian children. Here teachers intersperse periods of music and musical play throughout the day and children will learn by heart fifty or sixty songs or chants before they leave kindergarten. In standard elementary schools, children receive music lessons twice weekly. From the fourth year onward, they have required choir rehearsals where two-part singing and canons of up to four parts are regular features.

There are also schools with specialized music training that add daily music instruction to regular choir rehearsals. In either type of school, the students experience songs as exercises in the development of aural skills and music reading capabilities, while the choir rehearsals offer opportunities to learn repertoire all the way to the level of a polished performance. Singing is central in Hungarian music education, and Kodály convinced his communist comrades that the voice was the most accessible musical instrument for leading students to knowledge of their cultural heritage.

❖ BREAK POINT 4.7 Music for the Very Young

Attention to the education of young children in preschool settings has grown rapidly in recent years. Musicians trained to teach in elementary schools are being hired to offer musical experiences in early childhood settings that embrace singing, the playing of classroom rhythm instruments, attentive listening, movement, and creative expression. Often, preschool teachers have come from early childhood education programs where music is an important component of their training. Make arrangements to visit a preschool, to learn of the musical components of the curriculum and to determine how you might become involved in enriching their curriculum in musical ways.

Secondary school music instruction is much like that of standard and specialist music schools. Vocal music is emphasized, and choirs perform standard literature by Hungarian composers and others from Europe and the world. Instrumental music is pursued voluntarily by students in special afternoon music schools, where from the ages of six through twenty-two students receive two private lessons weekly as well as ninety minutes of solfege/sight-singing. Chamber music and music history are also options from which to choose. These afternoon music schools are a part of the general public educational system of Hungary, and all students are eligible for admission. For those with high interest and talent in music, there are fifteen conservatories where students between the ages of fourteen and twenty-two can study instruments, voice, music theory, choral conducting, and composition either as they attend high school or following their high school graduation.

The major Hungarian university for the study of music is the Ferenc Liszt University of Music which offers degrees in performance, conducting, composition, and music education. Pedagogical Colleges for general classroom teachers in grades 1–5 offer specialized study in music; music specialist teachers receive training at the Liszt and other universities. Teachers of the special afternoon music schools are trained at one of several music teacher training colleges.

In the same year that Hungary published the country's national standards, the Ministry of Education published in 1998 a list of basic musical instruments and equipment for all schools. Music theory classrooms that comply with these stipulations are equipped with five computers and assorted programs, digital instruments, and musical instrument digital interface (MIDI) systems and sequencers. An adequate budget for equipment and salaries comes jointly from the national budget and local governments, but fund-raising activities have become increasingly important in recent years to aid the realization of locally determined musical goals. Hungary has shifted gears to a free economy and a society that is recognizing its own diverse population of not only Hungarians but also Romanians, Slavs, Roma (Gypsy), German, and other nationalities. As such, curricular content and method will continue to shift to accommodate these economic and social transformations.

Japan

Japan, an island nation in northeast Asia, has imported arts from elsewhere in Asia, and yet the Japanese have succeeded in forging a uniquely Japanese identity where sameness, unity, and sensitivity to and reliance on the group are valued in the music that is made and taught in schools. Music was used to promote patriotism in the years leading to World War II. In the postwar years, music education became *joso* education, in which music was taught for its own sake to elevate students' aesthetic and moral sensibilities. The single activity of singing was then expanded to include instrumental study, composition, appreciation, and theory. By 2002, however, the Japanese Ministry of Education, Science, Sports and Culture put into effect a new National Curriculum Standard intended to develop students' musicality through performance and appreciation. Rather than cultivating national heritage and allegiances exclusively, the current curriculum is intended to promote children's expressive and creative abilities through compositional activities. The repertoire for listening and performance is often Western or mixed Western and Japanese, although there is a movement to put greater emphasis on Japanese traditional music and music of the world's cultures.

A general classroom music education is provided to children in the elementary grades while band, orchestra, and choir are extracurricular club activities. The National Curriculum Standard sets the contents of textbooks and instructional activity. The music to be taught and learned is prescribed, as are specific concepts and musical symbols, and they encompass Western art repertoire and traditional folk songs from not only Japan but also other parts of Asia, Europe, Africa, and the Americas. Expectations of the number of standard units or lessons per grade level that all students must have are uniform across all schools. Government-sponsored workshops, as well as those funded by private organizations, have aided in-service teachers in implementing the required curriculum through the presentation of materials and model lessons. These have been particularly important in clarifying the nature of creative music making and sound composition influenced by successful British models. Despite the uniform way the curriculum has been explained and demonstrated, the ministry has recently allowed for greater flexibility in the content and method of the lessons.

Where music is a part of secondary school curriculum, the content is more Western than Japanese, emphasizing analytical listening to symphonic forms, choral masterpieces, and chamber works of Bach, Beethoven, Brahms, and Mozart. The aims and activities of the music curriculum differ between the lower grades (7, 8, and 9) and the upper grades. For the younger adolescents, some in-school music programs consist of group lessons in Japanese traditional instruments, a development from earlier appreciation courses that could be taught by nonperformers. In recent years, teachers are being encouraged to lead students in learning to sing and play Japanese instruments as well as other instruments of the world's cultures. The "creative music making" lessons at this level also demand more of a teacher's musical expertise than in the past, so that teachers can clarify the details of the compositional process through the performance of suggested techniques as well as completed student models. Music in the upper grades typically is considered an elective subject within a period of integrated arts study and may consist of courses in traditional Japanese music, music technology, and even music of the Kabuki and Noh drama. There are instrumental and choral ensembles that rehearse at school but outside of class time (for example, after school and on Saturdays) as extracurricular activities, and some ensembles are stunning examples of highly regulated training where nothing less than performance perfection is demanded and delivered.

Some Japanese children learn music through privately funded Suzuki programs, where the very young learn to play on pint-sized violins (as well as on piano, cello, flute, and other orchestral instruments) through teacher demonstration and student imitation. The Yamaha Corporation is also significant in the musical education of Japanese children who learn keyboard, note-reading, and improvisation skills (on Yamaha pianos) outside school. The phenomenon of karaoke, the style of singing to prerecorded instrumental music, has motivated some young people to develop their voices independently and outside of school for solo pop-song singing. Finally, culture schools offer after-school and weekend lessons to young people in some of the music, dance, and drama forms of traditional Japan. These outside-school experiences have influenced teachers and curriculum writers to include in school programs music and music education methods that are relevant and meaningful.

❖ BREAK POINT 4.8 Embrace and Transfer

Some musical approaches and techniques from Japan have been widely embraced in the world of music education. Search out the phenomena of Suzuki violin training, Yamaha's keyboard-centered comprehensive musicianship training, the first-rate secondary school instrumental ensembles, karaoke or "music-minus-one" singing to an instrumental track, the attention to techniques that develop absolute (perfect) pitch. Brainstorm ways in which these approaches and techniques can be adapted in a school like yours.

South Africa

More than most African nations, South Africa has had a long effort in the formalized musical education of its students. Colonization led to the oppression of traditional ethnic cultures in South African society and its schools, and the creation by the Nationalist Party in 1948 of a policy of apartheid forced the separation and unequal treatment of ethnic groups. There were limitations to the students who could study music as well as the types of music that could be studied; music education was for nearly a half-century chiefly a curricular offering in Western classical music for the all-white students enrolled in private independent schools. Yet even in those times music permeated the lives of black South Africans and other people of color, where participation in singing and dancing (and sometimes instrumental play) was not only encouraged but expected as part of the personal and social development of every child—and still is. The resonant South African choral sound is a development of early European Christian missionary influence, buoyed also by influences from African-American spirituals and gospel songs. It is distinguished in its own vibrant way of including movement and dance, and improvisation atop rich textures. Singers are as comfortable reading the sol-fa notation as they are in producing the full chordal harmonies. Popular styles such as *iscathamiya, mbube, mbaqanga, township jazz,* and *kwaito* (African rap) emerged when South African musicians raised their voices and instruments in protest against the social inequities of the society. When music was not an option in the schooling of most South Africans, it was still a deep and abiding presence in their family and community lives.

The South African government supported the practice of musical and cultural traditions among black South Africans during the apartheid period, which perpetuated their segregation and prevented them from modernizing. With the election of Nelson Mandela as president in 1994 came the end of apartheid and the transfer of governance from the white minority to the black majority through democratic elections. Along with changes to social structures came the development of new education policies, and the government moved to redistribute funding to address the needs of youth—mostly underprivileged black Africans—whose schooling to that point had been severely undersupported. The full implementation of curriculum structures in 2005 includes music for the first ten years of schooling as one of the targets for transforming South African society according to its new constitution.

There are eight learning areas in the curriculum, and music is integrated with dance, drama, and the visual arts in an Arts and Culture Learning Area. There are recommendations for teaching music in an arts-integrated fashion as it would be experienced in black African cultures, but it can also be studied for its subject-specific knowledge, skills, and techniques. Specific outcomes are identified for musical learning: the development of music-making skills, the use of creative processes for developing social and interactive skills, an understanding of the origins and functions of music, the ability to reflect critically on musical experiences, the use of music to develop self-esteem and promote healing, and the acknowledgment of historically marginalized musical practices. These and other outcomes are spread across the arts and are intended to move beyond the Western paradigm of music and to see music as a cultural expression largely anchored in community activities.

Most teachers in South African schools have come from university programs steeped in Western European art music and Euro-American music education methods; one of the key challenges for them is to learn to teach music as it can best be learned. Children and youth of every cultural experience are capable of learning to read music notation, but literacy may not be relevant in learning all music. In teaching much of the music of Africa, South African teachers need to be able to facilitate the orality, co-creation, and improvisation processes that authenticate the experience. Repertoire is more easily changed than transmission and learning, and yet the inclusion of African "materials" will become meaningful when the appropriate process is carefully studied and applied by teachers in their classrooms. University programs in teacher education are undergoing reform to ensure that students develop the sensitivity and skills to begin using culturally sensitive (and musically authentic) pedagogical practices.

❖ BREAK POINT 4.9 Co-creation

One of the most exciting musical ventures for young people is their co-creation of a song, instrumental piece, or mixed-media music event. Discuss ways in which children and youth might invent their own music in a composition or improvisation project, and how ownership grows as a result of participation in musical invention. Think through and try out a project that allows students co-creation opportunities.

The United Kingdom

Partly motivated by the desire to improve congregational participation in churches, music in the form of group singing was introduced to the primary schools of the United Kingdom (England, Northern Ireland, Scotland, and Wales) early in the nineteenth century. The development of singing and aural training was furthered through the pioneering efforts of John Hullah, Sarah Glover, and John Curwen, whose tonic sol-fa means of solmization met with widespread acclaim throughout the kingdom. The syllable system of Glover, modified by Curwen, was adopted in Europe and North America, and their hand signs form the basis of the "Kodály hand signs" today. By the mid-nineteenth century, the British government was encouraging singing classes in schools, and instruction in instrumental music was rising along with the formation of choirs and orchestras as extracurricular activities for those with a special musical interest. Curricular and extracurricular music instruction continues today, although the in-school instruction has expanded far beyond the one-time emphasis on singing.

The arts—music, the visual arts, dance (within physical education), and drama (within English)—are included in the National Curriculum as foundation subjects, funded and supported by the Department of Culture, Media and Sport and the National Arts Council. This curriculum was introduced into the schools of England and Wales; Scotland and Northern Ireland operate their own related national systems. The arts in the National Curriculum are compulsory study for students in Key Stages 1–3 (ages five through fourteen) and optional for students in Key Stage 4 (ages fifteen to sixteen). The music curriculum set into motion in 2000 stipulated that "listening, and applying knowledge and understanding are developed through the interrelated skills of performing, composing, and listening." Four content areas are named: (a) controlling sounds through singing and playing—performing skills, (b) creating and developing musical ideas—composing skills, (c) responding and reviewing—appraising skills, and (d) listening, and applying knowledge and understanding.

❖ BREAK POINT 4.10 Key Stages

> Education tends to be conceived in stages that apply to the developmental levels of children and youth. Into how many schools and stages do districts subdivide grade levels? Within an elementary school, how are children further classified according to their intellectual, emotional, social, and physical development? Discuss how curriculum diversifies according to stages and developmental levels.

For children in the first three key stages that encompass primary school and the lower secondary school grades, instruction in performance and composition are central to classroom activities. Singing and playing classroom instruments are common occurrences, as is listening to recorded music and live performances of visiting artists and each other's music. Composition is a featured curricular component throughout the United Kingdom, partly due to the considerable influence of British composer-educator John Paynter as early as the 1960s. It manifests itself in song-writing and sound explorations of the voice, the percussive sounds of the body, available instruments, and "found sound" objects within the environment. From the earliest grades, children are led through experiences of increasing complexity intended to suggest elements, themes, and structures they can experience and manipulate for their own expressive purposes. By the time they reach Key Stage 3, ages eleven through fourteen, children in sequential programs of music study are developing full-fledged and sometimes sophisticated compositions that they can perform, notate, and replicate on call. The presence of Kodály, Orff, and Dalcroze practices in British classrooms is not widespread, largely because music in the lower grades is often taught by classroom teachers with minimal training in music. With grants from local authorities as well as Arts Council England and its regional councils, residencies by artists and composers are important components of school music programs.

When students reach the age of fourteen, the school curriculum in music parallels the demands of school-leaving examinations. The music content of programs at this level is increasingly remote from students' interest in popular music, as music-specialist teachers devote continued attention to activities in performing, composing, and listening to the Western art music that comprises the bulk of the exams students take at age sixteen for the General Certificate of Secondary Education (GCSE). For two additional years, students specialize in more intensive study of selected subjects, and those with a particular aptitude for it will select music. The course is an intensive program of harmony, counterpoint, history, analysis, and performance—again with an emphasis on Western art music, which culminates in an Advanced level ("A" level) examination.

Choirs, bands, orchestras, and other ensembles are organized in some schools but are less often a part of the curriculum than they are after-school opportunities. Sometimes on the school premises, but also in other community venues, the activities of ensembles and private and group instrumental instruction are appreciated as important to the general ethos of the school climate and the holistic development of children and youth. Trained music teachers, musicians without pedagogical training, and "community musicians" teach and rehearse students in recorder ensembles, jazz bands, steel drum ensembles, and percussion groups. Increased activity, supported by government funds, is found in the development of community programs that offer instruction and coaching in popular/rock music. Along with wind bands, the British brass bands draw young people into youth and mixed-age performance opportunities, while youth choirs and orchestras are assembled in various cities and communities throughout the United Kingdom. A particularly British route for the musical education of youth has been its tradition of choir schools, in which a rigorous approach to musicianship frequently features daily practices for chapel and church performances of Evensong and Sunday services.

Conservatories, universities, and colleges of higher education in the United Kingdom offer three- or four-year undergraduate courses in a variety of musical fields, from performance and academic music (history and theory) to a wide spread of fields that include ethnomusicology, the psychology of music, music therapy, popular music, and community music. For some music teachers, a one-year postgraduate diploma in teaching follows their undergraduate music degrees.

A small ensemble of high school singers.

North America: The United States and Canada

In the North American nations of Canada and the United States, music in school programs can be traced to the interactions between church and community. The Roman Catholic clergy organized choirs in Quebec as early as 1626, and singing and piano lessons were offered in convents. Singing schools arose in the American colonies early in the eighteenth century, when traveling singing masters would come to town for a few weeks of intensive vocal training and the development of a repertoire of sacred music for church services. The first instances of public school music, spearheaded by Lowell Mason in Boston in the 1830s, were oriented toward group singing and the formation of choirs. Vocal and choral music remained prominent in Canadian and American schools through the first several decades of the twentieth century, after which instrumental music became more popular. In the last several decades, a more equitable balance between choral and instrumental music has been reached, even as new musical offerings have come forward.

Instrumental music training in North America was first offered in Protestant-backed music schools, beginning with the first community music school established in Montreal in 1789. Private academies in the United States offered lessons in violin, cello, and piano. Instrumental music appeared in the school curriculum in the late nineteenth century, as the popularity of small-town bands and orchestras was brought to the attention of school boards who saw the extramusical outcomes of school spirit and entertainment as a convincing rationale for including instrumental instruction in schools. With the return of bandsmen from World War I, coupled with the sponsorship by instrument manufacturers of contests and festivals, bands and orchestras rivaled and even surpassed vocal and choral music activity in schools. Americans established a national school band competition, which also contributed to the rapid expansion of instrumental music. In Canada, the establishment of local music examinations based on the practices of the Associated Board of the Royal Schools of Music in London ensured that students were guided toward high performance standards.

A "general music" curriculum was developed for elementary schools, emerging from the once all-vocal music practices to encompass listening, movement, classroom instruments, composition, and improvisation. Listening experiences came to classes of music for children as the technology evolved to include RCA Victor gramophones, and music education through eurhythmic movement arrived in the 1920s with the influence of the European Dalcroze and modern dance techniques. European imports, including the Orff and Kodály methods, have been embraced by American and Canadian music teachers since the 1960s, and the certification of teachers in these pedagogies is deemed highly desirable for those who teach children. (Another import, the Suzuki method approach to string education, has steadily grown in the elementary school instrumental curriculum.) There are occasional cases of creative composition activity (more so in Canada than in the United States), and improvisation has begun to surface beyond jazz ensembles and Orff-based levels. Group keyboard and guitar instruction offer alternatives to the standard school ensembles, as do drumming, marimba, and steel drum ensembles. A recognition of the multicultural populations of cities like Chicago, Los Angeles, Toronto, Miami, New York, Houston, and Vancouver, as well as the legacy of the First Nations/Native American peoples, have brought an expansion of music materials and repertoire in the last several decades.

Musical study in American and Canadian schools has gained and lost ground since its first inception and is often dependent on whether the times regard the arts as necessary—or not—to children's development. Its presence is also linked to the federal, state, and local tax base, so that the arts are maintained during periods of financial stability but are reduced or cut altogether when funds are low. Schools are locally controlled for the most part, and so curricular decisions are often in the hands of school boards and even the site groups for each school. The justification for music in schools in North America has run the gamut from "music for music's sake" to its role in developing citizenship, building team spirit, providing leisure time skills, and supporting achievement in academic areas. Competitions continue to drive much of the performance activity, as music programs train their marching bands, concert bands, choirs, orchestras, jazz bands, and jazz, show, and swing choirs for interscholastic adjudicated festivals and appearances in select performance venues.

Although no nationally mandated curriculum exists in Canada or the United States, the National Standards in the Arts were drawn up as guidance for American music teachers in 1994 (see Figure 4.1). These standards followed the national movement in the early 1990s to assess student competence in the core subjects of math, English, science, history, and geography. The passage of Goals 2000: Educate America Act brought such attention to world-class standards in the arts that they were at least recognized as a fundamental academic subject. The National Standards made recommendations for the knowledge, skills, and understanding that all students in grades K–12 can acquire in the four arts disciplines—music, visual arts, theater, and dance. Three groups by grade level (K–4, 5–8, 9–12) are considered, with attention given to stages of human musical development as well as curricular content in elementary and secondary schools. For grades 9–12, when not all students elect to study music, "Advanced" levels of achievement are identified for those who choose specialized courses while "Proficient" levels are expected for those without further training. The National Standards for the Arts document is widely used by state and community groups to develop guidelines and benchmarks.

1. Singing, alone and with others, a varied repertoire of music.
2. Performing on instruments, alone and with others, a varied repertoire of music.
3. Improvising melodies, variations, and accompaniments.
4. Composing and arranging music within specified guidelines.
5. Reading and notating music.
6. Listening to, analyzing, and describing music.
7. Evaluating music and music performances.
8. Understanding relationships between music, the other arts, and disciplines outside the arts.
9. Understanding music in relation to history and culture.

Figure 4.1 • **National Standards for Music Education in the United States.**

Synthesizing the Systems

Understanding the varied educational systems by which music is taught may be of central interest to those who are planning to teach. A meta-view of national systems can provide specific ideas for what to do when faced with teaching, administering, developing curricular content, articulating ideas to principals and boards, and communicating to parents and the public at large. Figure 4.2 displays some of the principal points of national policies for music education as well as some of the common practices, showing the diversity of possibilities that are available to teachers who wish to shape a program uniquely tailored and highly relevant to the needs of their students.

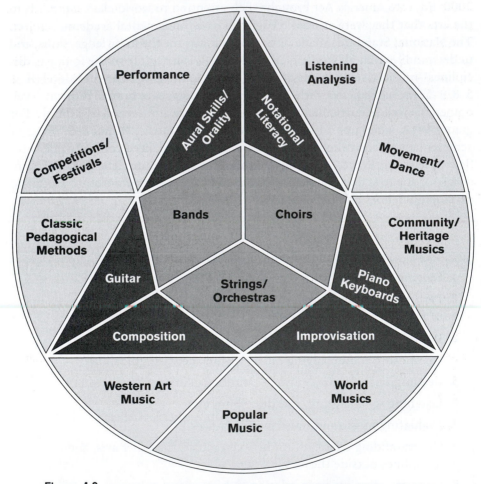

Figure 4.2 • Principal points of national policies for potential application by music teachers at large, in any system.

REFERENCES AND RESOURCES

Comte, M. (1994). *Music Education: International Viewpoints*. Perth, Australia: Australian Society for Music Education. An assessment by twenty-six music educators from twenty nations of the significant features, strengths, and weaknesses of music education within their national system.

Consortium of National Arts Education Associations. (1994). *National Standards for Arts Education: What Every Young American Should Know and Be Able to Do in the Arts.* Reston, VA: Music Educators National Association. Rationale for and specifications of the standard curricular goals for students in K–12 programs in music, visual arts, dance, and drama in the United States.

Gardner, H. (1989). *To Open Minds: Chinese Clues to the Dilemma of Contemporary Education.* New York: Basic Books. An examination of training, education, and schooling in the music and the visual arts in China, with a view to the lessons to be learned and applied to schools outside China regarding traditional or progressive approaches, rote learning or spontaneity, discipline or freedom.

Gates, J. T. (1988). *Music Education in the United States.* Tuscaloosa: The University of Alabama Press. A survey of philosophical stances and practical issues surrounding the practice of music education in elementary and secondary schools, and music in higher education, within the United States.

Hargreaves, D. J., and A. C. North. (2001). *Music Development and Learning.* London: Continuum. A compilation of music education policies, practices, and cultural traditions in fifteen countries and regions, with attention to goals, curricular content and method, and student issues.

Herbst, A., M. Nzewi, and K. Agawu. (2003). *Musical Arts in Africa.* Unisa: University of South Africa Press. Essays by music scholars, educators, and artists concerning African indigenous knowledge systems and content in the musical arts (including music, dance, theater, and storytelling) that interface with what and how music may be taught and learned in schools.

Lepherd, L. (1995). *Music Education in International Perspective: National Systems.* Toowoomba, Australia: University of Southern Queensland Press. A concise overview of nine national systems of music education, with attention to aims, administration, finance, structure and organization, curricula, and music teacher education and teachers.

chapter 5

Music in "Your Local"

Eighth-grade student A: Are you going to JFK for high school next year?

Eighth-grade student B: Nope.

Eighth-grade student A: But why not? JFK is where it's at, man. And it's the closest school to our neighborhood. If not JFK, where?

Eighth-grade student B: Jackson. Where else?

Eighth-grade student A: That's across town. What's your reason?

Eighth-grade student B: Number 1: the marching band. Number 2: the concert band. Number 3: the jazz band. All first-rate.

Eighth-grade student A: Hey, high school is about more than just band.

Eighth-grade student B: Band is the source there. Oh, and number 4: the band teacher. I've seen him work, and I've heard the trombone section. I need to be at Jackson.

Eighth-grade student A: Yeah, but I repeat: school is more than just band.

Eighth-grade student B: Music is tight at Jackson. They live, eat, think, and breathe music. They play assemblies, festivals, games, half-time shows, gigs in town . Everybody gets it, that Mr. Newton's program is awesome. There's no question about it: music makes the school.

Local Schools within Earshot

In the rural villages of northern England, residents still head out to the pub around the corner for fish and chips, or bangers and mash (sausage and potatoes), or a curry chicken and rice meal. They wash it down with their drink of choice and sit together at long tables to share the news of their small farms and gardens, their family activities, their mutual friends, and the politics of their community, nation, and world. This is their "local," short for their favorite restaurant that is within walking distance from their homes. The local is the hub of activity, where people come to relax, connect with their friends, exchange ideas, and learn something new. There is a local for every community and neighborhood, from England to Australia, Korea, India, and the United States.

Schools are local, too. They are centers of community activity. In a town or a city neighborhood, they are the places where children and adolescents are delivered daily, 180 days of the year, typically in North America from late August or early September until the middle of June. Schools are more than physical representations—logos—of learning, although that is their principal function as houses of instructional activity. They also serve as gatherings for after-school and evening groups of Boy Scouts and Girl Scouts; community basketball, volleyball, baseball, and soccer leagues; community choral and instrumental ensembles; book clubs; and a considerable variety of enrichment opportunities for adults and children. Schools are a central fixture in the life of a community.

Further, schools comprise their own community of young people and their teachers, each with its own rhythm, pace, and pitch. This community is a culture of shared values, attitudes, and behaviors. The community values of school are expressed in the content of the curriculum as well as in the methods and materials through which it is taught and learned. They are expressed also through the spaces that have been devised for learning: the size and contents of the classrooms, the decorative features of the school and its exterior. Values are in plain view of all who take in the student dress code, the body language, the verbal expressions, and the interactions of students with teachers. School communities are shaped by young students and their teachers.

Values of a local school community are also within earshot. Consider the teacher, his or her credentials and commitment, and whether there are multiple members of a music teaching staff. Look to the ensembles that are available at the school, whether required or as elective courses. The number and extent of choral and instrumental music reflect school values, as does the repertoire they perform. Whether they are standard school ensembles—bands, choirs, and orchestras—or whether they encompass a wider variety of performance possibilities—mariachi, world percussion, "global voices"—these, too, are emblematic of school values. Courses in composition and song-writing, and in keyboard and guitar signify the interests of the school community, as do private and small-group lessons on school time, or just prior to or following classes. The values of a school and the community that supports them are much in evidence in the makeup of the school music program.

❖ BREAK POINT 5.1 Your Local

Describe your own "local," the schools where you learned music. Imagine yourself as a visitor from another planet: What would you see and hear as defining your local schools, at large and in music?

Following are portraits of music programs of three schools in three very real North American communities. The teachers, the students, the parents, and the wider world of their schools and communities are briefly described for the music education aims and accomplishments that are in some cases individually inspired and in other cases collectively determined. None of these programs is the standard by which all other programs can be measured, but each affirms important principles in creating and continuing music education for young people in the schools.

Jackson High School

Not quite ten minutes by bus from the downtown commercial district of a large metropolitan city, Jackson High School sits high on a hill above an older urban neighborhood of homes, stores, and busy streets. The homes are single- and double-family two-story structures of wood, brick, and aluminum siding, most of them built in the 1910s and 20s and many now in need of repair. Apartment houses of brown and yellow brick, steel, and glass line the streets just a few blocks from the school, above the stores and restaurants that operate at street level. The community is a little rough around the edges, with litter in the streets, graffiti on building sides and signs, and more than a few empty bottles in yards, alleys, and occasionally on sidewalks. Buses grind up the hill to the school, and the subwoofers of car radios thump out the drum-and-bass sound of hip-hop, techno, and pop-punk music. Students of every shape, size, and hue stream up the steps to the sprawling three-story red brick building, across the lawn and under the trees to one of four entrances to the school. The century-old building does not look its age due to recent renovations made to preserve its Colonial Revival front and the utilitarian interior of intersecting hallways, classrooms, and offices. Set as a crown to what was once viewed as a community removed from the city itself, Jackson High School has commanding views of the neighborhood and the urbanscape of the city just beyond.

A little over 1,800 students are enrolled at Jackson. They enter the ninth grade out of several urban "feeder" middle schools and spend the next four years there, typically from the age of fourteen to their late adolescence. The average socioeconomic level of their families, many of them single parents, is at the low end such that over half the students are on the free and reduced-price lunch plan. The ethnic-cultural diversity of the student population is considerable: 54 percent African American, 17 percent Latin American, 13 percent Asian/Pacific Islander, 11 percent white, 1 percent Native American (and 4 percent self-declared as "other"). For nearly two-thirds of the students, Jackson is the last formal schooling they will have. Some 12 percent don't make it to graduation, while just 40 percent head from graduation to college or technical, business, or professional training institutes. Just over 10 percent of the student population is bused in from elsewhere in the city to take advantage of particular academic courses and the highly regarded music and theater programs.

There is an academic tracking system at Jackson High School: the college preparatory and the SRO (state requirements only) strands. Academic courses for the college bound include math, science, language arts, and social science courses that are standard requirements for admission to universities. In addition to this strand, there are AP (Advanced Placement) courses for high achievers, such as college-level calculus, chemistry, and physics that will transfer directly to their record on admission to college. The phenomenon of AP and other academic courses for college-bound students is that the majority of students enrolled in them are disproportionately white and Asian, bused in from more affluent neighborhoods in the district, and coming from families of medium to high socioeconomic income levels.

Students have a way of walking and talking at Jackson. They are cutting-edge urban youth, sporting loose-fit and low-hung pants, collarless T-shirts with fits both snug (especially girls) and oversized (especially boys), with everything from all-season sandals and colorful tennis shoes to heavy combat boots. Hairstyles include close-cropped cuts, slicked-back long hair, single and multiple ponytails, and a few examples of shoulder-length dreadlocks. Scarves, caps, and hats are creatively fixed to top off "the look." Where urban-area students once code-switched from home and street-style English to constructions of the language acceptable at school, many now bring their natural dialect into class discussion. The school is known for its history of gang activity, with groups often based in the ethnic enclaves of the larger community, and there are visible signs of these divisions in the walking, standing, and slouching styles, and in hand gestures. The gang style is often subtle, but the insiders understand who's who from the colors of a jersey to the way a cap is set on the head. The relatively few students who are bused in for the AP programs (many of them also attracted by the school's music and theater programs) are the standouts in the crowd, as they sport a more preppie look of belted pants, or rolled-up jeans, layered tank tops, and collared but loose-fitting shirts. They appear a culture apart from the Jackson mainstream, and due to their enrollment in the high-octane academic classes, they are indeed separated for most of the day from the majority population of the school.

Music at Jackson High School has had a long history of excellence, and for decades has been one of the leading programs across four counties within the metropolitan region. There are three full-time teachers of music at Jackson, several adjunct teachers, and an array of instrumental specialists hired under contract to teach private and small-group lessons. Mr. Newton built the band program over twenty-five years, including several levels of concert, marching, and jazz ensembles. Mr. Wenner's orchestral program began with a string ensemble twenty-two years ago, and has multiplied into two orchestras, a class period of four string-quartets, a mariachi band, a keyboard class, and an AP theory course. The choral activities are under the direction of Ms. Kantowski, who has in seven years maintained the Jackson Singers (the advanced chorale), a mixed choir (of mostly tenth and some eleventh graders), a freshman choir, and a triple trio (of girls), adding a vocal jazz group and group guitar instruction. Along with the full-timers, there are two adjunct teachers hired to teach the freshman-level jazz lab, the small jazz combo ensembles, a world percussion ensemble, and a course in world drumming.

The principal and teachers at Jackson take music for granted within the curriculum, only partly because two of the three full-time teachers have been on faculty longer than most of the staff. Their seniority is meaningful and their positions are revered, especially by a few of the faculty who were once students there themselves and have come back as teachers. The booming voice of Mr. Newton in staff meetings repeatedly reminds teachers of the school's reputation for musical excellence, as does the consistent press coverage of Jackson's ensemble ratings at district, regional, and national competitions. No other activity—academic or athletic—has the parental support in volunteer service and financial backing that the music program enjoys. Music is in an enviable position at Jackson, and the long-term commitment of its teachers, along with the long days they spend there, have made it what it is.

Enter the performing arts wing of Jackson High School, built during the school's renovations in 1997–98, and the music sails from the rehearsal hall, two classrooms, and practice studios. The theater department is also located there, with its black box theater and a classroom of wood floors for dance and staging practice. At the end of the hall is a 500-seat auditorium for concerts, assemblies, and occasional rehearsals. There are eight pianos distributed through the department (including three grand pianos), lockers to house student instruments, and music stands in every nook and niche. State-of-the-art audio equipment and video systems equip the halls and classrooms, and a small audio engineering/recording studio is located at the back of the auditorium. There is a library of band, choir, and orchestral scores, along with sound recordings, and four small offices, one for each of the music teachers and the drama teacher around the corner from the rehearsal hall.

A conversation with the music teachers reveals much of their philosophy in action, reasons for the success of their program as well as challenges they face

(Figure 5.1). Mr. Newton, age fifty-three, is a tall and wiry African-American man, renowned for his knowledge of jazz as well as his innovative repertoire of challenging works and numerous commissioned works. He is a trombonist and occasional trumpet player who plays in pit bands for traveling shows and at jazz clubs in town, but engages in these "only when they don't conflict with" his teaching, the after-school performances, and the band festivals and tours. In his early forties, Mr. Wenner is a cellist who played in and then conducted a community orchestra in California before coming to Jackson. His orchestral program is widely acclaimed by string teachers across the state, and his ensembles have performed for mayoral events, the governor's ball, and numerous regional and national conferences of music educators. Ms. Kantowski is in her late twenties, full of energy, with a strong mezzo-soprano voice and a range that makes vocal modeling over two-and-a-half octaves plausible. She was hired to build up a program weak in the vocal area and caught the ear of her senior colleagues when, at her interview, she recounted her own considerably diverse musical experiences in vocal jazz, gospel, Bulgarian choral sounds, and Brazilian samba and jazz styles.

The band in session.

Q: What's unique about the music program at Jackson High School?

Mr. N: It's not so unique, really. At least, it's standard operating procedure around here. I suppose to an outsider (it's unique because of) . . . dedicated kids, supportive parents, the administration—even an outside community that's interested in kids that can play.

Mr. W: We think that we're able to pose musical challenges to our students that most programs could never do. They can play standard works, read new works, even premiere them in performance that is very high level. Why? Because the kids take practicing seriously.

Ms. K: I was drawn to teaching here because of what my colleagues have made of their programs. It is their own dedication that has made Jackson's music so good. It also helps that there are parents who care enough to volunteer their time to get the kids to private lessons, to fund-raise, and to chaperone at concerts and festivals.

Q: Who are your students?

Mr. N: Any and all of Jackson's student population. We think we offer something for everyone, and we find a good mix of students in our classes.

Q: There are a lot of white kids in some of the classes.

Mr. W: Not only white, though: Asian—in my orchestras. My mariachi band is mostly Mexican kids. But my keyboard class is a real mix. No one is rejected because of race, if that's what you're wondering.

Ms. K: I would say that it's out there, any of the music, for any of the students. I'm working to get a better balance in my choirs. My triple trio has four African-American girls, two Latin Americans, one Asian, and two white students, and my guitar class is all across the board.

Q: How do you work on recruitment to your classes? What are your strategies?

Ms. K: It's mostly word of mouth, kids telling kids about what we do. Plus I have a tendency to yank them in, I go up to them in the hall, the cafeteria, outside, if they're singing or dancing, and I talk to them personally. Plus, I send my students out as secret agents to drum up business for my choirs, lure them in.

Mr. N: They do like the trips, the tours. I work them pretty hard, but they seem to like the energy that flows in these classes.

Mr. W: If they play a violin before high school, this is one of the few places in the district that has an orchestra. So naturally they come here.

Ms. K: Don't be so modest. Half the high schools have orchestras, but your orchestras have been rated the best in the state for going on a generation. Sure, that's why they're here, because of you.

Q: What about the band program, Mr. Newton? Every school's got a band. But your bands are the ones people talk about.

Mr. N: Our bands swing, I guess. We work up the marching band repertoire starting the second week in August, run concert band from November onward, and have the jazz groups going every day all year (and after school for a good bit of the time). My kids get private lessons: either their parents pay for them, or I have them studying with folks I hire from the community. I gotta say, too, that when there's a big event coming up, we'll do before-school rehearsals at 6:30 and then take weekend time to work out the kinks and polish the music up.

Mr. W: You also hire in specialists to clinic your kids. So do we all.

Mr. N: There's nothing like getting the pros in to play with your kids, conduct them, adjudicate them in advance of the festivals.

Q: Where does the money come from?

Mr. N: Too many car washes. Lots of magazine sales, wrapping paper, entertainment books, chocolate bar sales. It takes everything you've got to get a budget going. But one thing leads to another. You start with heart-to-hearts with your principal to get your first funds. You work the kids to a level of musical skills where they can start to feel pride about what they do, and their parents come on board to help out. The more festivals you win, the better the funds—from parent-run auctions, benefit concerts (we being the beneficiaries), a bigger chunk of the school budget, and parent-funded trips. Our community concerts, too, like playing for the mayor. We took in $1,500 for a gig two weeks ago.

Mr. W: I would agree. Winning is not the goal, but festivals raise the level of public enthusiasm for what we're doing. They offer us credibility, and that's worth something in donations to the cause.

Mr. N: We get good deals from instrument makers, too. I bought a set of twenty keyboards for half the price, just because they wanted to have their instruments here. We got the world drums and percussion instruments at a break, too, for the same reason.

Q: What's your long-range plan for music at Jackson High School?

Mr. N: I've done it, me and Wenner here. It's up to her to give it direction from here.

Ms. K: I just want to keep it going, because it can't get much better than this . . . except that I'm still working on gearing up the choral program to be as fine musically as the instrumental programs. I'm thinking about a song-writing class, too, and would like to see how we can get kids in ensembles more into the finer points of how the music they perform fits into history and cultures.

Mr. N: Let's just say that we want everyone who wants to make music, to make music here at Jackson.

Mr. W: And to keep our eyes on the prize: musical excellence.

Figure 5.1 • **Chat time with the Jackson High School music faculty.**

The contents of Jackson's music classes and the repertoire of the ensembles is determined by the level of student ability, the standard and approved festival repertoire for ensembles, the teachers' interests, and democratically, the students' interests as well. The bands make remarkably expressive renderings of Francis McBeth's "Of Sailors and Whales," Percy Grainger's "Country Gardens," "Crown Imperial" (Walton, arranged by Duthoit), "Sketches on a Tudor Psalm" (Tull), and Ralph Vaughan Williams's "English Folk Song Suite." Mr. Wenner goes for gold in his orchestral programming, including Mozart's "Eine Kleine Nachtmusik," Tchaikovsky's "Serenade in C Major," "St. Paul's Suite" by Gustav Holst, and Vaughan Williams's "Fantasia on Greensleeves." The jazz ensembles do well with tunes like "Witchcraft" (by Cy Coleman and Carolyn Leigh), "Manteca" (Dizzy Gillespie and Walter Fuller), "Tutti for Cootie" (Duke Ellington and Jimmy Hamilton), and Dianne Schuur's "Deedle's Blues." The straight-ahead choral ensembles work through four-part pieces as prescribed by the competitions: Stroop's "The Pasture," Pitoni's "Cantate Domino," "Four German Folk Songs" (Johannes Brahms), "Dirait-on" (Alex Lauridsen), "Wonfa Nyem" (edited by Abraham Kobena Adzenyah), and Curry's four-part arrangement of "Down to the River to Pray." As for the other ensembles and class offerings, the repertoire tends to be a compilation of favorite pieces taken by the teachers from workshops, visiting artists, and recommendations from colleagues.

❖ BREAK POINT 5.2 Chatting with the Local High School Music Faculty

Arrange to interview the music staff at your former high school or another school that is accessible to you. Follow the interview questions in Figure 5.1 to ascertain the nature of the students enrolled in the music program, the current activity of courses and ensembles, the general financial picture for the program, and the long-range plan regarding staffing, equipment, and the curricular vision of the staff. How does your selected school compare with Jackson High School's status?

Daniel Webster Middle School

The "wolverines" of Daniel Webster Middle School live suburban lives safe in a community that from all appearances is happily bound to largely intact families and the amenities of a well-stocked public library, an expansive recreation center with an Olympic-sized outdoor pool, and a shopping mall that features center-stage arts and entertainment every weekend. Webster Middle School is the site of the old high school, and is located four blocks from the mall and across the street from three churches. The homes on streets running perpendicular to Webster's street are bi-level, tri-level, and ranch homes, some of them remakes of the originals built in the 1960s and others built in the last ten years on what were once open fields. The school grounds are lightly landscaped with maple and elm trees, a few dogwoods that bloom in the spring, and low-lying holly and mulberry bushes that line the exterior walls of the building. The building itself is about sixty years old and worn but generally neat and clean; it is three-sided, with a courtyard in the middle and several portable classrooms lining the athletic field. Students scattered inside and across the school grounds appear young despite the attempts by many to dress fashionably older and, while shy by themselves, take confidence (and become noisy with enthusiasm) in their membership in a social group.

There are 650 sixth, seventh, and eighth grade students enrolled at Webster, all of them in early adolescence, from "eleven-going-on-twelve" to fourteen years of age. They come from families of at least moderate means and some would even be viewed as affluent; most of their fathers and mothers have had some college experience. Over half of the mothers work, many of them in professional and managerial positions, like the fathers. Less than 10 percent are single-parent families, and even fewer qualify for free and reduced-price lunch provisions for their children. The school is more homogenous than most, with a population that is 68 percent white, 11 percent each African American and Latin American, 6 percent Asian, with the remaining 4 percent self-classified as "mixed" or "other." The lower level of cultural diversity has much to do with socioeconomic factors. One further statistic of musical interest characterizes the Webster students and their families: three out of four families have a musical instrument in their homes.

Like all middle school students in their transition from childhood to adolescence, the students at Webster have interests that spread widely across a spectrum of possibilities. Sixth graders adjust from their elementary school personas, bringing with them a wide-eyed wariness of what it means to be edging into their teen years. Many are in transition from dolls to dates, and from model planes to popular music and movies. They prefer fast food with friends to a sit-down meal with the family, video games over board games, and personal space. By the seventh grade, they are spending their free time on the Internet, e-mailing and instant-messaging their circle of friends. Eighth graders take on leadership roles at Webster as they look toward high school. They're working their way through various after-school activities in an attempt to figure out what appeals to them and "who they are," from arts to sports. If given a choice, they would prefer most to hang out at the mall, meeting their friends, checking out the latest clothes, jewelry, CDs, DVDs, and even books—most notably, sci-fi and graphic novels (for boys) and adventure and mystery novels with a romantic tinge (for girls). They are the middle school "in-betweens," uncertain, exploring, seeking their social circles and clinging to them.

For the last decade, the music program at Webster has been steadily catching on and growing in its strength and reputation. Mr. "C" (short for Castigiliano), age thirty-three, hit the ground running following the retirement of the last music teacher. When he came there were two bands, a small choir, an orchestra of sixteen students, and a general music/music appreciation class. While music is not a state-required subject, Mr. C was of the opinion that he could make music essential to his students. This he did by teaching with intensity, selecting repertoire that was neither too difficult nor too easy for students, at times familiar to students and other times new to them but nonetheless musically "catchy." He arranged for music students from the high school to visit often so that they might perform, demonstrate, and interact with the middle schoolers, and he organized small-group lessons with students from a university not quite ten miles away. Mr. C met with a few parents in his first year and helped lay the groundwork for a parents' music club. He planned twice as many programs than required by his contract, and tripled the concert dates by his second year, so as to entice students who would find the public performances more motivating than just going to class. He toured elementary schools in the district with his band, choir, and orchestra, and performed at the mall for a variety of functions throughout the year. In his third year, his principal said "yes" to a second music teaching position and Ms. Wilson was hired on.

Currently, almost 70 percent of Webster students are enrolled in music classes, a high-water mark for the school that sets it far above the standard enrollment figures in the region's middle schools. Mr. C has switched to instrumental-only activity and Ms. Wilson has taken on the choirs and other music courses. Over six periods, there are now beginning, intermediate, and "senior" bands, a sixth-grade orchestra, the Webster Symphony, and a jazz band for seventh- and eighth-grade students. Ms. Wilson teaches a sixth-grade chorus, a sixty-member "senior" choir (for seventh- and eighth-grade singers), two keyboard classes, and two world music performance classes. The music activities are located on the south side of the building, where there are two ensemble rooms with tiered levels, a smaller keyboard room, three practice rooms, a storage closet where drums and other percussion instruments are kept, and an office that Mr. C and Ms. Wilson share. An auditorium in the center of the building and across from the main office serves as the rehearsal space for the three bands and the Webster symphony.

The status of school music has risen in the eyes of the Webster students, their parents, and their teachers in the years since Mr. C joined the faculty. Ms. Wilson has given it further energy as she increased the music-making choices. Their approach to middle school music is to offer students the skills they need to make music of sufficient quality to "do them proud." Mr. C devotes a full fifteen minutes of his daily band and orchestra sessions to scales and drills, which he claims "pays off in spades" in developing students' musicianship: their motor facility and flexibility, their ability to sustain tones, and their capacity to listen with care, read what is notated, and perform with musical nuance. Likewise, Ms. Wilson gives at least ten minutes daily to sight-reading exercises and vocalises, from scales to arpeggios to phrases extracted from current repertoire. While neither teacher speaks negatively of the elementary school music programs that graduate students to Webster, they have each spoken wistfully of how greater attention to aural skills and notational literacy at an earlier age would be of considerable benefit to young adolescents.

Mr. C's band curriculum extends from the drilling to repertoire to fit the level of the group, with pieces like "Ancient Voices" (Michael Sweeney) and "Air and Dance" (John Kinyon) for his beginning band, "Old Churches (Michael Colgrass), "Kentucky 1800" (Clare Grundman), and more works by Michael Story for his intermediate group, and Frank Erikson's "Air for Band" and Frank Ticheli's "Cajun Folk Songs" for his senior band. His sixth-grade orchestra is playing arrangements of chorales and dances by Haydn, Beethoven, and Bartok, while the Webster Symphony is up to playing the Brandenburg Concerto No. 5 (Bach, arranged by Merle Isaac) and simplified arrangements of Vivaldi's "Fantasia for Strings," Copland's setting of "Simple Gifts" and other American folk songs, and Mussorgsky's "Great Gate of Kiev." His jazz band plays blues scales daily so that some of the students are able to play a few rounds in works by Victor Lopez ("Mixed Bag"), Jim Snidero ("Basie's Blues" and "Groove Blues"), and Duke Ellington ("In a Mellow Tone," arranged by Paul Cook, and "It Don't Mean a Thing," by Ellington and Irving Mills, as arranged by Mark Taylor). He tours his senior band, the Webster Symphony, and the jazz band, taking them to district and regional festivals for adjudications. The senior band has already "gone state," as it was featured at the state conference of music educators for two years in a row.

Ms. Wilson takes great pleasure in knowing that her choral program has taken good shape. She uses the sixth-grade choir to catch all the singers she can, getting them to sing with sensitivity to surrounding voices, to develop their vocal ranges, their breathing mechanisms, and their attention to the match of what they see (in notation) to what they hear and can vocally produce. By the time they reach seventh and eighth grade, she auditions them into her choir, with expectations that they can sing in tune alone and as she sings a harmony part, and read a simple G-major and A-minor melody of quarter-, eighth-, and half-notes. She features unison and two-part songs in the sixth grade choir, and only introduces three-part music in the second half of the year. The more advanced choir typically sings three parts, too: soprano, alto, and "changing voices" (which she calls "the bass section" even though they are not all quite there yet). The balance is reasonable, too, but not without plenty of work to gain and keep the boys. They all like the songs with considerable rhythmic interest: "Siyahamba," "Shosholoza," "Mi Dan Pasteles," and arranged show tunes. There are also the classic standards that Ms. Wilson feels obliged to introduce, and so the choir climbs the steep learning curve to works like J. S. Bach's "Duet from Cantata No. 37, 'I Will Praise the Lord,'" Brahms's "In Stiller Nacht," Schubert's "Heilig," as well as "Follow the Drinking Gourd" and "The Lion Sleeps Tonight" (both three-part mixed) and a Cameroon Processional called "Praise, Praise, Praise the Lord."

Students in Ms. Wilson's keyboard classes read from *Contemporary Class Piano* (by Elise Mach), and an evening recital in the spring allows them to perform solos or duets or even their own compositions for their families. As for the world music performance classes, "anything goes": West African drumming, Brazilian samba, Afro-Cuban and Puerto-Rican styled percussion, Chinese *luogu* (drum and gong ensemble), Japanese *taiko* (large barrel-shaped drums), and Korean *samulnori* (farmers' drum and gong ensemble). Ms. Wilson mixes and matches Latin conga drums with Ghanian *djembe* drums, using both of them in some of the Asian ensembles, but makes the point that the experience is only partly about ethnic-cultural authenticity and much more about developing a sense of what the music entails even if the instruments are changed. Thus, the performance class works off recordings of various ensembles, and after sufficient listening to even a single piece, "the students are working it out on whatever we have."

❖ BREAK POINT 5.3 Inside the Middle School

Arrange to visit your former middle school, or another that is accessible to you. Examine the curricular schedule of the teachers for its substance, enrollment, diversity of students, repertoire, and strategies employed by the teacher(s). What similarities are notable between the site observed and the circumstances at Daniel Webster Middle School? Are there aspects of Webster's program that could be adapted reasonably well into your selected school?

Maplewood Elementary School

Well within the municipal boundary of a thriving metropolis, Maplewood Elementary feels like a small-town school. The district recently rated Maplewood as the number one neighborhood elementary school, praising it for the commitment of parents and teachers to children's development of comprehensive academic and social skills, achieved through an unusual give-and-take of ideas and energy at school and at home. Contained within its neighborhood of residential homes and few commercial businesses down the street (a small grocery, a fast-food and a sit-down Mexican restaurant, a coffee shop, a dry cleaner, a video/DVD rental store, and gas station), parents see one another on a regular basis and chat about Maplewood, its teachers, the classes, and the after-school activities. The schoolyard is newly paved, with basketball courts and four-square games redrawn on the black surfaces, and the school itself was transformed with new floors, walls, windows, and ceilings over a year's renovation during which the children were bused to other schools. Now children, teachers, and parents are pleased and proud to have their school back, and the buzz of the little community is brighter than ever in the cheery surrounds of Maplewood.

The award-winning school houses almost 400 children from kindergarten through grade 5. From the ages of five to eleven, children spend their days from 8:30 in the morning until 3:15 in the afternoon at Maplewood. Over three-quarters of the children come from two-parent families, and a surprising number of these families include a grandparent (if not two). Many of the families are young, so that mothers may be at home with children not yet of school age; in some cases, mothers work while grandparents take on the child care duties. The Maplewood neighborhood is a working-class community of mostly service workers, with the population spreading across several major ethnicities: 44 percent white, 28 percent Latin American (mostly Mexican), 12 percent African American, 9 percent Asian American, and the remainder (9 percent) "mixed" or "other." While many families attend the local Catholic and Methodist churches, it is the school itself that appears to be the heart of this community.

From the later stages of early childhood, through middle childhood, and on to the brink of adolescence, children in elementary school are in constant—and often rapid—development. Yet they are also who they are at the moment: kindergarteners grappling with crayons and paints and shapes to put together and take apart, full of exhuberant chatter; primary grade children learning to read, to address mathematical concepts with wooden manipulatives, to write block letters and then graduate to cursive script; children of the intermediate grades who are reading novels with thick plots, tuning to current events locally and in the world, and working with pre-algebraic concepts. Maplewood children are keenly interested in their toys, and some wear with pride their "Toys R Us" T-shirts to proudly celebrate their enthusiasm for everything from Elmo to action figures, and Barbie to matchbox collectibles. They play with high energy and enthusiasm on swings, slides, and wood-and-steel playground structures, delight in the tether-ball and basketball activity, and cluster to share secrets among their small groups. The Maplewood school grounds are alive with their daily squeals and shouts, and it takes the constant attention of teachers to settle them down to focused attention on academic assignments and tasks.

Ms. Lee has served as the music teacher at Maplewood School for two years. She knows that in a staff meeting the year before her arrival, a few classroom teachers supported a trade-off of the music position to fill computer needs or a position for a second reading specialist. However, the principal held firm that the Maplewood children need their twice-weekly diet of music. Ms. Lee teaches in a basement room across from the supply room next to a janitor's office and down the hall from two kindergarten classes. Her room is spacious, half carpeted and half new hardwood floors. There is a wide selection of equipment: a new spinet piano, floor-to-ceiling shelves and cupboards stocked with instruments, books, and recordings, twelve electronic keyboards, a set of risers against another wall, and a closet full of drums, xylophones, marimbas, guitars, and nonpitched percussion instruments. There is a teacher's desk, computer, and filing cabinets, thirty stackable student chairs, a long work table, and space for movement on the wood floors. This is the ideal setting for an elementary music program, and Ms. Lee is well aware of it. An instrumental teacher, Ms. Howe, visits on Tuesdays to offer group instruction in violin, trumpet, trombone, flute, and clarinet, and beginning orchestra for fifth-grade students.

The music schedule allots three twenty-minute sessions for each of the two kindergarten classes. From first through fifth grades, children come to music twice weekly for thirty-minute music sessions in grades 1–3 and forty-minute sessions in grades 4–5. But that's not all: a grade 2–3 choir meets on Wednesday afternoons and a grade 4–5 choir meets on Friday afternoons, each for a forty-five-minute session. There is a before-school marimba band open to children in grades 3–5 on Mondays and Thursdays, a recorder consort on Tuesdays, and a guitar ensemble on Wednesdays and Fridays.

Ms. Lee's classes are filled with occasions for singing, listening, movement (or outright dancing), creating, and instrument playing. At first glance, these may appear as a hodge-podge of active things to do. On a more careful examination, the activities are aligned with particular goals that underscore musical facets to experience and to be represented by notational symbols. As many as five or six songs, some familiar and at least one that is brand new, appear in her lessons to demonstrate a common rhythm or melodic phrase. These songs may be rhythmically chanted in a kind of speech play or accompanied by body percussion (such as clapping or patting), and they are often enjoyed for the game that may be associated with them. She mentions songs that are "absolutely central": "Bounce High (the Ball to Shiloh)," "Hey Betty Martin," "Charlie over the Ocean," "Little Sally Walker," "This Old Man," "The Alley Alley-O," "Kye Kye Kule" (for younger children), and "Skye Boat Song," "San Sereni," "The Gypsy Rover," and "Uncle Jessie" (for older children). She sets up xylophones and metallophones on the work table and is consistent about allowing at least one song to be accompanied by her choice of ostinati and drones—and sometimes, children's own made-up accompaniments. There is also a listening experience in every lesson—a CD player pumps out Mozart or Debussy or samba

Many aims can be met through recorder-playing, from notational literacy to improvisation, with a fair measure of fun mixed into the process.

or gamelan as the children enter, and Ms. Lee leads them in movement followed by a brief question and answer session about the musical features they hear.

The music programs at Maplewood tend to be "informances" more than performances at the December, March, and May meetings of the PTA group, when several classes and an ensemble share what they are learning in music class. In addition, there is a spring concert that features Ms. Howe's school orchestra as well as Ms. Lee's two choirs, the marimba band, the recorder consort, and the guitar ensemble. Occasionally, Ms. Lee works with classroom teachers toward the production of a school assembly, such as those that happen for Veteran's Day and Martin Luther King Day. In April, the Maplewood music ensembles join with the band and choir ensembles at the middle and senior high schools to perform at the all-district arts festival, an all-day affair of music, visual arts, and food booths that brings parents, teachers, school board members, and even the mayor. The community celebrates Cinco de Mayo at the school, with home-made tacos, burritos, and tamales, games and raffles, and a mariachi band for dancing. The guitar students sit in with the band for "La Bamba," strumming away to keep up with the more professional musicians, making real the year's worth of group instruction.

❖ BREAK POINT 5.4 Triple View

Compare three elementary school music programs: recollections of your own elementary school, Maplewood Elementary School as described above, and a local school you choose to visit. What do the three schools have in common—and how do they differ—regarding the physical setting for music study, instruments, equipment, and enhancements, teaching schedules, and programs? How do their teachers' philosophical views and instructional strategies differ from one another? How much of this is due to their personal style, the community in which they teach, the age/grade levels of their students? Contemplate your personal reactions to the three "locals": Where would you want to be teaching, and why?

Music in the Community of School

A music education program is what it is as a result of the people who participate in it. The trained and experienced teacher knows to size up the school, its composite population, and the community that surrounds and feeds it. A school's legacy spells out much of the program to new teachers who come in to an established program, and what is working may need only to be maintained. Yet communities change as families come and go, as homes and apartments are built, torn down, and rebuilt, and as commercial developments emerge or change. Five years, ten years, or twenty years on, a nearly nonexistent music program can rise due to the energy and ideas of teachers who know their schools and the communities that support them. (Unfortunately, the reverse can happen, too, as successful teachers with strong programs depart and new teachers lack the competence and community consciousness to motivate students to learn or parents, principals, colleague-teachers, and the wider public to stand behind and believe in the multiple benefits of a musical education). Mr. Newton, Mr. Wenner, Ms. Kantowski, Mr. C, Ms. Wilson, and Ms. Lee are pseudonyms for real teachers who are making a difference in real schools. They are sensitive to their situations, understand their students' needs, and are tireless in their daily commitment to making music in the best and most deeply meaningful ways they can muster. They serve as models for music education ideals with universal appeal.

REFERENCES AND RESOURCES

Abrahams, F., and P. Head. (2005). *Case Studies in Music Education*. Chicago: GIA Publications. A critical look at real-world issues in context, including matters of performing and learning, discipline, and assessment, with descriptions of thoughtful decision making by teachers and the long-term impact of these decisions.

Cox, G. (2002). *Living Music in Schools 1923–1999: Studies in the History of Music Education in England.* Aldershot, UK: Ashgate. Snapshots of music education in the United Kingdom at twenty-five-year intervals that profile music in British schools and society, offering recommendations for the future.

Peshkin, A. (1982). *Growing Up American: Schools and the Survival of Learning.* Chicago: University of Chicago Press. A masterful revelation of the upfront and hidden curriculum of schools in the United States across subjects, and the processes by which young Americans learn and are taught.

chapter 6

Theories of Musical Thinking and Doing

University student A: We keep getting lectures about psych-this and psych-that, and what's "developmentally appropriate," and when kids can keep time, and how the brain and body work with music. It's such a huge gap between theory and what teachers really do.

University student B: Unless what happens in the classroom is somehow connected to these theories?

University student A: Such as . . . ?

University student B: Well, maybe teachers are making their long-range plans because of what they know about the typical behaviors of kids at certain ages.

University student A: Like choosing repertoire based on age?

University student B: Well, sure, and planning lessons because of what they know that kids can do in second grade versus seventh grade, and so on.

University student A: OK, granted. But how does this help the day-to-day stuff?

University student B: Maybe teachers make snap decisions based upon what they know about these psych-based learning styles and sequences.

University student A: Maybe so. We're in the thick of it, that's for sure. I hardly think I'll remember any of this stuff past the test.

University student B: Oh, you will. And do you know why?

University student A: Because deep in my subconscious memory, I'll need to dig out Piaget and brain theory to survive-and-thrive?

University student B: Could be. There is a theory, you know, that says that we retain what is relevant . . . to our survival.

University student A: Who said that?

University student B: Check out the psych readings for Friday's class.

Music as Human Behavior

In recent decades, music teaching and learning has been greatly advanced through the efforts of psychologists. There are educational psychologists, child psychologists, social psychologists, and even music psychologists, all of whose specialized study of human behavior contribute to music education's many realities and activities. Other contributors are specialists in sociology, anthropology, and ethnomusicology. The research of psychologists has helped to clarify human musicality, psychoacoustical processes, and physiological and affective responses to music—who we are musically, how we process and give meaning to music, what we feel within the musical experience, and why we like the music we do. Specializations in educational psychology and the psychology of music have led to the development of research-based theories of music learning and instruction. There is a burgeoning literature in cognitive psychology on matters of aural perception, learning, memory, concept formation, and problem solving, all of it useful in understanding the human processing system. Theories frame the research of psychologists, and the results of their research direct the development of frameworks for effective avenues in music education. Well armed with an understanding of how music is processed, at what ages and in what contexts it is differently processed, and which factors may be more beneficial to learning than others, teachers take the vital third step: to apply this knowledge to their classrooms for the benefit of their students.

What makes children "tick musically"? What can be expected of adolescent musical expression that is not possible among younger children, and how are their skills tempered by their motivation? What do young people hear, and when do they understand what they hear? Are there points in their development when certain musical behaviors typically come into focus? Do they perceive, perform, compose differently over time and as a result of "styles" that are innate or conditioned? When is a teacher's role tied to the direct transmission of knowledge and skills, and when is it more a task of facilitating and guiding the growth of musical expression? How does instructional theory help the design and delivery of successful classroom and ensemble experiences for children in elementary and secondary schools? These are important questions for music teachers.

Who They Musically Are

Children and adolescents have qualities that make them musical. They listen at a deeper intellectual level than do other mammals; they also enjoy music for its visceral effects, its social-emotional facets, and its ability to enhance ritual and bridge to the spiritual. Not all young people will achieve high levels of technical proficiency as singers or players, but they all have the capacity to perceive, under-stand, and respond to music, and to participate in its creation as performers, composers, and improvisers. Anthropologists and ethnomusicologists who study music in and as culture have documented the presence of music in every known culture, and there are numerous descriptions of music in the celebrations, cere-monies, and daily lives of young people. They take music in, even if they are not directly involved in singing, playing, and dancing it because music is almost uni-versally present. Those in deaf culture or with severe retardation are drawn to and respond to music, too, and may be active participants in the music making, for it is the human thing to do.

There are different types and levels of musical involvement, and both nature and nurture are responsible for shaping the extent of our musical experience and expertise. Some people are more adept as singers, due to the strength and width of their vocal cords, the capacity of their lungs, and the shape of their oral cavity to produce a resonant sound. Top-ranking wind and brass players tend not to have extreme overbites that might be detrimental to their embouchures. "Born" pianists and string players may have been gifted with greater dexterity than others, and drum-set players may have more coordina-tion of their hands, arms, and feet than most people. Still, musical proficiency is largely learned. A few physical qualities may limit the development of partic-ular types of high-level musical competence, but most people become skilled because of their deeply personal interest in music, the support and encourage-ment they receive, and the attunement of their learning styles with the teacher's style of transmission so that "the connect" can be made between them.

Young people are musical because they are biologically disposed to hear sounds as organized, and because they are attracted to music's sensory proper-ties. There is the belief that music is cultural rather than natural, and that the perception and creation of musical forms and meanings are mediated by where children live and with whom they interact. Music is widely seen as the expres-sion of socially conditioned factors that cannot be generalizable across cultures, which thus argues against a biological basis for musicality. Through this cul-tural lens, children are viewed as growing into their musical values, skills, and understandings through enculturation, in which shared experiences are pro-vided by the culture of their elders, including their parents, grandparents, sib-lings, and various members of their community. They are socialized into music and are active agents in this socialization, making decisions about which music they prefer and which they will choose to make themselves. So where does this leave the premise of music as a biological entity?

An important factor in human musical expression that crosses cultures is its regular temporal organization—the pulse, or beat. Listeners tap to the beat, subconsciously and without thought, whether they know the music or not. The universality of this reaction argues for music as a natural and biologically driven trait. Another aspect of music that crosses cultures is the octave, possibly because this is the first and easiest tone to hear in the overtone series. Pitches within the octave are divided differently in various cultures, with much Asian music using intervals considerably smaller than the half tones of Western mean temperament; but the octave seems to be constant across cultures. The presence of both pulse and octave in almost all cultures seems to suggest that these are basic to human perception.

The music that young people make and their potential for developing musicianship is a result of both genetic heritage and environmental factors that include education and training. As members of humankind they have the capacity for musicality far beyond the basic biological sense of discernible beats and octaves.

What They Hear—and How

Sound vibrations happen with or without the presence of people to hear them, but when humans are there to receive the auditory sensations, perceptual processing occurs. The rate of vibration is a series of cycles called a frequency which, when perceived by humans, is called pitch. Amplitude is another property of vibration that relates to its strength, so that more powerful vibrations are perceived as stronger, louder, and with greater amplitude. The human perception of timbre is a result of hearing the multidimensional property of particular waveforms, and the extent of time a tone lasts is the basis for human-perceived rhythm—the durational relationships of sounds and silences. These acoustical properties of sound vibrations are "humanized," converted by human perception into the four main psychological constructs of pitch, loudness, timbre, and duration. From vibration comes sound, which is organized by performers and listeners alike as music in all its structural and sensory glory.

Infants react to sound, startled by loud sounds and soothed by soft ones. They recognize timbres as familiar or not, and they are able to discriminate among pitches and durations in their first months of life. In fact, fetuses develop auditory capacity by the sixth month after conception. As we hear, the outer ear captures the air pressure waves of sound, which then make their way down the ear canal to the extremely sensitive membrane of the eardrum. A highly complex operation happens as a series of muscle actions move the vibrations along to the cochlea and the organ of Corti of the inner ear, where minute hairs rapidly change their length to enhance signals that are sent along the auditory nerve to the brain (see Figure 6.1). The auditory sense develops after the tactile sense, while the visual sense is still making improvements and becoming more fine-tuned for days and even weeks after birth. The hearing mechanism is an amazing feat of engineering, and it is through its most sophisticated process that sound vibrations are transmitted and perceived by the youngest little humans for the various qualities that emanate from speech, music, and other facets of the environmental soundscapes that surround them.

Children perceive the sensory information that comes to them and use it to make their way in the world. Perception leads to cognition, their packaging of the auditory information they receive, and their storing and retrieving what is useful to them while discarding the rest. Guided by parents and family members, and later by teachers and others, they grow to understand, appreciate and use music—or at least certain types of music. Through the course of their development, they go from hearing durations to knowing rhythm, from the rise and fall of higher and lower pitches to full-gauged melodies, and into the musical realms of tonality, texture (such as harmony), style, and form. By the time of their adolescence, young people have developed their own personal and social subcultural preferences for the music they will listen to, perform, learn more of, and express creatively.

❖ BREAK POINT 6.1 The Science of Sound

Explore the science of sound so as to develop an understanding of the complexities of sound, how it is humanly heard, and what sense is made of it. Arrange to visit the facilities of a physics or acoustics lab, or invite a specialist from physics, speech and hearing, psychoacoustics, or psycholinguistics to share ideas.

The Range of Their Feelings

A prime feature of the interaction of teachers and students is that teachers care not only about what music they teach students but also about how students receive the music. The responses of children and youth to the musical experiences of a teacher's carefully crafted performance sessions and listening lessons are key to the educational process, and so the question "How do you feel?" hovers alongside "What do you know?" as a significant point of information. Yet feeling is variously defined, and may imply a spectrum of responses that range from the deeply aesthetic—almost spiritual—experience of music, to the

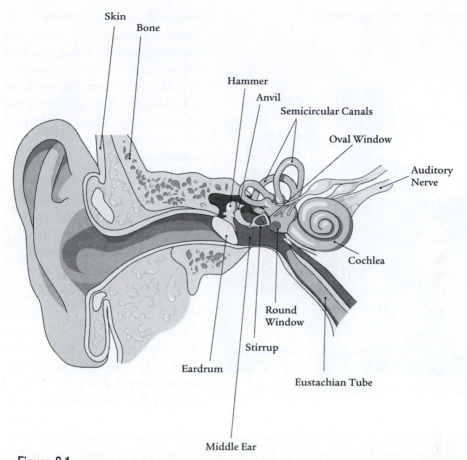

Figure 6.1 • **The hearing mechanism.**

affective responses of music's impact on one's mood and emotional state, to the physiological reactions that are felt by the body. Music has ways of moving its makers and its listeners, and its sensory power as well as its psychological meaning produce a range of "feelingful" responses by children and adolescents.

While teachers aim for positive responses to their lessons, the music they select can have an impact all its own. A musical selection can make students anxious, calm, excited, happy, sad, and tense, and may induce a great many more emotional responses. The particular qualities of the music can arouse or tranquilize listeners, and can affect performers' emotional states as well. Faster tempos, denser rhythms, louder dynamic levels, and staccato passages are stimulative qualities that tend to activate and energize students. Slower tempos, minimal rhythmic activity, softer dynamic levels, and legato passages have a

Listening and feeling the musical sound.

tendency to calm them. The musical qualities of music for marching and dancing will vary considerable from the qualities of lullabies, just as the music of a wedding is distinguished from a funeral dirge. Music's functions are certainly wrapped into the sound of the music itself, and teachers may find themselves designing lessons and the content of performance programs based on the character of the music and its impact on both their young performers and their audiences.

Young people make choices of the music they listen to and even the music they make. There are the short-term choices, called musical preferences, and the long-term valuing of music that is embodied in their musical taste. These choices and values are influenced by a wide variety of factors that include the characteristics of the music itself as well as the variables that belong to the individual and his or her social circumstances. Thus the acoustical properties, complexity, referential meaning, and performance quality of music can make or break the listener's attention and attraction to the music. Meanwhile, the musical choices of peers, family members, and teachers are also persuasive influences. To complicate things further, the individual's own musical sensitivity, past experience and training, age, personality, gender, ethnicity, socioeconomic status, and memory are important in choosing one musical genre, or specific selection, over others. Teachers do well to concern themselves not so much with altering the preferences of their students but in guiding them to experience a musical selection, process, or genre repeatedly and in participatory ways that then clarify for them the details of its components. In this way, teachers need not fight the rock, rap, and country music that so attracts young people but can instead broaden and deepen their musical experiences for these and other genres that are increasingly removed from the familiar.

Music can cause physiological changes, so that there is truly some measurable evidence of "goosebumps" and other bodily reactions that result from listening to music—let alone making it. For teachers attuned to how the music "feels" to their students, this is a relevant subject for their consideration. These responses may exist separately from deep affective feeling, although they are sometimes enhanced by the listener's training and experience. Scientific measurements have been taken of music's effects on heart and pulse rate, galvanic skin response (the subtle electrical charges on the surface of the skin that, when magnified, can lead to "sweat"), respiration rate, blood pressure, muscular tension, blood volume or density, skin temperature, gastric motility (or stomach constrictions), oxygen in the blood, and hormonal secretion. These physiological changes are what some refer to as the "human passion" for the music, and yet there seems to be no certain connection between what the body feels and what the mind thinks—between physiological reactions and psychological states. Much of the research on these measurements has not been able to verify that particular musical characteristics will cause predictable bodily effects, and students cannot be counted on to share similar physical feelings on hearing the music. Still, it is clear that there are powerful visceral effects to music's presence.

❖ BREAK POINT 6.2 Pumped-Up by Music

Discuss a conversation overheard between middle school students on music's physiological effects. What music has been known to "shake you up" physically? Can a teacher ever facilitate such an experience? Is the experience ever social and connected to performing or listening with others, or is it personal and singular?

Sixth-grade student A: Whenever I hear that song, I get so pumped.

Sixth-grade student B: You mean your heart gets pumped up with music?

Sixth-grade student C: I think she means her heart beats faster. That happens to me with all my favorite songs. And I breathe faster on the fast songs, too.

Sixth-grade student A: Yeah, that's what I mean. Even when I'm not thinking about it, music does something to my body, to my insides, and I can't really explain it.

Sixth-grade student B: Well, for me, most of the music I know is just about feeling better. Because I do, when I hear it.

Sixth-grade student C: I would say that there's just the right music, the right songs that match my moods—every one of them.

Developmental Schemes

Over time, as babies become toddlers and as preschoolers become schoolchildren, their abstract, internal representations of knowledge about music evolve. These developmental schemes include children's grasp of melody and rhythm and are ways that cognitive psychologists use to explain the refinement of their musical understanding and skills. One example is the way children develop a frame that shapes their conception and performance of song and singing. Young preschool singers will hear a song that initiates their learning of it: first singing a song's "outline" or general shape into which rhythm and a melodic contour are progressively incorporated, then graduating to the particular pitches of the melody, and eventually perceiving tonality that reaches across the individual phrases to tie the song together in a musically sensible manner. Schemes are like building blocks of knowledge that change as children assimilate new objects and events, and they are developmental in that they are age-related. The song frames of a three-year-old are filled in, so that by the age of five the child may well have a repertoire of songs that sound like the standard nursery rhymes and children's songs of the culture. As children grow, they become more capable of discerning the pitch and rhythm content of the songs they sing, and thus they can use their developmental schemes not only to make sense of the music that comes to them but to express themselves musically. Children produce (sing) only as well as they perceive music, and the singing of even a simple song requires the perceptual skills of melodic and rhythmic discrimination, and memory for tones and rhythms.

Children's melodic development is notable both perceptually and conceptually. In their first four years, they develop the ability to recognize familiar songs based upon the dimensions of melodic contour and rhythm. From their entrance into kindergarten (if not sooner), children are able to conceptualize aspects of pitch and melody as high and low, upward and downward—although it may be the task of the teacher to define and clarify any confusion of terms. In the primary grades, children can identify discrete aspects of pitch motion such as steps, leaps, and repeated tones, and by third to fourth grade they can recognize melodic sequences. As children reach the age of ten and eleven, they are building concepts of scale and mode. Their greater sensitivity to the components of melody occurs through their sense of discovery and experimentation that is both natural and guided.

The rhythmic development of children begins in the womb with the sound of the mother's heartbeat and continues in their infancy as they rhythmically sway, rock, and bounce in their cribs and crèches (and in the arms and on the laps of their parents and caregivers). Children vocalize and perform dance-like movements in irregular and gradually more regular rhythms in their early child-hood, and by the age of three to four years they are tapping in time to a regu-lar pulse and replicating short rhythmic patterns. Beat competence is typically internalized by first grade, as is children's capacity to distinguish fast from slow tempos, and long from short rhythms. They can perceive "getting faster" and "getting slower," too, and they grow from beat competence to perceiving and performing subdivisions of the beat by the age of eight or nine. Metric group-ings are felt by children as early as three or four years, but as they reach third or fourth grade, they are sufficiently experienced that they can recognize and even conduct various meters. Much of children's rhythmic development is tied to their movement sensibilities, just as they develop their melodic understand-ing through experiences in song.

As children grow their awareness of pitch and duration into a full-fledged understanding of melody and rhythm, they also mature to the stage of reading and writing what they hear and can perform. Notational literacy is a valued tech-nique which comes with formal lessons in music at school and in private stu-dio situations. Too often, however, symbols are thrust upon children prior to their ability to discriminate musical concepts and the fine gradations of pitch sets and rhythm patterns. Children who have had ample exploratory experiences in music are able to comprehend the notation that represents specific sounds and sets. Ideally, the earlier the experiences, the smoother the transition from aural images to their symbolic representation. Even as notation is introduced, whether in first, second, or third grade (seldom earlier and rarely later), the sonic experiences of listening and responding to the music help to clarify the mean-ing of the symbols.

❖ BREAK POINT 6.3 Natural or Nurtured?

> Much of what young people can do musically is a part of their natural devel-opment, and yet musical skills and understandings are taught and learned, too. Which is which? Enumerate qualities of musicianship that are innate and not affected by training and education, and those that are enhanced by them.

By the time children graduate from elementary school, they are on their way to further adventures in music through their adolescent years. If they have had strong and positive musical experiences at home and a thoroughgoing educa-tion at school (or training in private lessons), they may continue their musical involvement in middle and high school. For some, adolescence is a time to catch up and surge ahead on skills for singing, playing instruments, listening analytically, reading musical notation, and learning to express themselves as composers and improvisers. At ages twelve or thirteen, and in the years beyond that, they are at the stage of truly understanding the expressive nuances of music. They can more easily produce the dynamic shadings, the rubatos, and the articulatory subtleties of the music they perform. The logic of musical structures become clear to them, too, so that they are able to make sense of the music they perform and will compose. Of course, some will drop out of formal music instruction when it becomes their choice to do so, even though music continues to be meaningful to them as part of their personal identity and a marker of their membership in a social group. Others will continue to develop their musicianship in elective musical courses, and the extent of their effort and time spent at practice will determine the level of their musical accomplishment.

Theories of Learning and Teaching

Nearly all music experiences in school and outside it revolve around theories of learning, teaching, and instruction. Theories derived from the research of psychologists and educators can enhance the instructional practice in classrooms and ensembles, since they help to explain how young people learn and how teachers maximize their learning through various processes. All theories of instruction consist of instruction (a set of events provided by the teacher), learning processes of the student (including attention, perception, memory, rehearsal, recognition and recall), and learning outcomes (the student's demonstration of verbal information, intellectual skills, motor skills, cognitive strategies, and attitudes). Theories direct the music teacher in providing appropriate and well-organized instruction that fits the needs of the learners, offering direction for initiating attention to the learning task, providing steps through which the task is learned and remembered, and suggesting ways the learner may demonstrate that learning has occurred. Teaching without theories in mind is like driving into new territory without a road map. Theories provide direction and frameworks, even though each must be adapted to a particular context. There are theories of teaching and learning that are relevant to the practices of music classrooms in elementary and secondary schools, including those classified and grouped according to their emphasis on stage development, modes of representation, socialization, reinforcement, constructivism, learning styles, and instruction. Samples from these theory groups are briefly described below.

The stage development theory of Swiss biologist Jean Piaget is one of the most influential frameworks for the study of age-related changes of intellectual growth of children from infancy to adolescence. As a classic model of cognitive development, it is grounded in the precepts of organization, the tendency of individuals to integrate all their personal and social experiences into a structured system, and adaptation, the development of this system through the interaction by individuals with and investigation of the environment. Four stages of thinking occur in Piaget's cognitive model, each of which is characterized by new learning in the form of assimilations and accommodations: (1) sensorimotor (from birth to two years of age), learning through motor activity and direct sensory experience; (2) preoperational (two to seven years), learning through actual events and the manipulation of objects, noting the consequences of these events and manipulations and internalizing them for future use, thus transforming stimuli to symbols; (3) concrete operations (seven to eleven years), classifying objects in concrete and systematic ways, and discovering relationships among them; (4) formal operations (from eleven years to adulthood), learning abstractly using logic and deductive reasoning. Stage three, the period extending from grades two to five, is a turning point due to the emerging concept of conservation, which refers to children's ability to recognize objects as unaltered in spite of possible rearrangements. The classic example of conservation is the conserving child's judgment of glasses of two different shapes or sizes as holding the same amount of water, while a musical illustration is a child's identification of the general invariance of two melodies despite the fact that one is performed in major and the other in minor modality. The essence of Piaget's stage development theory is in its puzzling-out the simple-to-complex learning that evolves in the maturation of the child. Piaget's final stage begins at the onset of adolescence, when sophisticated conceptual thinking is possible.

Harvard psychologist Jerome Bruner centered the development of educational theory around the importance of mental structure in learning and its transfer to other situations and concepts. He drew attention to the readiness which children have for learning at various age levels, the nature of intuition as important to children's immediate apprehension of an idea and its balance with analytical thinking, and the importance of motivation—the desire to learn. His modes of representation have been found useful to teachers, as they design their delivery of information to students in one of three modes: enactive, through a set of actions; iconic, through images; and symbolic, through abstract constructions that go beyond what is immediately perceptible in the environment. These modes are illustrated in a process for learning to read music notation, where children may begin with body movements to represent the highs and lows of a melodic contour (enactive), proceed to line graphs to trace these contours (iconic), and graduate to the reading and writing of notation itself on the staff (symbolic). These modes are typically dependent upon the age of the learner, but are also successfully applied to the learning of concepts that are new to students of various maturational levels. See Figure 6.2 for a comparison of Piaget's and Bruner's theories.

In his theory of socialization, the Russian social psychologist Lev Vygotsky established the adult, whether parent or teacher, as the primary influence in the social process of bringing the child into encounters with a set of valued intellectual concepts. The adult transmits these concepts, including music, to the child, and participates in the child's discovery and manipulation of the music to be acquired. Cultural "signs" such as verbal comments and facial expressions are communicated by the adult to the child as indication of approval of appropriate learning behaviors as well as reinforcement of specific elements of an experience. These signs draw children into knowing their social group and their culture (such as their musical culture) while also shaping their understanding of the cultural object (such as the music). As young learners grow in ownership of a song or a musical principle, they become familiar as well with the elements of the musical tradition. Vygotsky's theory extends to the interaction of experts and novices in learning situations, such that at any age, including among children and adolescents, there are always more experienced learners who can interact with less experienced learners in grappling with concepts and skills. Thus, teachers may bring together one student who is skilled on an instrument or in note-reading to help another student learn these skills.

❖ BREAK POINT 6.4 All That Theory

Discuss an exchange heard between two teachers on the merits of the ideas of two psychologists, Lev Vygotsky and B. F. Skinner, on getting children to make the most out of their music class. What further ideas might you offer the teacher who is having "a hard time" that is in line with theories of instruction and learning?

> **Teacher A:** I am having a really hard time with that third-grade general music class. They simply will not settle down.
>
> **Teacher B:** What's your reward system?
>
> **Teacher A:** You mean that old Skinnerian stuff? Are you serious?
>
> **Teacher B:** Yep. And what about the Vygotsky trick, pairing more experienced and less experienced kids in collaborative projects?
>
> **Teacher A:** You *are* serious. Maybe there is something to all that theory stuff.
>
> **Teacher B:** Works for me.

A	B
Piagetian Stages	**Brunerian Modes**
sensorimotor *(<2 years)*	enactive *actions*
preoperational *(2–7 years)*	iconic *images*
formal operations *(>11 years)*	symbolic *notation*

Figure 6.2 • **Piagetian developmental stages and Brunerian learning modes.**

Reinforcement theory is the culmination of decades of experimentation in behavioral psychology, the offering of American psychologist B. F. Skinner. An outgrowth of earlier theories of Pavlov, Watson, Guthrie, and Thorndike, Skinner's operant conditioning is at the core of behavioral change, including learning. The premise of operant conditioning, or reinforcement theory, is that behaviors that are reinforced are likely to recur. A three-part instructional process occurs as manifestation of all learning behavior: a stimulus is presented to the learner, which triggers a response by the learner, which is then followed by the presentation of another stimulus to reinforce the response. Thus, stimulus-response-stimulus is the kernel, or process, that undergirds behavioral change. Stimuli operating in the environment, including the verbal and nonverbal approval of a teacher, have an impact on the learning behaviors of students, so that the teacher's smiles and positive comments are likely to maintain or increase the accuracy and refinement of their singing and playing skills. Along with the shaping of performance skills and academic knowledge, reinforcement theory is also the basis of the classroom management system called behavior modification. This classic system of keeping students on task by contingent rewards—from smiles to stars and from free-choice to field trips—for good behavior has been heavily employed by teachers at all levels, in all venues.

❖ BREAK POINT 6.5 As Easy as 1-2-3

Continuous interactions between teachers and students mean continuous opportunities to observe the stimulus-response-stimulus behavioral sequence. In a typical classroom setting, the teacher provides information, or a question, or a cue to perform (the first stimulus); students respond to that information (the response); and the teacher provides feedback by way of a comment, a gesture, or a facial expression that offers approval or disapproval (the second stimulus). Sometimes, the sequence is incomplete, consisting of only the first two steps, but it is the teacher's response that solidifies the exchange and then leads to further sequences. In some circumstances, a lead student may provide the first stimulus, followed by responses by other students and/or the teacher, and then feedback by the lead student. Take five minutes in various instructional settings to record the frequency of this behavioral sequence, including "who" and "what" details of the behavior. See the example in Figure 6.3 and expect that many exchanges of this sort are rapid and multiple, even in a short period.

Constructivism is a process of learning that results from the reconstruction of principles of a subject by students themselves, allowing them to shape their experiences into new information that is both relevant and meaningful to them. American psychologist-educator David Jonassen is among the proponents of this theory of instruction, which directs attention away from the teacher to the student as active seeker of ideas from multiple sources. Teachers act as facilitators, providing environments that are conducive to learning, and standing by but also stepping aside so that students may engage in experiences that lead to the acquisition of principles, skills, and understandings. Constructivism is behind the student-led evaluations of their vocal and instrumental performances, and their choices of what to improve through student-led rehearsals that work out "the kinks" and lead to musical interpretations that they can call their own. A constructivist approach is also at work in the experimentation by children with instruments and musical motifs in small-group collaborations that lead to their collective compositions. The learning process is less restrictive and more personally meaningful than many others, and it is the teacher's frameworks at the start and guideposts along the way that ensure the acquisition of knowledge and skills by students.

The human personality is complex, and students have many individual differences, so their various learning styles call for many instructional strategies. Among theories that have inspired teaching tailored to learning styles is the notion of hemispheric specializations (popularly referred to as "split brain theory") and the spectrum of learning modalities. For several decades, interest has been directed to the different but complementary tasks of the brain's right and left hemispheres. Cognitive psychologists have referred to cerebral dominance, suggesting that some individuals are "left-brain convergent" thinkers who respond better to verbal, sequential, and linear processing, while others are "right-brain divergent" thinkers who are inclined toward nonverbal, spatial-visual, and simultaneous processing. While there may be inclinations for individuals to prefer one learning style more than another, teachers have tended to gear their instructional practice to both "brains" because rapid and complex communication between the two hemispheres is likely to enhance overall learning.

A second theory of learning styles concerns learning modalities; it claims that the learner's most efficient processing of information rests in one of three sensory channels: visual, auditory, or tactile/kinesthetic. Visual learners absorb

Setting: Ninth Grade Band (1 teacher, 40 students; warm-ups)			
	Stimulus	**Response**	**Stimulus**
(1) Who What	T "Anyone who still needs the music?"	S Nods meaning "no"	T "Great. Glad you're so organized!"
(2) Who What	T "Let's play slowly but very steady. Ah-1-2-3-and . . ." (cue)	S Playing begins	T "Wait a minute: you're dragging."
(3) Who What	S "Can we take the tempo a little faster?"	T "Sure, how about like this?" Taps his baton on the stand.	S "That would be good."
(4) Who What	T "OK. Let's go. Ah-1-2-3-and . . ." (cue)	S Playing begins	– –
(5) Who What	S "My reed is chipped."	T "OK. Get another one."	S "OK."
(6) Who What	T "Let's start again. Ah-1-2-3-and . . ." (cue)	S Playing begins	T "Pretty good."

Figure 6.3 • Behavioral sequence in band practice.

The joy of creative musical expression.

information by seeing, reading, and observing demonstrations; auditory learners by orally delivered examples and directions; and kinesthetic learners by touching, moving, and engaging in physical action. Learning modalities are thought to be relatively stable over time, but students may grow out of one preferred modality into another and to blend modalities as well, so that teaching becomes most successful when lessons involve stimulation of all the modalities. More than most theories, this one merits continuous attention by teachers in the design of their lessons, class sessions, and rehearsals to fit the needs of their students.

A third contribution to learning styles is Harvard psychologist Howard Gardner's theory of multiple intelligences. Rather than considering intelligence as a single phenomenon that is limited in its compass, Gardner saw multiple pathways for the learner's processing of the world: linguistic, musical, logical-mathematical, spatial, bodily-kinesthetic, interpersonal, and intrapersonal. He has recently added consideration for "naturalist" and "existential/spiritual" perspectives as well. A student may find particular strength in one domain and more moderate capacities in others. Each intelligence is a learning style that calls for specific instructional strategies which, when carefully considered by teachers, can make a tremendous difference in the student's learning and development of ideas, concepts, and skills. Figure 6.4 shows the three modes of learning.

Instructional theories take into account the interactions of teachers and learners in the presentation and delivery of knowledge and skills. Among them is Robert Gagné's description of eight "events of instruction" or "conditions of learning," which offers a progression of sensory information from perception to concept formation. Eight steps feature the behaviors of teacher and students in successful instructional experiences: the teacher's gaining and maintaining of student attention; preparation for instruction; presentation of material; and providing learning guidance; the student response to the material and learning experience; and the teacher's feedback on the student response, evaluation of retention, and facilitation of the transfer of student learning to new tasks. Each step in the hierarchy becomes increasingly complex in the interactions that should occur between teacher and students, and the final step requires considerable ingenuity in problem-solving through the use of concepts and skills in new experiences. The application of Gagné's steps to music by Edwin E. Gordon formed the basis of his "music-learning theory," a sequence of perceptual activities that graduates to greater generalization, application, and understanding by the student. The focus of this hierarchy is on the achievement of musical understanding through the development of *audiation* or silent hearing—the

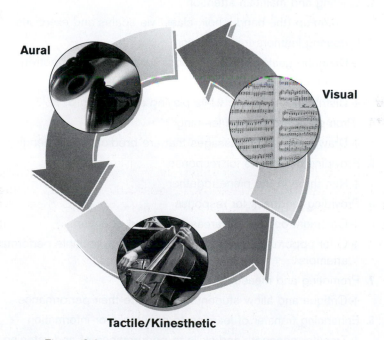

Figure 6.4 • Multiple modes of learning styles.

ability to hear sounds that are not physically present. The eight levels begin with aural or oral reception and transmission and culminate in improvisation and music theory as the final two steps. These levels address the sequential nature of acquiring basic discrimination and music literacy skills, and the use and transfer of these skills to bring about more sophisticated possibilities for music learning. Like Gagné's theory, Gordon's model is an instructional theory that addresses the contributions of teachers and learners in a working classroom.

⟡ BREAK POINT 6.6 A Series of Eight Fortunate Events

Observe the events of instruction that occur in diverse classroom settings, for example, in a children's music class, a middle school instrumental ensemble, a high school choral ensemble, and a keyboard class. Be specific about what constitutes the event, that is, what precisely happens within the event. See the eight events and illustrations below. Discuss modifications of the sequence, the circumstances of the modifications, and how they moderate the effectiveness of the lesson.

1. Gaining and maintain attention
   - ❖ Warm-up (the band, choir, class) via scales and exercises
2. Preparing learners for instruction
   - ❖ Describe goals and expectations for the lesson or activity
3. Presenting the material
   - ❖ Distribute new music while playing a recording of it
4. Prompting and guiding learning
   - ❖ Draw attention to passages that are predictably challenging
5. Providing conditions for response
   - ❖ Run through the piece together
6. Providing feedback for response
   - ❖ Comment on specific areas of needed attention
   - ❖ Offer opportunities for corrections through multiple performance attempts
7. Promoting and measuring retention
   - ❖ Critique and allow students to evaluate their performance
8. Enhancing transfer of learning to new tasks or information
   - ❖ Transfer concepts and skills to performance of and listening to unfamiliar music

Research to Practice

A veritable explosion of research within the social sciences and the health sciences has occurred in the last two decades on music perception, cognition, and performance. A greater understanding of the human brain has led to questions of how music is processed, how it is acquired, and how it is retained over the long term. Music appears to be associated with specific regions and functions of the brain, and this revelation has led to scientific experimentation to discover how and when these regions are activated. The continuing study of music and teaching and learning behaviors within psychology and its associated fields will lead to the refinement of our knowledge of how music is heard, thought, felt, and communicated. Systematic and sustained investigations, paired with theoretical considerations for instructional practice, will lead to improved opportunities for young music thinkers and performers who depend upon thoughtful and well-prepared teachers.

REFERENCES AND RESOURCES

Eysenck, M. W. (1984). *A Handbook of Cognitive Psychology*. London: Lawrence Erlbaum. A guide to understanding the processes that are set in motion in human perception and cognition, which lays the groundwork for the study of human growth and development.

Hodges, D. A. (1996). *Handbook of Music Psychology*. San Antonio, TX: University of San Antonio Press. An introduction to music as it is heard, perceived, learned, and understood, with contributed chapters by music educators and psychologists on musical memory, music listening behavior, music learning and development, and neuromusical issues.

LeBlanc, A. (1982). "An Interactive Theory of Music Preference." *Journal of Music Therapy* 19:28–45. This article set the course for studies of musical taste and preference for a generation; it features a model of sources of variation affecting the individual musical choices that music listeners make.

McAllester, D. P. (1984). *Becoming Human through Music*. Reston, VA: Music Educators National Conference. Based on a symposium dedicated to the study of music learning and transmission. This volume includes accounts of music in schools, at lessons, and in family settings in Bulgaria, Iran, Polynesia, among the Venda of South Africa, and elsewhere.

Merriam, A. P. (1964). *The Anthropology of Music*. Evanston, IL: Northwestern University Press. Long viewed as a cornerstone for understanding music in culture. This book deciphers human musical behavior in the act of performance; it includes a chapter on music learning and transmission.

Radocy, R. E., and J. D. Boyle. (2003). *Psychological Foundations of Musical Behavior.* Springfield, IL: Charles C. Thomas. A thoroughgoing description of music's psychoacoustical foundations, melodic and rhythmic perception and cognition, music ability, learning, and affect.

chapter 7

Teaching Music to Children

Fourth-grade student to a visiting university student: My cousin doesn't have music in her school. I feel sorry for her.

University student: Why so?

Fourth-grade student: Because you get to do fun things in music like playing instruments and making up songs, stuff you can't do anywhere else.

University student: So you like your music class?

Fourth-grade student: Sure. Next to Fridays when we have field trips, our music day is the best day of the week.

Children as a "Choice"

There are some who relish the thought of teaching music to children. They look forward to the possibilities of guiding children in learning to sing in tune and to dance in time. They imagine year after lively year of creative movement-to-music with five-year-old kindergarten children who whirl and twirl, shuffle and skip, stretch and "shrink" on cue. They see themselves among energetic fifth-grade children who are old enough at ten years to have honed listening and per-formance skills and young enough to be playful with them. They have thoughts of guiding children in their performance of multipart xylophone pieces, of lead-ing them in singing a wide repertoire of unison and part-songs, of providing them with their early analytical listening experiences in the music of Mozart and Mali, of Bach and Brazil. They understand the importance of a solid musi-cal education in the elementary years—in itself, and for sending musically com-petent students onward to secondary school programs. For some who consider music education their professional pathway, their thoughts turn immediately to images of smiling children making joyful music.

Just the same, there are those who resist the prospect of teaching music to children. They find the thought of working with them puzzling at best, if not even pointless. Childhood is a long way from their lives, and between then and now are the warm memories they hold of performing well within their high school and university (and even professional) ensembles. For them, elementary school music experiences are often but a dim memory, and sometimes not a highly positive one. Little faces looking every which way, little bodies twittering with excitement, tiny reed-thin voices, shrill shrieks from overblown recorders and dull chordal twangs from out-of-tune autoharps, many "exposures" but rarely experiences that can be called educationally valid—these are their images of teaching music to children. When the choices are making music with highly motivated, self-selected secondary school students who already have a rich set of skills versus starting from scratch with a mandatory, nonselect mass of unfocused "rugrats," some declare no contest: the latter option has little appeal.

There are pros and cons, flavored by personal preferences, personalities, and past and present experiences in how teachers view their prospects of teaching music to children. One secret of successful music teachers is in finding the individually determined balance between "music and people," and then striving toward mastery of the skills that are necessary to communicate and facilitate meaningful musical experiences for them and with them. Some teachers choose the challenging path of leading the wee ones, as musically untrained and inexperienced as they may be, through their wonder years in turning even a single melodic line into a beautiful sound and a profound experience. These teachers know that there are tremendous joys in teaching music to the little people in elementary schools even as they also know there are challenges to be met so that both children and teacher may have a sense of genuine accomplishment. Children are inherently musical, but it takes well-trained and perceptive music teachers to design and deliver for them a learning environment and the

Children's performances on classroom instruments need not be dull, and may even inspire dancing to the collective rhythms and timbres of a percussion ensemble.

sequential instruction that brings their musicality to the surface in the songs they sing, the pieces they play, the music they listen to, move to, and create. While the music selected by teachers for experience and study by children may not typically be sophisticated, the pedagogical techniques for developing their skills as performers and thoughtful listeners are complex and take time to master. For elementary school music teachers, the benefits of the job are in the beauty of children singing together, playing in their first instrumental ensembles, and dancing with delight to the rhythms and forms of the music they hear. They know the importance, too, of making connections to parents (who can foster children's musical development at home while also supporting their education and training at school) and to classroom teachers (who can integrate music into their subjects). Moreover, there is considerable fulfillment in recognizing that with a little help, children are beginning their long lives as musicians in the little elementary school lessons that teachers can offer them.

Musical Children *au Naturel*

All children are musical, more or less, and in a myriad of ways. This statement becomes real and apparent on listening and watching children at play, in conversation with one another, and as they bond and band together through events and projects. Outside the influence of teachers, they sound off to hear themselves, to think aloud, to vent emotions, to expend energy. They socialize through music, making their own communal "jams" of jump-rope songs, hand-clapping chants, singing games, and rhythmic raps. Many of their utterances are musical, too, consisting of pitched and rhythmic fragments that carry along an idea, a call, a cry, a tease, a demand, or even a reprimand. Beyond their playful experiences, children also choose melodies to sing, hum, wail, and whistle while they work—from the homework they do to the housework to which they contribute. Their melodies, newly invented or selected from what they already know, help their chores along, and their rhythmic movements are often what drive their choices.

Before and beyond the influence of adults, children have a musical lore all their own, one comprised of traditional and popular songs, chants, dances, and musical games. They have created this repertoire or they have varied and shaped a repertoire received from adults and other children to fit their needs. They create parodies of songs and poetry they have learned, and they devise couplets and verses to accompany their games and pastimes. They may hold some music intact, too, including seasonal, patriotic, and "school songs," and the music their families have given them. In North America, their traditional songs more often than not include standards like "This Old Man," "Clap Your Hands," "Kumbaya," "Frere Jacques," "The Ants Go Marching In," and "Down Down Baby," and they are keen to pick up and learn the latest mediated music—songs from popular movies, videos, TV programs, tapes, and CDs. They hear plenty more music than they may save, discard much that may not appeal to them, and develop their lore to encompass their perceived needs for particular melodies, rhythms, and rhymed texts.

Along with the music they sound, children's musical nature can also be seen in the ways they move rhythmically. They bounce, sway, rock, nod, and groove to the sounds they hear or make themselves, using their hands, arms, feet, heads, and whole bodies in ways that demonstrate their inherent feel for the beat and its subdivisions. Their rhythmic movements can be simple recurring patterns that may align with the syllables they speak or the functions they perform. There are also the complex cross-rhythms they create alone, hands in one rhythm and feet in another, and the polyrhythms they make together as they rap, hand-clap, and jump rope.

❖ BREAK POINT 7.1 Children at Musical Play: Music Heard and Seen

How do children behave musically, "naturally," while at play or leisure, beyond the direct influence of a teacher? Find a setting where children gather (a playground or schoolyard, a preschool, a community center), seek out the permission of parents or teachers, and sit casually by for thirty minutes to listen and watch for the music that may appear. Listen to their vocalizations, from song to melodic phrases, to rhythmic chants. Watch their movements for recurring rhythms as they swing, hop, and skip. Observe them for the ways in which toys and other objects take on musical sounds as the children manipulate them. Notate some of the musical fragments that you have heard and seen. Write up your observations and share them with your colleagues.

Children have music in them, and it appears to be a natural characteristic of their childhoods to hear music, respond to it, store it, and make use of it in standard and inventive ways. As they grow through infancy, toddlerhood, and into their school years, they are musically enculturated by their parents, grandparents, siblings, extended family, neighbors, and friends. The music of home and family is the sonic fabric of children's musical lives, through which are woven further threads of musical experience they will later come to know outside their first familiar environments. If the society in which they live accepts the concept of musicality as a natural human trait that can be advanced through further education and training, then all children will grow more musical as part of their curricular activities at school. A school music program by its very design can continue the natural development of children's capacity to listen, perform, and create. Music teachers who accept children as innately musical and with the potential to become ever more musical will thus take them further—all the way to the limits of their ability and interest.

Children's Enhanced Musical Development

Just what can children do rhythmically and melodically as a result of a strong and continuing school music program for them? Alone, together, and with the guidance of music teachers who model, stimulate, and propel them forward from one developmental stage to the next, they can make amazing musical inroads from an early age. At the preschool ages of three to five years, they are singing spontaneous songs that sometimes span an octave or more of imprecise pitches. As preschoolers they can replicate small-range and simple melodic phrases and rhythmic patterns that are modeled for them, singing them and playing them on nonpitched percussion instruments. Ask these young children to tap, pat, and clap, and they will, with the teacher's guidance and modeling behaviors, thus demonstrate their feeling for pulse, for meter, and for regularly recurring rhythmic patterns. Kindergarten children begin to conceptualize durations and pitches as same and different, and an understanding emerges early of high and low, fast and slow, and long and short. With regular—even daily—classroom experiences in song, rhymes and rhythmic chants, and directed listening experiences for their movement responses and focused attention, young children in early childhood education settings grow more able to perform music and to understand it holistically and in some of its component parts.

In the primary grades (1 through 3) of elementary school, children undergoing regularly scheduled music education sessions at ages six through nine make the great leap forward in their rhythmic and melodic development. Teachers initiate pathways for their music literacy, because by first grade children are capable of transferring their performance and listening experiences into notation that they can read and write. Once children have been directed to sing and listen to a host of selections of live and recorded music, then components such as quarter-notes, eighth-notes, and half-note rhythms and basic melodic patterns in the pentatonic scale of *la-sol-mi-re-do* make sense and can be read with ease, and written, too. Children learn to identify notation for ♩♫♩♩ (ta ti-ti ta ta) and ♩♩♩ (ta ta toe), and for *sol-la-sol-mi* and *mi-re-do* because they have heard it in singing games and children's songs, and in the music of Haydn and Copland (and of mariachis and gamelans) and have internalized it prior to being shown symbols that have no meaning to them. The key is that music instruction at this early age should be carefully sequenced with these sound-before-sight processes so that children can have full-fledged music-making experiences prior to learning notational symbols. Children have typically heard and performed for years, in "children's music" and popular styles, lively syncopations of dotted-quarter and eighth-note patterns. Teachers can introduce symbols for reading and writing these rhythms when children are only eight or nine years old.

Laminated cards, "big books" readable by the whole class group, blackboards and whiteboards, overhead transparency projectors, CDs, individual student books and handout sheets, and various manipulative objects that are iconic representations of concepts, are utilized by teachers to teach note-reading to children who have been readied for it through strong and continuous experiences with sound. As children's singing range expands from a fifth (d–a) in kindergarten to an octave and a fourth (B♭–E♭') by third grade, their sense of tonality and of pitch relationships also develops. Teachers who sing often with their classes (and with attention to posture, the breathing process, and the articulatory mechanism) can help to develop the greater range, intensity and volume, and accuracy of their children's singing voices. Their musical perception deepens and they become "beat competent" through singing games and rhythmic play so that they are able to keep a steady pulse as a group, thus also ushering children into their earliest experiences in ensemble performance. In these early school years, children can refine their ability to imitate as well as to read notation for ever-longer phrases on xylophones and nonpitched percussion instruments, from wood blocks and triangles to djembe drums. By the end of their primary grades, children are able with guidance to learn to detect major and minute changes in tempo, texture, rhythm, meter, and melody in the music they hear, and they can learn to express themselves at increasingly more sophisticated levels. Without a teacher's guidance, these developments unfold more slowly for children, if ever, particularly in building aural skills, creative musical expressions, and notational literacy.

Children continue their musical growth through the intermediate grades (4 through 6), so that beginning at age nine or ten to the onset of adolescence at age twelve, they can through training become musically competent in what they sing, play, and create. They learn to understand intellectually smaller divisions of the pulse, all the way to sixteenth-notes (including dotted eighth- and sixteenth-note patterns) that they can perform, read, and write. As children can recognize by listening the various metric possibilities at this age, including cut time, compound meters (9/8 and 12/8), and even asymmetric meters (5/8 and 7/8), they can also learn to perform them. They can identify aspects of pitch motion, including steps, leaps, and repeated tones; recognize melodic sequences; and conceptualize and perform in various scales and modes by the time they are eleven or twelve. Their singing range increases to as much as two octaves, and with steady vocal training they can sing independent parts in a variety of harmonized song forms. The development of their small muscle coordination allows them the potential for performing polyrhythmically on various drums and percussion instruments, as well as playing layers of harmonies within xylophone ensembles, and on recorders, guitars, and even beginning repertoire for brass, wind, and string instruments. By the end of their elementary years, children may have already begun to function as expressive and thoughtful independent musicians. They may have fully arrived at the edge of the "big" musical cultures that stretch well into adulthood: string orchestras, multipart choral music, rock bands, and various other sophisticated adult-style genres, leaving their world of musical childhood behind them.

Music teachers make children more of who they musical are, and guide them to all they can become musically. They understand children's natural propensity to make music and to respond to it, and they know of children's intellectual, social-emotional, and physical development. They are aware that some children learn best by seeing (shapes, icons, graphic representations, or notation to represent the ABA form of a minuet to which they are listening), others by doing (moving to a rhythm pattern that is to be learned, or playing it on a hand drum), and still others through listening once or repeatedly to internalize the melody of a song or theme. Music teachers combine what they learned in their music theory, history, and culture classes to shape the most comprehensive musical experiences they can for their children. They choose goals, materials, and activities to fit the needs of children of varying ages and experiences, because first graders learn differently from fifth graders. They interact with classroom teachers to learn what children are learning in language arts, social studies, and math so that some of their music lessons can integrate knowledge and skills acquired in these subjects. They understand what children are musically able to do without training and how a consistent and rigorous musical education can enhance their musical development. Through carefully crafted lessons, music teachers offer children a broad musical development that goes well beyond what comes naturally.

Methods for Teaching Music to Children

Children learn music in schools through methods that teachers acquire in their undergraduate programs and certification studies as well as through specialized in-service training. Teachers know that the action "ing" words—singing, playing, moving, listening, and creating—are the ways and means to children's musical understanding. Their methods typically mix and match these activities to accomplish goals of music literacy, aural skills, vocal production, instrumental performance, creative composition and improvisation, and all-around musicianship. Teachers know a little about a lot of methods, or sometimes a lot about a single method, but in the end they are likely to fashion a method that is personally suited to their own musical strengths and preferences in music and instruction. They may teach from the philosophical frameworks and practical perspectives of the Dalcroze eurhythmics, the Kodály sequence, or the Orff-Schulwerk—all European methods with American applications. Some may teach from a number of other specialized and more localized approaches, while others choose an eclectic approach that combines techniques from across the pedagogies. These methods are briefly described here but require observation, demonstration, and do-it-yourself experiences in order to be more clearly understood.

In the midst of a singing game.

Dalcroze or Dalcroze eurhythmics is movement-based pedagogy that was devised by Emile Jaques-Dalcroze (1865–1950) in his work as a professor of theory in Geneva, Switzerland. He viewed his students as rhythmically wooden and decidedly deficient in their intonation, phrasing, and expressive qualities, and sought to elevate them from their mechanical performances to those that were more musical. His three-part approach of eurhythmics, solfege (and solfege-rhythmique), and improvisation were intended to raise each person's musicality to its fullest potential. Dalcroze eurhythmics is centered on simple-to-complex kinesthetic reactions to music so that the attentive student may hear, process, and immediately respond through movement to rhythmic phrases, melodic movement, harmonic changes, and musical phrases and forms. Live music, usually performed in improvisatory fashion by the teacher at the piano, stimulates and inspires movement that is purposeful and reflective of the music's components; occasionally, other instruments, including drums, and recorded music are also used. The student who moves eurhythmically is not dancing in an artistic manner or performing a creative movement, but is rather responding with immediacy to the music as it sounds. Movement is the means to musical understanding rather than the end-point, and those who practice Dalcroze allow their students to make the brain-body connection to the music they hear.

Hungarians call it "the Hungarian method," but the name of the composer who inspired the next pedagogical approach is Zoltán Kodály (1992–1967). The Kodály Sequence is a well-ordered and logical system of materials and techniques that lead students to the development of performance skills, hearing, and notational literacy. The fundamental premise of the approach is that music belongs to everyone, and that daily—or at least regular and consistent—instruction in folk, traditional, and art music is critical to the musical well-being of children. The accent is on singing songs from national (and increasingly, international) traditions as a way to develop musically independent individuals who can read and write music as surely as they can perform it. Highly visible in the practice of Kodály educators is the use of relative or movable *do* for solfege exercises (in which the tonic of the scale and key, whichever one it will be, is always *do*), the application of hand signs that correspond to scale tones, and the use of the French Cheve system of rhythmic mnemonics for chanting melodic rhythms. Thus, *do-re-mi*'s, *ta*'s and *ti-ti*'s, and closed- and open-fisted gestures are some of the means for getting into the structural details of folk songs and other music. Step by small step, children who listen and perform songs with attention to their melodic and rhythmic "kernels" will be able to absorb and transfer these phrases and patterns to new and unfamiliar music. In a Kodály-oriented program of music lessons, children graduate from elementary school ready for the reading ahead in their middle and high school ensembles (see Figure 7.1).

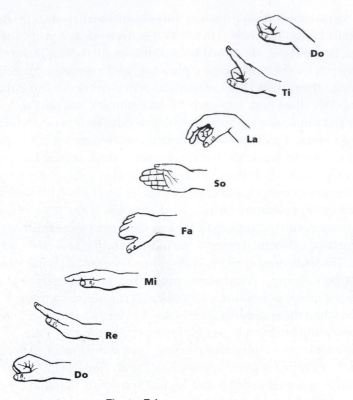

Figure 7.1 • Kodály hand signs.

The process that weaves the natural behaviors of singing, saying, dancing, and playing with improvisation and creative movement is known as Orff-Schulwerk. The German composer, Carl Orff (1895–1982), brought attention to the integrated manner in which children mix music playfully with speech, dance, and movement. The Schulwerk, or "school work" that has evolved from observations of children in their natural play and exploration is a music education process that features folk and folk-like songs in pentatonic mode, ostinati, drones and bourdons on small-sized xylophones and metallophones, rhymes that are chanted rhythmically, and movement that spans the spectrum from body percussion (such as *patschen* or lap-pats, hand-claps, finger snaps, and foot stamps) to creative full-body expressions and formations. The Americanized version of the Orff approach has four stages: imitation, exploration, literacy, and improvisation, so that oral/aural learning and exploration of the sonic possibilities of classroom instruments are key to the process, and note reading and improvisational projects develop from these child-centered ways of learning. Much has been made of the xylophone ensembles in the Orff practice, so that children can accompany their songs with a full complement of synchronized melodic and harmonic phrases as well as create their own compositions in question-answer phrases, ABA, and rondo forms. Recorders, various drums, and small nonpitched percussion instruments are used by Orff teachers, too, to round out the songs that are sung and played. Orff-Schulwerk is embraced by teachers who are drawn to the possibilities for integrating playful child-centered experiences into their method.

At play on the ubiquitous classroom instrument.

✣ BREAK POINT 7.2 Prelude to Standard Pedagogical Practices

✣ *Dalcroze Eurhythmics.* As one colleague/classmate improvises a melody, a bass line, or chord changes at the piano, others walk the pulse and conduct the meter. On the player's cue (a verbal call to "change" or a musical call by way of a high-pitched chord cluster), listeners begin to clap only the first beat while continuing to walk and conduct. On additional cues, they shift to clapping only the second, third, or fourth beats. In another round of playing, combine some of these responses (walking, conducting, clapping) with the challenge to listeners-walkers to change directions at every new musical phrase.

✣ *Kodály.* Choose a familiar melody (for example, Beethoven's "Ode to Joy," "Amazing Grace," "Auld Lang Syne," "La Raspa"). Sing it with solfege syllables. If known, use the Kodály-Curwen hand signs to physically represent these syllables and their pitches. Chant the melodic rhythm using "ta"s and "ti"s. In small groups of three and four colleagues/classmates, select one or more short melodic and rhythmic phrases that may work as vocal or instrumental ostinati, and prepare a musical rendition of the melody with ostinati for the class to hear.

✣ *Orff-Schulwerk.* Choose short poems, proverbs, famous quotations, or even colloquial expressions to speak in a rhythmic manner. Chant them repeatedly, feeling the metric accent, the rhythm of the syllables, the flow of the phrase. In small groups, create a body percussion piece to perform while chanting. Find a simple melody for the chant (using just three pitches, such as *do-sol-la*), and sing it until it is memorized. Add a bourdon (fifths, such as in C major the simultaneous C and G pitches for tonic and the simultaneous G and D pitches for dominant qualities), and simple ostinati on various xylophones and metallophones to accompany the newly learned melody; rehearse it for class performance.

Other approaches found to be effective by thoughtful and well-trained teachers are Edwin Gordon's Music Learning Theory and the classic and still influential Comprehensive Musicianship. Embedded within the Gordon approach is the goal of audiation, or hearing music in the mind when it is not physically present. A hierarchy of musical skill-building steps begins with aural and oral means of acquiring musical phrases and patterns, points toward literacy, and progresses to the final stages of creativity (and improvisation) and theoretical understanding. The thrust of Comprehensive Musicianship, a broad and sweeping vision that is applied as much to conceptualizations of undergraduate programs in music as to curricular development for school music programs, is the

combined effect of experiences and studies in performance, theory, history/
culture, composition (and improvisation). Children are actively involved in listening to and performing the music of many historical and cultural traditions
(art, traditional, "new," and popular), so that all performance classes include
historical/cultural and theoretical concepts just as all listening classes have
applied performance and composition activities. The intended result of the
method, of course, fits its name: comprehensive and complete musical understanding through the many techniques by which music can be known.

The Teacher of Musical Children

The teacher of children in the elementary school music program is a walking,
talking, multitasking phenomenon. Model artist-musician, composer, impro-
viser, arranger, conductor, and certainly compassionate communicator, the
music teacher is central to the musical, artistic, and expressive life of the school
(see Figure 7.2). She (or he) is responsible for the musical lives of children in
school and knows that many of the skills and understandings children develop
in the music program will follow them far beyond their elementary years and
into their secondary school bands, choirs, and orchestras. He (or she) understands that children are not mini-adults but playful little people in the process
of exploring their world of sonic and expressive possibilities, of finding meaning in it, and of balancing what they already know with what they can learn.
The music teacher plays the critical role of shaping the vocal and instrumental
skills of all children, their conceptual knowledge of how music works, and their
coming-to-grips with how they might express themselves through the music
they create and re-create.

Teachers vary in their teaching styles, in their explicit educational aims, and
in the methods and materials they choose. These variances are affected by their
own musical expertise and training, their personal preferences for repertoire and
pedagogical techniques, and the contexts in which they teach. Meet three teachers of music to children, all of them employed as full-time specialists in elementary schools, all successful yet with challenges that continue to keep them on
their toes in their interactions with children.

SINGER OF SONGS

Chris is in her second year as music teacher at Jefferson Elementary School in
a suburban school district that prides itself on "arts for all" from the early ages
through the award-winning high school band, choral, and orchestra programs.

She always knew she would teach music, and that as a vocal major with piano background, she would work with choirs. While her first preference was high school, the Jefferson position came open and Chris decided that she could do worse than to work with young singers. Her curriculum is song-based, and her goal is that children at every grade level will learn fifteen songs a year, every year, until they have about seventy-five songs that they know well enough to sing alone or together. She selects the songs from several sources that were recommended to her by teachers in the district and her former methods course instructor, including *American Folk Songs for Children* (Seeger, 2002), *Sally Go Round the Moon* (Langstaff and Langstaff, 1986), *First Steps in Music* (Feierabend, 2000), and *Roots and Branches* (Campbell, McCullough-Brabson, and Tucker,

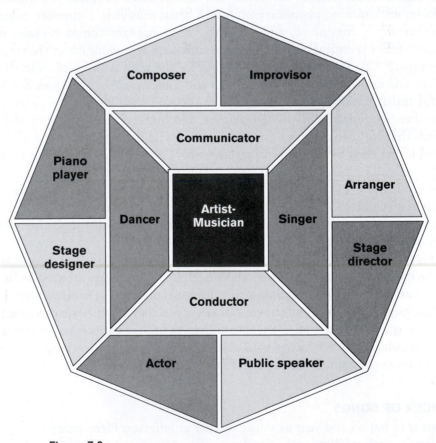

Figure 7.2 • The many facets of a teacher of music to children.

1994). Chris meets every class of children twice weekly in thirty-minute periods for grades K–3 and forty-five minutes for grades 4–6, in a large carpeted room at the end of the first floor. The room is well-equipped with a piano, an exceptional audio system, a VCR, two guitars, a dozen xylophones and metallophones of various sizes, over fifteen congas and djembe drums, and literally dozens of small percussion instruments. Despite all of the equipment, however, it is the songs that Chris keeps in constant focus when she teaches. She sings an introductory song in every class to the younger children, works in vocal warm-ups at the start of classes for the older children, vocally improvises in recitative style some of her instructions and conversations, and typically features three or four songs per class period. Her classes of children learn a new song every other week and spend class time not only singing the song's melody but also clapping its rhythm, singing a selected phrase or two in solfege, accompanying them with various instruments, creating vocal ostinatos (or singing bona fide harmony parts), playing associated games, and creating simple movements that go with the rhythms and forms of the song. Her biggest accomplishment so far in the program was the spring concert at the close of her first year of teaching, when every class group of children stood up to sing—and sang well—for the parents and teachers. Chris started a select choir this year so that fourth, fifth, and sixth graders could perform unison and two-part songs, and thinks that she will enter them into the regional choral festival in May "just for the experience"—theirs and hers (and because it is one more opportunity for parents to hear them and learn why music is an important subject for study!). She talks regularly with the middle and high school choral music teachers and is always open to a visit of their choirs for a performance at Jefferson Elementary School for the musical models they present to her students.

MEDIA MAN

Although he played clarinet and saxophone in his high school band, Jeff also sang lead in the senior class musical, played bass guitar in a weekend band in college, and has dabbled with synthesizers and various music technologies for as long as he can remember. Jeff now teaches music at Spring Street Elementary School in an urban neighborhood of multiple races and religions, just up the bus-line from "the projects" (federally subsidized housing). He has been at Spring Street School for eight years. This is a school on the move: a public school in a large urban school district, it has been "adopted" as a corporate project by a local bank. The eighty-year-old building has been renovated, every classroom is wired, and a budget has been provided for teachers to purchase traditional and high-tech instructional resources as aids to their teaching. It is a dream come true for a school that was marginally surviving at the edge of a community too strapped to help it along. Jeff has a large music room, partitioned off into an area for fifteen keyboards and wood floors for movement and dance; there is a VCR and two monitors, an audio system with speakers he has dreamed of owning for himself, and multiples of every sort of drum imaginable. A corner of the room is devoted to computers, and because he believes in technology-assisted instruction in music, he has extensive software for his students to use during class, at recess breaks, and before and after school: Making Music and Music Ace (for composition), Practica Musica (for ear training), Sibelius (for sequencing and printing), and ECS Time Sketch Series (for music history), and Band-in-a-Box (harmonization). Jeff knows the kids like music, and they like the way he teaches it, too, in a hands-on manner that keeps them focused on the interactive process of making music together as well as the mechanical know-how for building skills and developing their abilities to think and "do" music independently. He is guided by the National Standards in the lessons he designs and is careful to aim for the development of performance skills (#1—singing, #2—playing instruments), but also creative-composition (#4) and music reading and writing (#5) skills. He believes in his students' ability to make music, is interested in *their* music, and is aiming to make the connection between what they like and what they need. He has established a lunch club for children to learn West African and samba drumming, and an after-school "Song-Riders" program to assist children in song-writing, using technology in creating and recording raps, songs, and instrumental pieces of children's own choosing. He admits that he's giving a lot of his time to support the interests of older children at the school but notes that even his first graders can play various melodies on the keyboards, beat patterns on the drums, and play singing games across the wood floor. Jeff is like a kid in a candy shop with all of his new resources, but he seems to have maintained his focus on what counts as truly musical experiences for children.

THE INTEGRATOR

Four years into her first teaching job, Shannon is at home as the music specialist at Raymond Hill Elementary School. The community is supportive of her work, and her PTA programs of musical skits and costumed productions are peak experiences not only for the children but also for their parents, grandparents, and extended families. Shannon has learned to tune into the community and school cultures, the lifestyles and goals of the families of her children, the overarching goals of her team of teacher colleagues, and the curricular themes that emerge across the grade levels. Raymond Hill is a small school in an orchard town of peach farmers and apple pickers, where school attendance fluctuates according to points in the growing season and only three of five students make it to high school graduation. Shannon and her colleagues know that if children are to acquire basic academic (and artistic) skills, it will likely need to happen through a consistent school program rather than in the home. There are few resources in the basement music room, aside from shelves of decades-old music textbooks and song collections, an upright piano, a portable "boom-box" CD and tape player, tone bars, several colorful metal xylophones, a box of recorders, and a cupboard filled with sticks, jingle bells, tambourines, cowbells, and maracas. Hardly the latest gear, and yet the children come to her classes enthusiastic for what they might experience. Shannon keeps up with what they are studying with their classroom teachers so that she can underscore and illuminate subjects and concepts through music and the related arts. (After all, she is the school's only arts teacher, so she is in a position of responsibility to bring a broader awareness of all the arts to children—and their teachers.) Sometimes Shannon will devise listening lessons that complement stories and poems, or lead children in turning a folk tale into a musical drama complete with songs and instruments. She meets the benchmarks for National Standards (see Figure 4.1) in various ways: Her one-minute listening experiences are followed

One child's song, with the full support of her teacher.

by "What did you hear?" worksheets for the children (National Standard #6); her half-page historical and cultural descriptions of the music her children perform go out weekly to the classroom teachers (National Standard #9); and her children invariably spend a few minutes—or more—of nearly every class session improvising upon the new pattern or style they are learning. She will extend children's study of patterns in mathematics to experiences in detecting symmetry, repetition, and variation in the visual arts and in the music they may hear and respond to, or create themselves. When she learns that children are studying a geographic region or culture in their classrooms, Shannon will draw together relevant songs, stories, and recorded music to reinforce their learning of the land, people, and their traditions. There is so much for the Raymond Hill children to learn in school, including catching up to prepare for a more socially and economically mixed middle school, and Shannon believes that the music lessons she provides can help them to grow aesthetically while extending their understanding of other subject areas. She works overtime, spends a good bit of her personal budget on items (music, puppets, storybooks, instruments, and small prizes for children's good behavior), and is often exhausted in her attempts to link music to the other subjects that she knows less well; but she knows it's all for a very good cause: the children.

❖ BREAK POINT 7.3 The Ideal Program

> What would be the best-case scenario for teaching music to children? If you had an unlimited budget, what equipment would you purchase? If you had maximal time with children, for example, three 30-minute lessons with every classroom group of children each week, what objectives would you aim for? What strategies, concepts, and repertoire would you include in your teaching of children in a primary and intermediate grade? Compare your ideal program with those of your colleagues.

The music teacher plays an important role in raising musical children within school programs who will be guided by the interest their teacher has in particular types of music, musical activities, and pedagogical strategies. He (or she) is responsible for teaching music *and* teaching children, and ensuring that not only teaching but also learning is underway in their classes. The dynamics of working well with children—playfully, inventively, enthusiastically, of knowing what music is best in given circumstances, of coming to grips with one's own personal styles and preferences, of fitting into a faculty of teachers of other subjects, of sizing up the community for its interests and aims, all contribute to the making of a successful teacher of music to children. It takes an individual with comprehensive musical skills, imagination and curiosity, high energy, and a certain nurturing sensibility to take on the challenges of the position, but there are deeply personal rewards to be had in making children's lives more meaningful through music.

Teacher's Duties, Children's Rights

There is more than meets the eye in the work of an elementary music teacher. There are the larger curricular goals that must be considered, daily lessons to plan, and seasonal and thematic programs to put together. All along the way, the music teacher is guided in curricular content by national, state, and/or district standards for the attainment of musical goals and objectives, which is good reason for her (or him) to know the means and methods of evaluating the children's musical growth, tracking their progress, and then communicating their progress to parents and classroom teachers. There is the overriding and pressing need for the teacher to be able to articulate that while school music classes for children may seem at times to be mere "noise," sometimes chaotic, or simply "prep-time" for classroom teachers, it is in fact one component of basic knowledge and bona fide experience—different but equally valid—which all children should have as young members of American society. All children deserve equal rights to know music as part of their cultural heritage, and to develop their aural, artistic, and expressive capacities to the fullest degree. This is a teacher's duty, to move children more deeply into their musical selves and outside themselves, too, to the music that sounds in their world.

REFERENCES AND RESOURCES

Bjorkvold, J. R. (1992). *The Music Within: Creativity and Communication, Song and Play from Childhood through Maturity*. New York: HarperCollins. A neoliberal view of music in infancy, toddlerhood, and through middle childhood. This book pays tribute to the importance of music in the child's world of home and family as well as at play with friends and in study at school.

Campbell, P. S. (1998). *Songs in Their Heads: Music and Its Meaning in Children's Lives*. New York: Oxford University Press. An exploration of the meaning and value of music in children's lives, based upon their expressed thoughts and actual musicking behaviors in school and at play.

Campbell, P. S., and C. Scott-Kassner. (2005). *Music in Childhood: From Preschool through the Elementary Years.* Belmont, CA: Wadsworth Group/Thomson Learning. A delineation of music and instructional approaches suited to the perceptual-cognitive, physical, and affective development of children in early and middle childhood, with sample models and graphs to illustrate techniques and systematic methods for teaching musical concepts and skills to children.

Choksy, L., R. M. Abramson, A. E. Gillespie, and D. Woods. (2000). *Teaching Music in the Twenty-First Century.* Upper Saddle River, NJ: Prentice-Hall. An examination of the processes of four pedagogical methods prevalent in the teaching of music to children in North America: Dalcroze eurhythmics, the Kodály sequence, Orff-Schulwerk, and Comprehensive Musicianship.

chapter 8

The Choral Classroom

An early-morning rehearsal in Mr. Mitchell's choir room. The concert choir is just finishing their first rehearsal on a new piece.

Mr. Mitchell: OK folks, let's take just the last three bars. As you approach that final chord, you need to maintain your breath support under the tone. Think of the weight of a glacier, slowly, but powerfully moving forward till it finally comes to rest.

The choir sings and the teacher holds the final chord for a very long time.

Mr. Mitchell: Excellent! Good first rehearsal on that piece. See you tomorrow.
Jessica: Mr. Mitchell?
Mr. Mitchell: Yes, Jessica.
Jessica: What just happened?
Mr. Mitchell: What do you mean?
Jessica: When we held that final chord I got shivers and I felt like I was going to cry. It seemed like the whole choir just locked in together as a single voice. It was so beautiful!

Singing is the oldest and most fundamental form of human musical expression and musical vocalizations occur in infants almost from birth. This widespread ability to sing is apparent even in public gatherings. People of all cultures have historically included music as part of important ceremonies, events, and even casual gatherings. But while no one expects someone to pick up a trumpet and play along with the band, people often sing along with music at the ballpark, the rock concert, or around the campfire.

Choral music education has its roots in informal community singing and in music for the church. The church influence can be seen even in today's school choirs. Much as bands often wear uniforms indicative of their military origins, many choirs wear robes reminiscent of their ecclesiastical roots. The role of the amateur, too, has had implications for how choral music in the schools is viewed. It is both a great strength and a weakness that choral programs typically welcome members even if they have very little musical training. There are often not the same expectations of early training or even private study for choir students that are frequently associated with band or orchestra participation. The strength of this approach is that choir classes are more accessible to students at a variety of levels of musical training. This allows the choral program, more than any other ensemble at the secondary level, to draw students into musical participation at any point in their academic career.

This accessibility for less-trained members is also a weakness that appears most clearly in the common belief that "there are *musicians* (i.e., instrumentalists) and there are singers." Nothing could be further from the truth. While the ability to sing may develop in individuals without a lot of formal training, the necessary skills for an accomplished choral musician require a level of vocal and musical ability well beyond most amateurs. The magic of choral singing however, is that because of the intuitive and imitative nature of singing, a few highly trained voices in each section can have an enormous impact on the sound and skill of a much larger ensemble.

What are the skills that choral teachers should be developing in their groups and how can they do so while maintaining the accessibility that has become a hallmark of choral education? The answer lies in a comprehensive view of the choral program that welcomes all levels of musicians but rewards advanced training and achievement with greater levels of musical challenge.

❖ BREAK POINT 8.1 Informal Participation in Singing

Think about the last time you sang or heard singing at a public gathering. Was it a formal event like church or just singing along at a sporting event or in the car with friends? What music was sung? Did most people participate?

The Comprehensive Choral Program

At first glance the choral curriculum may appear to be just a set of pieces programmed for the concert. When music education students first go out to observe choir classes, they often describe the teacher's objectives in terms such as, "To rehearse *Shenandoah*." They are focused on the surface level of *what* is being rehearsed rather than looking at *how* the rehearsal teaches skills and concepts through *Shenandoah*.

The choral curriculum is built on the skills and knowledge central to the art form. Chief among these are development of the singing voice, development of musicianship—both technical and expressive—and a historical and cultural knowledge of repertoire being sung. These curricular elements may take different forms depending on the grade and skill level of the singers, but all are crucial to the success of the program. The goal of the curriculum is to offer secondary students a comprehensive education as performers, listeners, and creators of music with choral music as the medium of instruction.

THE DEVELOPMENT OF THE SINGING VOICE

Most choir students do not take private voice lessons to supplement their training. For that reason, their development as singers is largely dependent on the training they receive in the ensemble. Vocal training takes place throughout the choir rehearsal but is addressed most directly in the warm-up period at the beginning of rehearsal.

Warm-ups should be thought of as a group voice lesson where the fundamentals of singing are reinforced and tied to the challenges of the literature being rehearsed. Fundamentals include breath and posture, resonance, vowel formation, range, flexibility, and intonation. One of the advantages of choral

High school singers doing vocal warm-ups.

music is that the "instruments," while having different ranges, share almost all the basic elements of sound production. Daily exercises on fundamentals are as important to an experienced singer as they are to a beginner. Most conductors use warm-ups at the beginning of a rehearsal to establish a supported sound, increase vocal flexibility, and build long-term vocal technique. This can be done through a series of exercises that the conductor has found to be effective in those areas, and the exercises may remain relatively unchanged from day to day. A more contemporary approach is to use a variety of warm-ups to build vocal technique that are tailored to the demands of different styles of music. By customizing warm-ups to the literature being rehearsed, a conductor can prepare a choir both vocally and musically. The basic principle behind this approach is that a choir should never sing without some kind of musical goal or intention. More detailed sources for effective warm-ups are listed at the end of this chapter.

One important consideration in teaching adolescents to sing is the phenomenon of the voice change or vocal mutation. The vocal instrument actually changes shape and size as the young singer grows and matures. This creates a special set of difficulties for the choir teacher. It is well known that boys' voices change or "break" during adolescence. This voice change results in an eventual octave shift in range that can create problems for boys in using their singing voice and for teachers trying to program appropriate music. Girls, too, experience a voice change from the child voice to the adult voice, but they may not be aware of it unless they are singers. The change is subtler, but it still creates difficulties in vocal tone, range, and breath support for adolescent girls that choral teachers must understand. Guiding boys and girls through the voice change requires a teacher who is informed, understanding, and patient. Figure 8.1 outlines the ranges and tessituras associated with the more dramatic stages of the voice change for boys as characterized by Barresi. Because students are negotiating these physical changes,

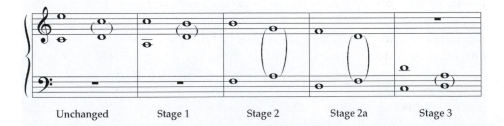

Unchanged Stage 1 Stage 2 Stage 2a Stage 3

Figure 8.1 • **The stages of the boy's voice change with total range and comfortable range.**

changes that often affect their usable singing range, group vocal training and repertoire have to be adjusted to meet different needs.

Despite the potential challenges of the voice change, it is important for young singers to continue to sing throughout adolescence. While all children's voices eventually mature, those who have maintained a connection with their singing voice and practiced good fundamentals will emerge from early adolescence with a stronger, more pliable singing voice. Middle school choirs can, with solid vocal training and appropriate literature, make incredible music.

THE DEVELOPMENT OF MUSICIANSHIP

Developing good singing technique is an important part of choral training, but it is only one facet of a comprehensive curriculum. Choral directors have a responsibility to develop well-rounded and competent musicians as well. Once students enter the choral ensemble at the secondary level, it is often their only source of school-based musical training. Thus the choir director is not just their *choir* teacher, but their *music* teacher. While it would be ideal for every child to experience training in singing and playing instruments throughout their school years as they do in elementary school, such broad training is nearly impossible at the secondary level given the increasing limitations on the number of electives students may choose.

The comprehensive choral program must teach students the fundamentals of music including the skills of music reading, stylistic awareness, critical listening, and expressive performance. Of these, the most challenging and least taught seems to be the skill of music reading. Here again, singing's greatest strength is also a weakness. Because singing is so intuitive, because students can learn so much music so quickly by ear, they can often avoid the more difficult task of accurately reading music at sight. To help understand why this skill of imitation is a strength, imagine a concert band rehearsal where students had to learn to play their parts simply by listening to them over and over and playing by ear. While it could be done (and *is* in garage bands and some jazz groups), it would be a very cumbersome and time-consuming process that would reduce the amount of literature performed to one or two pieces a year. Yet entire choir programs are run this way. In contrast, learning to read music on an instrument is often a much more straightforward and external process of connecting a written note to a corresponding key or finger placement on the instrument. Not to minimize the accomplishment of instrumental sight-reading, but consider if instrumentalists couldn't see their hands, or their instrument, but had to connect a written note to producing a particular pitch merely by thinking it. That is what sight-*singers* (and eventually all good sight-readers) must do.

How do choral directors, then, teach singers to read music? Fortunately, there are numerous effective approaches to teaching sight-singing in choir. The biggest obstacle is usually the teacher's own experience. Many choral music teachers were not trained in choral programs where sight-reading was taught, so they have no models on which to base their instruction. The evidence for the power of this influence comes from observing choral teachers from states where music reading is taught in school choirs because it is a requirement for choral contest. Beginning choir teachers who were trained to read music in their own high school choirs include music reading in their programs when they go out to teach, even when they go to teach in another state.

A choir teacher leading a sight-singing lesson with hand signs.

TEACHING SIGHT-SINGING

There are a few basics that can illustrate why teaching sight-singing is a very attainable and important curricular goal for any choral program. Often at least some students in a choral ensemble will have little or no experience reading musical notation. These "prenotational" singers are often the biggest challenge for choir teachers, particularly new teachers, who wonder where to begin the learning process. The choir teacher should begin with the *sound* of the music before the *symbol*. While students might not be able to sing a major scale from solfege syllables, they are very familiar with the sound of a major scale and can easily imitate a variety of pitch and rhythm patterns. The process of imitation provides the means for connecting familiar sounds to the new symbols that are needed for music reading.

Another important consideration in teaching music reading is the development of a consistent approach to reading a new piece of music. Choral teachers eventually want their students to be able to pick up a piece of music, study it, and sing it independently, so they must teach them an approach to music reading that will support that goal. The song learning sequence in Figure 8.2 provides a good foundation for such an understanding. At the prenotational level, information on meter and key will be provided by the teacher, but as students progress in their skill development and musical knowledge, they will be able to determine the meter and key information on their own.

There is no concrete evidence that any one system of music reading is better than any other, though teachers will strongly advocate their favorites. The most important factors in choosing a reading system are that the system make sense to the teacher and, ideally, build on the students' previous experience. If the system doesn't make sense to the teacher, he or she will not teach it well or enthusiastically. In teaching these skills, the teacher's own ability as a sight-reader is not as important as one might think. First of all, teachers should not be sight-reading during the lesson. That is, they will have chosen the examples and studied them prior to the lesson, and even practiced the solfege and rhythm patterns

Rhythm

❖ Identify the meter and starting beat.

❖ Scan for difficult and repeating patterns.

❖ Set a steady tempo and chant the rhythm while keeping the beat.

❖ Evaluate.

Pitch

❖ Identify the key signature, tonality, and starting syllable.

❖ Scan for difficult and repeating patterns.

❖ Establish sense of key through tuning up, perhaps sing difficult patterns.

❖ Set a steady tempo and chant or sing solfege (or other syllables) in rhythm.

❖ Evaluate.

Figure 8.2 • A song-learning sequence.

to be sure they are modeling accurately. Two of the most important factors in students' eventual success are a positive teacher attitude and consistency in teaching music reading every day.

While music reading is a key component of musicianship, it is not the only skill that must be taught in choir. The National Standards make it clear that music education at all levels should include instruction in composition, improvisation, listening skills, and historical/cultural knowledge. Many of these elements are easily incorporated into daily rehearsal through guided listening, performance evaluation, and a diverse approach to repertoire. Composition and improvisation opportunities often require a more direct approach, but a number of teachers have accomplished this through composer residencies, choral arranging experiences, integration of computer technology, and the inclusion of repertoire that allows for a more improvisatory approach to singing. Choral teachers need to be sure that the musical experiences in their classroom, while centered on the choral experience, go well beyond the rehearsal and performance of specific repertoire.

CHOOSING APPROPRIATE REPERTOIRE

The development of vocal and musical skills culminates in rehearsing the repertoire chosen for performance. The repertoire of choral music, like the robes, is rooted historically in the Christian church, though it has expanded considerably over time to embrace a wide variety of sacred and secular music from many cultures and styles. Over the last twenty to thirty years, repertoire choices have expanded to the point that an enormous variety of music from different musical cultures and styles is available and accessible for any level of ensemble.

So how do choral teachers decide which pieces out of this vast repertoire are best for their students? Next to the teacher's own skill, repertoire choice may be the single biggest determinant of the eventual success or failure of a choral program. If the music doesn't fit the students' ability level, then no amount of effective teaching will result in success and either boredom or frustration will eventually take over. Boredom is a risk if the music chosen is too easy. While this is a less frequent problem, it can happen if the teacher targets repertoire to the weakest members of the ensemble rather than attempting to balance the needs of diverse skill levels. A more common occurrence is that the director, especially an inexperienced teacher, will choose music that is too difficult, or choose too many difficult pieces for a single program. In this situation, even a very good choir can become frustrated and disheartened. The reason this mistake is more common in new teachers has to do with the teacher's orientation. When a new teacher has just finished his or her college training, the primary reference point for literature is the sophisticated and highly technical music of the college choir. Everyone wants to teach music with which they are comfortable and familiar so sometimes teachers go first to literature that's comfortable for *them*, but too difficult for their students.

A second consideration in choosing appropriate repertoire is to balance difficulty across a program. Sometimes teachers will choose a piece that stretches the choir in a particular area like rhythm or tone but is otherwise not beyond the singers' abilities. The problem comes when every piece on the program fits that description and the students are given no real opportunities for comfort and mastery of any of their pieces. Repertoire that is simpler technically allows the teacher to explore the expressive aspects of choral singing in more detail and polish elements of tone, blend, and balance in ways that are impossible when the pitches or rhythms are still in doubt. A unison piece, for example, can provide many wonderful opportunities for teaching singers about tone, blend, phrasing, and expressive singing.

When programming repertoire, teachers should seek a balance of difficulty, of styles and cultures, and of tempos. Programming a concert has been compared to planning a formal dinner, one has to balance appetizers with entrees and too much dessert can be bad for you. In addition to repertoire variety, it is important for a teacher to know the group's strengths and weaknesses from year to year: will there be more men, are there more beginning readers? Do you have certain solo voices? How many high sopranos are returning? All of these factors can contribute to intelligent programming. Consequently, less-experienced teachers would do well to choose only a handful of pieces at the beginning of the year to help familiarize themselves with their groups' abilities before completing a full program. In addition to the group's particular strengths, there are some general considerations in choosing appropriate repertoire. Figure 8.3 offers a list of questions to ask about any piece of music before choosing it for the ensemble.

Having answered these questions and identified a group of appropriate pieces, the teacher must now look at how they fit together. Does this piece fit with the other choices thus far? Are the choices balanced for difficulty and style? This is extremely important both for the enjoyment of the audience and the education of the singers. Even if the demands of a particular piece can be met, teachers must be sure that the time required will not overwhelm the needs of the other pieces. A good rule of thumb is to do more with less in terms of both the number and difficulty of the works chosen for the program. Teachers should choose pieces that allow the conductor and the singers the opportunity to get deeply into the expressive and technical demands of the music and have the potential to yield the most polished performance.

1. Do the ranges and tessituras fit my singers?

If the singers can't sing the pitches of the piece or they are consistently out of their comfortable range, then they can never be successful. The teacher must be knowledgeable about the general range limitations of young voices at different age levels, and about the limitations of their particular group of singers.

2. Is the literature of good quality?

This question may seem very subjective and indeed some directors still have difficulty acknowledging the "quality" of any music that is not Western art music. What is meant by this question is, "Does the piece represent its style well?" For example, does the gospel piece have the characteristic piano accompaniment and voicing? Is the South African piece actually from the culture or composed to "sound like" South African music? Even within Western art music there are numerous "rearrangements" of classical works for smaller forces like two-part or SAB and some of them are better at preserving the character of the original work than others.

3. What are the musical challenges?

The literature is the curriculum. It is the vehicle for teaching the concepts and skills that will build good vocal technique and choral musicianship. The difficulty level cannot be so overwhelming that all of the rehearsal time is spent drilling pitches and rhythms. The challenges of any one piece should be at a level where the choir can be working on articulation, tone, and balance even as students are beginning to learn the work and polish their parts. This requires a thorough understanding of the structure of the piece and the challenges within.

4. Is the text of good quality and appropriate to the age/type of group?

Ideally choral directors should be knowledgeable about poetry and literature, as the text is one of the aspects that distinguishes choral music as an art form and adds an important layer of meaning to the musical experience. Consequently, choosing texts of good quality can enrich the learning and the lives of the students in choral ensembles. The marriage of a beautiful text and a sensitive musical setting can be a transcendent experience that deepens the understanding of both. This requires that the text be appropriate for the age level of the students and have literary value on its own.

Figure 8.3 • **Considerations in choosing appropriate repertoire.**

Choral Ensembles

We have discussed the various needs of the choral curriculum, but what does the comprehensive program look like in terms of the kinds of ensembles offered? Comprehensive instrumental programs must offer ensembles dedicated to certain kinds of music (e.g., orchestra, jazz band, or marching band) because each different style of music requires a different set of instruments. Choral ensembles on the other hand, can sing a great diversity of music within one ensemble. So the choice of which ensembles make up the choral program need not be determined by repertoire as much as by the function of each choir in the overall curriculum and variety of learning opportunities available to the students. There are any number of possible combinations depending on the individual situation. Whatever the ensembles offered, it is crucial that any student who wishes to sing have a place in the choral program. To meet this need, one or more of the choirs in a choral program must be nonauditioned and welcome singers of all levels. What follows are examples of the kinds of choirs and other offerings that can serve an important function in the comprehensive choral program.

THE LARGE MIXED CHOIR

Mixed choirs of forty to eighty singers are typically the foundation of the choral program and for good reason. They involve the most students and have the greatest variety of literature possibilities due to their size. A typical balance of literature for a large mixed choir would include selections from larger choral orchestral works, historical and contemporary works that feature six to eight parts, selections of popular music, gospel, or world repertoire and even arrangements or medleys of Broadway tunes. These groups usually perform in at least three larger concerts a year as well as in other smaller performing opportunities and participate in at least one large group festival or contest. From a curricular standpoint, the large mixed choir is where the fundamentals of choral singing described earlier are taught and developed. There should be at least two larger mixed choirs; a beginning and an advanced choir organized by ability. The beginning group allows the teacher to introduce fundamentals of vocal training, musicianship, and choral artistry that will be expected before students can join the advanced group. Beginning groups can also give younger students a chance for solo and leadership opportunities before they "graduate" into the advanced ensemble.

A high school chamber choir.

THE SMALLER SELECT CHOIR

Choral programs usually feature one or more smaller select ensembles of between sixteen and twenty-four singers that are by audition only. These smaller select groups, often called chamber choirs or madrigal choirs, offer an opportunity for additional musical challenges for the more advanced students. The curriculum in these groups focuses on learning repertoire more quickly, more varied performing opportunities, developing more independence as a musician, and greater vocal challenges with fewer singers on a part. In many programs, the select choir does not meet during the school day but as a before-school activity with all members required to be in one of the larger mixed choirs. This allows the teacher to offer more opportunities for advanced singers while retaining the leadership of those singers in the larger group. Another option is to have the small group meet during the school day but perform with the large group in addition to their chamber repertoire.

THE JAZZ OR SHOW CHOIR

One of the most common types of chamber ensemble is the jazz or show choir. These groups are often the most popular with students (and parents) and can be a great way to showcase a choral program, especially for recruitment. They offer opportunities for students to develop solo singing skills, improvisation skills, and even choreography. Students who came from a program that featured such a group will no doubt want to have one in their own program. There are several issues to consider before instituting such an ensemble. It is important that the director use the visibility of this group to support rather than obscure the other ensembles in the program. Since these types of groups often require significant resources involving equipment, costumes, and travel, it is important that their needs and financial requirements be balanced with those of the entire program. This means they shouldn't do too much more traveling than other groups, and other larger ensembles should feature some of the more popular literature on their concerts. Jazz or show choirs can be an important and enriching aspect of a choral program when balanced with the needs of all the students. Because of the comparatively narrow range of literature, some programs have the select chamber choir do madrigal and chamber literature at the beginning of the year and then become a show choir or vocal jazz ensemble in the spring, providing a greater variety of training for the advanced students.

WOMEN'S AND MEN'S ENSEMBLES

Most choir programs have a women's ensemble because there are usually more females than males interested in singing at this level and spots in the mixed choir are too few to meet their needs. Because of this, the women's ensemble can sometimes be seen as the "leftover" group from the mixed choir. Some directors have reversed this trend by making one of their small select ensembles a women's group. The repertoire for women's ensembles has exploded in recent years and there is a wealth of quality music, much of it written specifically for such a group.

While women's choirs are more common, both men's and women's groups can serve an important function in the choral curriculum. Single gender ensembles allow the teacher to tailor both the vocal and musical training more directly to the different needs of male and female singers. This is particularly important in middle school because of the different physical changes and vocal needs of adolescent boys and girls, not to mention social needs. The reason single-gender ensembles aren't more common in middle school has more to do with school scheduling than pedagogical practice. Finding separate times in the schedule, one open for all seventh- and eighth-grade boys and another for the girls, can be very challenging. Add to this the possibility that initially the girls' choir may number sixty and the boys' group only six and the challenge increases. Even so, teachers who have been able to institute separate training at their schools have reaped enormous benefits in terms of the progress of both their male and female singers and the number of boys attracted to their program. While the boys and girls may train separately, they can still perform many numbers as a mixed choir. If it isn't feasible to have separate men's and women's ensembles in the schedule, then the teacher should be sure to program some repertoire featuring each group out of the mixed choir to provide the experience of singing in such a group.

Another place where men's and women's choirs can function well is in the first year of high school. The teacher can focus the curriculum on the needs of each group of singers and provide more leadership and solo opportunities for young singers before entering the larger mixed ensembles with upperclassmen. It also allows the director to develop a foundation for students' musicianship training as a prerequisite to entering the more select ensembles while exploring a different literature.

OTHER POSSIBILITIES

There are a number of other offerings that could be part of a comprehensive choral program. Schools with madrigal choirs sometimes produce a traditional medieval feast or madrigal dinner every year complete with costumes and other entertainments from the period. Such events are excellent opportunities for curricular integration with other subjects such as history, literature, visual art, or theater. Many high schools produce a musical every year. While musicals typically involve students outside the choral program, the choir and theater teachers may choose to offer a musical theater class for the semester or trimester that the musical is being prepared and performed. This provides an opportunity for students to experience a different repertoire and set of performing skills that can be very positive.

Another class sometimes offered by choral teachers might be called *Karaoke*. It features students performing solos to prerecorded music much like the popular club activity but can actually function as an introduction to vocal performance. Students learn vocal technique, different styles of popular music, history of popular music repertoire, and performance skills such as stage presence and memorization. Other possible offerings for the choral program involve choirs focused on other kinds of repertoire such as a gospel choir or a world vocal ensemble. While such repertoire can be included in any ensemble, these choirs focus not only on a particular repertoire but also on traditional approaches to learning and performing music that is different from Western art music. More is said about these groups in Chapter 10, but they can be a valuable part of the choral program.

⊹ BREAK POINT 8.2 Design Your Ideal Program

Design your ideal high school or middle school choir program. What choirs will be offered, how often will they meet and perform? Will they be tied to a certain repertoire or be more flexible? Keep in mind the variety of skill levels you might encounter and the desire to encourage musical participation for as many students as possible.

Qualities of a Successful Choir Teacher

So what skills does a teacher need to be successful in meeting the diverse goals of the comprehensive choral curriculum? What qualities and skills identify the successful choral teacher? No two teachers are exactly alike and there are many roads to success, but there seem to be some attributes that are shared by most, if not all, successful teachers in this area. Below are the scenarios of three choral directors who arrived at choral teaching on very different paths.

THE SINGER AS CHOIR DIRECTOR

Eric had been in all-state choir since his sophomore year of high school; he'd had the lead in the musical and many solos with his choir. As a senior, he was elected choir president and part of his duties included directing warm-ups several days a week. This experience led him to pursue a music education degree in college. Despite his skills as a singer, he placed in the very bottom level of theory and piano class and realized that some aspects of his musicianship were severely lacking. During his first two years he took private lessons on piano in addition to his piano class and began singing bass in his church choir to improve his sight-singing skills. By his junior year he was named the section leader of the Concert Choir and began running sectionals and warm-ups for his college group.

His first job was in a top high school program that had a strong tradition of excellence. His first year was difficult because the teacher he replaced was a very strong pianist and the students were used to having accompaniment or parts played every time they sang. He was able to persevere by choosing some literature that better fit their reading level and by practicing the piano accompaniments a lot between rehearsals. He also implemented a music-reading curriculum in the lower grades and challenged the students to work more a cappella. By his second year he had gotten money from his boosters to hire an accompanist to assist on Fridays. His skills as a voice teacher and strong conducting ability were beginning to make a positive impact on the choir's sound. It didn't hurt that a number of his students did very well at solo and ensemble contests because of his strong vocal coaching.

THE "BAND GUY" AS CHOIR DIRECTOR

Allan is a self-declared "band guy." He is an excellent trumpet player who was one of the stars of his suburban school's band program. He played in multiple ensembles during college, played jazz and funk professionally on the side, and student taught in one of the top band programs in his area. He often complained during his undergraduate training about having to learn choral music methods and basic piano because he knew that his band teachers had never needed these skills to be successful. Allan's first job was in an urban school with a struggling music program that wanted to rebuild. In his first year he taught concert band, jazz band, two beginning piano classes, and . . . choir.

Because Allan knew what it required to be an excellent performer and band director, he felt woefully unprepared to teach choir. He knew that he needed to improve his vocal and keyboard skills in order to provide a quality experience for his students. He immediately started studying voice on the side and found out that he was actually a pretty good singer. More important, he began to understand what his singers needed to know to make a better sound. Allan had excellent musical skills and a strong interest in kids, so he was able to learn on the job and learn from his colleagues and students. His biggest challenge was getting familiar with the repertoire and the culture of choirs. To help with this he brought in experienced choral teachers as clinicians to work with his students from the very beginning and help him learn what he needed to know. He also allowed his students to explore a variety of vocal styles through small-group work and even produced several CDs featuring a number of student-created ensembles. Allan now has one of the top choral programs in the district and used his strong instrumental jazz skills to create an award-winning jazz choir at his school. He is sought after as a clinician for jazz choirs in the area.

THE PIANIST AS CHOIR DIRECTOR

Karen has been in choirs since middle school but often behind the piano as an accompanist. While this slowed her vocal development, it gave her an excellent view of what skills were needed to teach choir. She spent hours drilling notes in rehearsal for various groups and vowed that her choirs would never depend on the keyboard in the same way. She got into college as a music education major with piano as her major instrument but began taking private voice as soon as her schedule allowed. She improved enough to get into the college chamber choir by her junior year and began working as an assistant conductor-accompanist for a local children's choir.

Her first job was a middle school choir program that had a strong tradition but had declined in recent years. In her first year, she made time to visit all of the elementary schools and even hosted a choral festival at her school in the spring. She partnered with the other middle school choir teacher in the district to invite all the fifth graders to a concert where they sang two numbers with the sixth-grade mass choir. To help prepare them she offered several after-school rehearsals at the various elementary schools. She started a sight-singing curriculum with her sixth-grade choir that she planned to implement gradually in the upper grades as those students moved on. She joined a local community choir to continue to develop her knowledge of the singing voice and to continue performing at a high level. By her second year she had added ten singers to each of her choirs and planned to start a separate boys' ensemble in the third year.

Profiles of Success

All these teachers found success despite having very different backgrounds. What qualities did these teachers share that helped them succeed? All three had an understanding of how to communicate with students and parents and generate excitement and interest in their programs. They all possessed a set of strong musical skills in at least one area that could serve as a foundation for their continued growth as a choral teacher. They avoided a "one size fits all" approach by assessing the current levels of their students and developing a program that would be successful for both teachers and students. They were all willing to partner with other, more experienced teachers and seek help when they needed it from colleagues. Finally, they understood the importance of musical excellence and the commitment required to achieve it. This commitment and dedication to continued musical growth was critical in their eventual success. All of these teachers also demonstrated the following skills in varying degrees of proficiency.

KNOWLEDGE OF THE SINGING VOICE

Successful choral teachers know the voice and understand its development in children. This does not necessarily mean that they are great singers, but they have worked to understand their own voices and the physical sensations associated with a relaxed and well-produced tone. In addition they have studied the voice change and understand how to help students demystify this process and continue to participate in singing while the voice changes. Strong keyboard skills are also a plus in choral teaching because of the need at times for an outside pitch reference in rehearsal, but they are not a prerequisite.

REPERTOIRE

The successful choral teacher cares about presenting literature that is of good quality and compelling to the students. Finding quality literature takes time and dedication and many directors are constantly on the prowl for a good piece of music, even "rearranging" pieces to better fit their group's needs. One of the best initial resources for quality literature is the other experienced teachers in the area. Seeking their advice and attending their concerts is one of the best ways to learn what works and what doesn't in school choral repertoire.

MUSICIANSHIP

All of our directors made sure that their students were developing musical skills during their time in choir. Both Karen and Eric inherited strong programs but without a sight-singing tradition. They both introduced music reading in the younger grades and gradually built the curriculum and raised expectations over a period of years. It is important to realize that even though Eric felt that sight-singing was a weakness of his as a student, he did not shy away from prioritizing it as a teacher. Indeed some of the best sight-singing teachers are those who had difficulty learning to read music and are aware of the challenges their students face.

DEDICATION TO TEACHING

All of our directors showed that they cared about children and enjoyed being with them. Not surprisingly, this quality is shared by anyone who succeeds in teaching, regardless of the subject matter. Students can sense an individual who appreciates and respects them for who they are. Unlike the performance world, where the artist is in service to the music, in teaching, the music must always serve the needs of the students and help them develop their musical selves. The extra hours teachers spend in their first years setting up their programs will pay great dividends in the future.

While many choir directors come from a background of singing and being in choir for many years, some of the most successful choral directors did not start out on that path. They found themselves confronted with the challenge of teaching choir and, in responding to that challenge, they fell in love with the deeply personal experience of singing in a choir and the unique musical moments that come from the marriage of great text and great music. Teachers who find themselves in a school without a choir should take the initiative to start one so that students whose gift is singing will have the opportunity to continue their musical education. In doing so, they may find that they too have the qualities of a successful choir director.

✦ BREAK POINT 8.3 The Skills of a Successful Choir Teacher

Perhaps one of the profiles above mirrors your own background and experience. What skills do you possess currently that would be important to a successful choir director and why? Identify one area where you would like to have a little more preparation.

This brief snapshot of the comprehensive choral program gives a sense of the challenges and rewards that await those who choose this path. Music education students interested in teaching choir can begin working on many of these skills immediately. One of the best ways to learn how to teach a choir is by doing. Find any opportunity to lead a choral ensemble while still a student. Volunteer to lead warm-ups and sectionals for a college group, find a church or community choir that would welcome an assistant (likely unpaid), or see if any of the area schools have after-school choirs that could use help. Along with seeking these opportunities, begin to identify which of the skills listed in this chapter are personal strengths and weaknesses and start taking extra time to develop the weaknesses into strengths. As busy as college students are, first-year teachers are that much busier, so now is the time to develop personal musicianship to the highest possible degree. With the right instruction, students at all grade levels can achieve amazing success in choral music and those musical shivers, those glimpses of perfection students experience in choir, will stay with them the rest of their lives.

REFERENCES AND RESOURCES

Brinson, B. (1996). *Choral Music Methods and Materials: Developing Successful Choral Programs (Grades 5 to 12).* New York: Schirmer Books. An excellent comprehensive introduction to many of the issues involved in teaching choral music at the secondary level.

Demorest, S. M. (2001). *Building Choral Excellence: Teaching Sight-singing in the Choral Rehearsal.* New York: Oxford University Press. An overview of the issues and approaches involved in teaching sight-singing in the choral rehearsal. Provides information on current methods and materials and offers a number of practical lesson models.

Haasemann, F., and J. M. Jordan. (1991). *Group Vocal Technique*. Chapel Hill, NC: Hinshaw Music. A good introduction to group vocal techniques and to the process of using warm-ups for specific musical goals as well as vocal fundamentals. Supplemental exercise cards and a video are available.

O'Toole, P. (2003). *Shaping Sound Musicians: An Innovative Approach to Teaching Comprehensive Musicianship through Performance*. Chicago: GIA Publications. Contains a number of strategies for teaching comprehensive musicianship in the ensemble. Based in the Wisconsin Comprehensive Musicianship Project, it includes contributions from master teachers in choir, band, and orchestra.

Phillips, K. H. (1992). *Teaching Kids to Sing*. New York: Schirmer Books. A research-based overview of the issues and approaches to teaching young people the fundamentals of good singing with a wealth of exercises and detailed explanations of techniques.

chapter 9

Of School Bands, Orchestras, and Jazz Ensembles

Chung, a fifth-grader attending a concert by high school students in his elementary school gym: Wow! I'm going to play that one . . . that big instrument.

Ben, another fifth-grader: Why? It's way in the back. No one will see you.

Chung: But the sound was so cool. I could feel it with my insides.

Ben: Yeah, but I like that shiny one up front. That's my sister's friend playing it and she is really nice to me.

Chung: I like the uniforms, too.

Ben: Yeah, they're nice . . . and it will be fun to come back and play here again one day.

How Did We Get Here?

If school music were started all over again, right now, right from scratch, would it turn out anything like the instrumental program as it currently exists? That would be rather unlikely. The typical instrumental music program, with its various large and small, wind and string, indoor and outdoor ensembles, is a product of historical pressures and convergences rather than centralized planning (Humphreys, 1995). Across time, student-centered educational philosophy, high-visibility national performances by student groups, professionally sponsored national contests, intercollegiate athletics, the enthusiastic support of the music industry, and even international relations in the form of two world wars have provided opportunities for the widespread development—and astounding success of—band and orchestra instruction in the schools. Interestingly, despite the historical genesis of instrumental school music, little has changed since its appearance in the late nineteenth and early twentieth centuries. Describing the state of instrumental music in 1928, E. B. Birge wrote,

> The instrumental field includes first and second orchestras and bands and classes for instruction in all instruments, including the piano. . . . [T]he orchestras play the symphonies of Haydn, Mozart and Beethoven and many of the best overtures and suites, both classic and modern. The bands are of symphonic fulness [sic] in instrumentation and perform the standard selections of band literature. (Birge 1928, 168–169)

Writing almost seventy years ago, Birge is describing what is still considered the core of modern instrumental music education, particularly in places like the United States, Canada, and a number of other nations where instrumental music has become such a major component of school music.

On a large scale, the enterprise of instrumental music instruction in the schools has been tremendously successful for a very long time. On an artistic level, the musical distance between the best high school performing ensembles and their professional counterparts is less than that between those same ensembles and the school district's beginning band and orchestra classes. This speaks volumes about the potential for growth that young people possess as well as the effect quality musical opportunities and quality music instruction can have on aspiring instrumentalists.

The challenge of maintaining a quality comprehensive instrumental program is great. Instrumental music is one of a school's most expensive enterprises. School bands and orchestras typically require their own facilities—one or more rehearsal rooms, multiple practice rooms, and extensive library and storage space. Ensembles need specialized equipment that likely includes large instruments, concert and marching percussion, electronic keyboards, and a variety of amplifiers. Concert and marching ensembles usually need uniforms, often different ones for each group. All this needs to be kept up to date, maintained in proper working order, and replaced as necessary. And, of course, overseeing all this is at least one music teacher dedicated solely (or, at least, largely) to instrumental music instruction. This is a sizable investment for a school to make in a program that may serve only one-fifth of the student population, at best.

For students who choose to pursue instrumental instruction, a substantial investment is usually necessary as well. With few exceptions, students must provide and maintain their own instruments. Reeds, strings, sticks, and mallets break or wear out and need replacing. Uniform parts such as shoes, shirts, blouses, or ties may be the students' responsibility. Most schools, teachers, or parent groups now have programs in place to assist with expenses that financially troubled students cannot bear. Despite this need for significant contribution on the part of both the schools and the students, instrumental music programs not only still survive, but often thrive.

Even considering that a proportionally modest percentage of the student population participates in school ensembles, it is remarkable that in terms of sheer numbers so many students elect to join the band or orchestra. In many schools, the opportunity to join a beginning instrumental class in fourth, fifth, or sixth grade is the first time a student is asked to *choose* whether he or she would like to participate in music. But what does a fifth-grader know of bands or orchestras? Certainly these ensembles are historically part of Western culture—in the case of school band, particularly American culture—but they are not necessarily part of a young person's soundscape. Unless a parent was once a band member or a sibling played in the orchestra or the family holds season tickets to the local symphony, a child probably has only limited knowledge of the kind of instrumental music that exists in schools. She may have seen the high school band in a local parade or the jazz ensemble at the district open house. She may have seen a string quartet performing at a relative's wedding or watched a tuba player "dot the 'i'" during a college football game. Maybe she just heard that the band teacher is "cool."

On the other hand, maybe the student believes that joining the band will allow her to become a performing musician like those whose recordings she owns, whose songs she hears on the radio, or whose videos she has seen on television. The idea that bands and orchestras may play a different type of music from that done by a favorite contemporary performing artist does not register as strongly as the desire a student may have to join the ranks of "musicians." Nevertheless, that student is stepping into a particular musical world, shaped by tradition and led by educators who are charged with carrying that tradition forward and nurturing the creative and artistic spirit of young people.

The Shape and Size of the Instrumental Program

An instrumental music educator is expected to have expertise in a variety of performance arenas. The same individual who conducts the symphonic band may also need to direct the jazz ensemble and lead the marching band. After teaching the freshman string orchestra during last period, the instrumental music teacher may then be required to front the pep band at an after-school girls' basketball game. To be specific about it, school instrumental programs include some combination of the following: beginning instrument classes, large concert bands, string orchestras, full orchestras, jazz ensembles, jazz combos, marching bands, pep bands, chamber ensembles, percussion ensembles, and nontraditional ensembles.

Which is a teacher's favorite ensemble? Which does a teacher most enjoy teaching? In which did the teacher most enjoy performing? It doesn't matter, really. It is the task of the music educator to give each ensemble complete attention and enthusiasm. Recalling Chapter 1, Rob's passion for jazz may lead him into music education, but it will not carry him through the school day. Nor will it carry his orchestra, symphonic band, and marching band students through the year. Every musical experience gives students an opportunity to grow as musicians and to enjoy the unique activity of music making . . . providing that the teacher facilitates these experiences with commitment and professional integrity.

❖ BREAK POINT 9.1 Peak Performance

In which ensemble did you find your most "peak" performance experiences? In what ways did these experiences depend or not depend on the setting, the audience, or the type of literature you performed? Is there a specific experience that you had as a school musician that you would want to replicate for your own students?

While the *content* of the instrumental program is largely consistent from one school to another, the *structure* of instrumental teachers' days can vary widely. In some school districts each instrumental ensemble class is team-taught by two full-time instrumental specialists, significantly increasing the personal attention each student can receive while simultaneously allowing the full ensemble to remain on task. In other districts the majority of the instrumental teacher's day consists of brief private lessons, a series of weekly one-on-one teaching opportunities designed to complement the daily full ensemble class. Still other instructors find themselves spending each day of the week at a different school, helping beginning and second-year students develop fundamental skills. Other districts provide a more vertical distribution of responsibilities such that each instrumental teacher works with students at every level, from the most junior to the most senior.

Regardless of one's specific responsibilities, the success of an instrumental program rests on the ability of one or more music educators to construct a coherent, sequential, yet multifaceted experience for students. Strength in one area is often contingent upon strength in another. While one particular student's path through instrumental performance may look quite different from another's, all roads should offer the finest of music making along the way.

Becoming an Instrumentalist

Students may walk into beginning instrumental classes with little knowledge of the skill they are about to learn. In the case of the elementary choir, a child has likely already developed a love of singing and has, in fact, been doing it for quite some time, inside and outside the music classroom. But at the outset of beginning band and orchestra classes, the love of playing an instrument may only have been a love from afar. Not that musical instruments, in general, are unfamiliar. Many elementary programs engage students extensively in instrumental music making through the use of percussion, mallet keyboards (often referred to as Orff instruments), and recorders. These are instrumental ensembles in the truest sense of the word, but do not necessarily represent experiences shared by all beginning band and orchestra students.

To get students going in the right direction, it is beneficial to establish clear and open lines of communication between teacher and student, student and parent, and parent and teacher. As one who will have spent many years participating in, studying, and now teaching instrumental music, it would be understandable if the instrumental teacher overlooked the fact that fifth-graders and their parents may not really know what band is, what orchestra is, and what the difference might be between the two. Students and their parents may find it incomprehensible that an instrument so clearly popular as the guitar does not figure into any of the opportunities offered, or that the number of beginning percussionists has been limited to four. To understand the source of such confusion or, better yet, to head off conflicts before they arise, consider the varied perspectives from which the student, parent, and teacher view the beginning instrument experience. The *student* has been an active music maker all her life—singing, moving, listening, responding. For her, the beginning instruments class represents an opportunity to make music in a way that is new, more challenging, and perhaps more like she is used to seeing or hearing in the adult world. The *parent*, alternatively, has provided constant support for each new endeavor his child has taken on. He has sought out opportunities that he feels will contribute to his daughter's quality of life. Now the time has come for her to learn to play an instrument, a pursuit he reasonably associates with her becoming a well-rounded human being. The *instrumental music teacher* has as his primary concern assembling a class of beginning students that will provide a solid future for the band or orchestra program. The success of the upper-level ensembles depends on the teacher's ability to recruit a class of sufficient size and appropriate instrumentation, a program blueprint of which this student is an integral and very specific part.

Aside from the decision to join the instrumental program itself, the selection of an instrument is probably the most consequential choice a beginning student has to make. Why do students choose the instrument they do? The factors that influence this decision are numerous. Size, convenience, role models, sound, looks, peer pressure, adult pressure, teacher pressure, or just random chance may push a student toward or away from certain options. Stereotypes about who plays what kind of instrument, possibly established years earlier, may affect a student's opinion. Alternatively, a student might not even know which instrument is which (recalling one beginner who referred to every instrument as a "trumpet").

It is the teacher's job to decide what instruments will be available for selection and how that selection will be made. Figure 9.1 presents one possibility, a progressive approach to instrumentation that leads, among the band students, from a small array of instruments to a full complement. Beginning with fewer choices allows the teacher to divide her attention among fewer competing technical needs. It also allows students to help each other as they try to master skills unique to their own instrument group. In this particular system, because of the necessity of "growing" the range of instruments in the ensemble, it would be more accurate to say that students are being asked to select the *first* instrument they will play—the one on which they will begin—rather than the *only* one they will play.

For orchestra students, the composition of the beginning group is no different from that of a professional string orchestra. Switches are still likely, though they will be from a one-half or three-quarter size instrument to one that is full size rather than between different instruments. It may also be that, in time, a larger number of low voices—cello and bass, or even viola—will be needed than was originally selected. Different technical and musical demands necessitate the separation of beginning orchestra and band classes (as suggested by the solid line between the two groups in Figure 9.1) with full orchestra opportunities only emerging in later years. Unlike most beginning band students (though flute may be an exception), some beginning orchestra players will arrive in class with experience gained through Suzuki instruction. This internationally renowned method gives significant initial attention to performance through imitation rather than notation. While a number of teachers have adapted this method to class settings, strict adherence to Suzuki's principles of instruction necessitates a blend of private and group lessons, involving not only the teacher and student but parents as well.

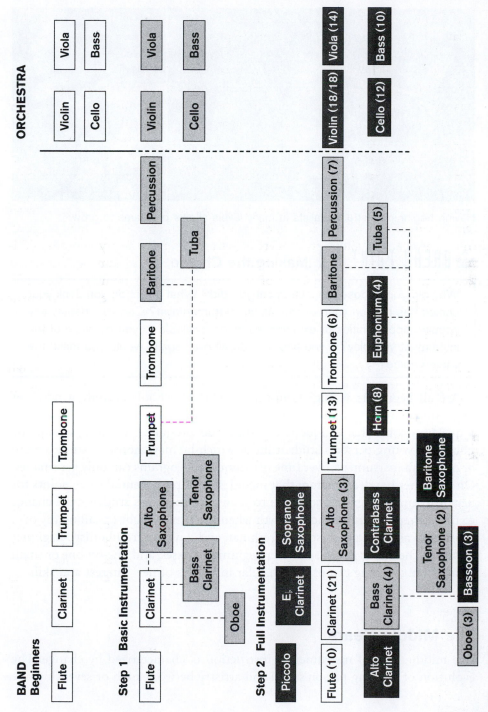

BAND

Beginners

Flute | Clarinet | Trumpet | Trombone

Step 1   Basic Instrumentation

Flute | Clarinet | Alto Saxophone | Trumpet | Trombone | Baritone

Bass Clarinet | Tenor Saxophone | Tuba

Oboe

Step 2   Full Instrumentation

Piccolo | E♭ Clarinet | Soprano Saxophone

Flute (10) | Clarinet (21) | Alto Saxophone (3) | Trumpet (13) | Trombone (6) | Baritone | Percussion (7)

Alto Clarinet | Bass Clarinet (4) | Contrabass Clarinet | Horn (8) | Euphonium (4) | Tuba (5)

Oboe (3) | Tenor Saxophone (2) | Baritone Saxophone

Bassoon (3)

ORCHESTRA

Violin | Viola

Cello | Bass

Violin | Viola

Cello | Bass

Violin (18/18) | Viola (14)

Cello (12) | Bass (10)

Figure 9.1 • A progressive approach to instrument assignment for large concert ensembles. Approximate numbers of players for full symphonic instrumentation are shown in parentheses.

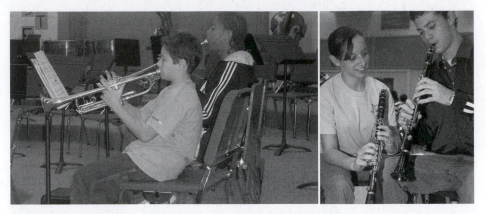

Having beginning instrumentalists at many levels allows programs to grow.

✥ BREAK POINT 9.2 Making the Choice

Why did you choose the instrument you did? What effect do you think your choice has had on your identity as an instrumentalist? Can you identify any specific opportunities or experiences made available to you because of the instrument you play? If you had it to do all over again, would you make the same choice?

Are all beginners young? Is upper elementary school the only window of opportunity to choose instrumental instruction? As noted in Chapter 8, this is a question somewhat unique to instrumental programs. If there is only one point in a young person's student life at which he may choose to study a band or orchestra instrument, over time instrumental programs can only get smaller. On the other hand, a program that includes multiple potential entry points for new instrumentalists can continue to grow. It also allows students the chance to take a step toward musical growth when the time is right (recalling my own experience as both a high school freshman and a novice trombonist). Beginner classes in the upper grades, summer beginning classes, and one-on-one or small group peer coaching can provide regular infusions of new interest and skill.

The Middle Years

The middle level of instrumental instruction is characterized by change. The evolution of a young person's skill and artistry between sixth or seventh grade and the beginning of high school is remarkable. It is not surprising that many veteran music teachers identify this as their favorite level to teach. Through the sheer accumulation of time, students who participate in band or orchestra for a second, third, fourth, or fifth year are demonstrating something well beyond a passing interest in learning to play an instrument. They are making a serious commitment.

Early adolescents are in the process of figuring out who they are. They are changing in appearance and personality, in the way they relate to each other and to the adults they encounter. Each is beginning to stake out his or her own individuality while still seeking support and approval from their peers. Their continued presence in instrumental music indicates that they have chosen to make band or orchestra membership part of their identity and that other ensemble members make up a significant part of their social circle. Participation in a performance group is changing them both as young musicians and as young people.

On strictly musical terms, the middle-level instrumentalist is one who moves away from the safe, sequential confines of the method series. "Music" no longer refers to the song on page 24 of the class instruction book, but to the stack of loose sheets she has been given in a folder. Each has a title and a part designation—second clarinet, first violin—indicating that there is much more information about this piece than can fit on a single sheet of paper. She must now make sense of how she fits in the emerging ensemble. The decision she made about which instrument to play takes on new significance as the different sounds and colors are segregated and assigned separate roles. Greater independent musical responsibility is required.

But even instruments may change at this level, too. The basic instruments from which beginners typically may choose are no longer sufficient to fill out the ensemble. Piccolos, bass clarinets, baritone saxophones, double reeds, French horns, bass trombones, and tubas—not to mention a whole host of new percussion—become options for student exploration. Reduced-size string instruments may now be laughably diminutive in the hands of growing adolescents.

As exciting as some of the changes associated with early secondary school can be, others pose significant challenges to the music educator. Moving into middle-level music classes usually means that students move from the elementary school environment to a middle school or junior high school campus. It may also mean that they must make a transition from their regular elementary music teacher and beginning band or orchestra teacher (if these are, in fact, different people) to an unfamiliar teacher—one who possibly stands on a podium and wields a baton. It is at precisely these sorts of junctures—moments of significant contextual change—that ensemble retention rates can drop precipitously.

New schools present students with new choices. They may wish to try out new experiences or distance themselves from things they now associate with "little kids." New teachers represent new social settings. The social structure of band or orchestra as students knew it is about to change and that change may seem intimidating or undesirable. An ongoing task of the instrumental teacher is to smooth these transitions so that the next level of music making does not seem foreign or forbidding. Visits to elementary schools by the middle school ensembles, joint performances between the beginning and intermediate groups, beginning-level section rehearsals run by junior high students, frequent guest visits by the secondary instrumental teachers to the beginning classes or by beginning students to secondary classes are all strategies that can minimize the gap between the different levels of instruction. Younger students get the chance to become familiar with the middle-level setting, to meet the middle-level instructor and see middle-level students making music and taking on positions of leadership—students they may see as older versions of themselves. The activities of older students are often the goals toward which younger students aspire.

The Many Faces of the High School Instrumentalist

THE CONCERT ENSEMBLES

The large concert ensembles are generally viewed as the heart of the instrumental music program. They are thought of as the central hub around which other ensembles revolve, the core from which other groups draw strength. From a broad perspective, these are the destinations to which all roads lead, starting from the beginning classes through the middle-level bands and orchestras. The symphonic band and the symphony orchestra are often considered the most musically "serious" ensembles, playing the most substantial literature in the most formal settings. Even at high schools where second- or third-level concert groups exist, their function is largely preparatory, getting students ready to step into the top concert organizations.

For the music educator, the top high school concert ensemble presents the greatest opportunity to step into the role of conductor. With the very best high school ensembles, the musical challenges posed to the teacher—much like those faced by the student performers—require significant study and analysis. The results can be sublime, producing musical performances that reach toward the level of professionals.

There are good reasons to think of these organizations as occupying the center of the instrumental picture. First, among the high school ensembles, they tend to involve the largest number of students and the most diverse instrumentation. Second, the symphonic band and orchestra are the modern equivalents of the ensembles that served as the historical starting points for instrumental school music, with other performing groups gaining curricular status and popularity later. Third, beginning method books are clearly designed to introduce and refine skills uniquely tied to symphonic ensemble performance. From the instrumentation available to the selections included in the lessons, from the stylistic emphasis of the content to the type of note-reading expected, these materials prepare students for success as performers of concert literature.

Even with the special status afforded these ensembles, the symphonic band is much more prevalent in the school curriculum than the orchestra, with incidence of the latter ensemble varying widely by region (Smith, 1997). This may seem surprising given that the local or professional symphony orchestra is a more common and more visible institution than the local or professional band, if there is such a thing. But it begins to make sense when one considers the greater variety of functions the band can perform, particularly as the marching and jazz organizations are drawn from this ensemble. Perhaps also relevant is a perception that the orchestra is a more socially elite organization or, at least, representative of a more socially elite cultural institution.

Ensemble format at this level requires consideration. Many orchestra programs move to full symphonic instrumentation at the high school level. While this allows students access to some of the best-known repertoire in the Western classical canon, few pieces provide wind and percussion players the level of engagement offered by band literature. Similarly, some programs feature a wind ensemble—with players placed one on a part—as the highest level of band experience. Such an ensemble offers an entirely unique challenge to students, necessitating a high level of independence.

THE JAZZ ENSEMBLE

Among the mainstays of the instrumental music program, the jazz ensemble is the newest arrival. This is remarkable given that the jazz idiom came of age chronologically in tandem with, or even ahead of, instrumental school music. In its earliest days, jazz was associated with lifestyles and social contexts deemed to be at odds with the prevailing view of better living. The earliest jazz performers shaped their art by synthesizing a broad variety of musical influences, while subsequent generations of players learned by sitting alongside these veterans on the bandstand, in the clubs, and in the recording studios. Formal educational institutions played little part in the development and transmission of the jazz style and actively excluded jazz from the acceptable musics of the academy.

The more recent view of jazz as a sophisticated art form worthy of serious contemplation and scholarly study coincided with its disappearance from the mainstream of popular culture as well as the appearance of jazz studies programs in a number of colleges and universities. School jazz ensembles, originally known as stage bands or dance bands and granted only club or extracurricular status at best, are now typically part of the formal instrumental program at the secondary, middle and, in some cases, even primary level.

There is little question whether school band music or school orchestra music is, in fact, band or orchestra music. However, there is less agreement whether, for all young jazz players, school jazz music is always jazz. The format of the performing group—the big band or combo—certainly echoes the jazz tradition. But for students to truly learn the art of jazz, they must attend to matters of style and improvisation. On the page, students may note that jazz looks quite similar to concert music. Its realization, however, requires a different set of performance practices. Tone, technique, articulation, and interpretation all take on a new character in the context of a swing, bop, or Latin chart. Improvisation is the heart of jazz playing, yet these opportunities may come to only two or three "solo chairs" of an eighteen-member big band. Successful jazz music selection and lesson planning allow all students the unique experiences of jazz performance—its particular styles and skills. Few other school music activities offer such a rich opportunity for students to explore an entirely different musical world.

Jazz's original status as a music (and even a lifestyle) on the periphery of accepted social norms sometimes affects the personality of school jazz ensembles. There is often a distinct identity—an air of confidence, even a mildly defiant swagger—among jazz ensemble members when they are on the way to or from a rehearsal or gig, especially if students from the school's other ensembles are present. Where concert and marching ensembles typically have uniforms or strict dress codes, jazz groups tend to take on a more eclectic appearance. Rehearsals seem more relaxed with far less distance—both physical and personal—between the players and the teacher. Overall, there is an element of "coolness" that students associate with membership in a jazz ensemble that is as attractive as the performance opportunities such membership affords. This strong ensemble personality can become increasingly unsettling to members—particularly female members—to the point that they may choose to end their jazz performance careers (McKeage 2004).

THE MARCHING BAND

With few exceptions, there is no more visible school ensemble—instrumental or otherwise—than the marching band. The presence of a marching band at school athletic events has become "as natural as having a choir in church" (House 1965, 154). The appearance of a marching band signifies that a truly important community event is about to take place. To many outside the music department, the marching band *is* the band program. As a teaching colleague inquired one December, "So what do you all do now that football season is over?"

Such notoriety is not always well received by the music teacher who may wish that greater attention were paid to the concert ensembles, groups that she may consider the artistic heart of the program. Nevertheless, the marching band commands more public attention than virtually any other segment of a school's academic curriculum. Admittedly, this sometimes results in music being seen as "un-academic," more closely related to the athletic programs it supports than the fine arts programs it represents.

There is no question that the marching band can take up an exorbitant amount of a teacher's time and what some may consider a disproportionate amount of a school's or booster group's financial resources. But that is not to say it must. The difference between a band that begins its season a week before school opens and performs at four home football games and one area festival, and a band that holds a three-week summer band camp, performs at four home football games, four away football games, and eight major competitions in three states has nothing to do with the marching band, per se, but the values of the director and, in turn, the expectations of the community. That is not to say that either of the above scenarios is inherently problematic. In either case, the prime considerations are whether the experience the students are having is in line with their educational needs and personal resources (including time, attention, and energy) and

Excellence is not specific to any one style. History has produced a variety of marching performance traditions.

whether the activities of the marching band are in balance with the rest of the music program.

There is no single answer to the question of just what a marching band should be, how it should perform, what set of traditions it should follow. Some advocate giving greater attention to the marching band's sound than to its movement, in a sense presenting the marching band as a symphonic band on a field. Performances from recent Drum Corps International events featuring adaptations of symphonic wind literature may seem to support this depiction. Of course, when considering performances at this level, it would be a regrettable oversight not to acknowledge both the detailed complexity and precise execution of the drill. On the other hand, there are significant marching traditions in which energy and range of movement are the distinguishing variables among ensembles, traditions in which the distinction between sound and movement becomes essentially meaningless.

Exactly how a marching band relates to students' educational needs has been the subject of some question. Marching bands have been criticized as offering little in the way of musicality. If, by musicality, one means nuanced performances of substantial works of aesthetic beauty and complexity, then perhaps there is some truth to this argument. But if one means performances that adhere to an agreed-upon array of stylistic expectations and that evoke an emotional, social, or even physical response, then marching bands offer the possibility of a unique and highly musical experience. Marching bands are integral components of many social rituals including athletic events, holiday celebrations, civic festivals, and public ceremonies. They can personify a school's or community's identity. While these functions certainly fall under the category of service, they can also be viewed as opportunities for authentic music making.

THE SMALL ENSEMBLES

Small instrumental ensembles range from chamber groups to jazz combos to percussion classes. These ensembles are flexible and mobile—the pep band or strolling strings, for example—and may also encompass a broader range of musical styles as in the case of fiddle groups and mariachi bands. While groups like these are often seen as existing on the outermost periphery of the instrumental program, a strong case can be made that the musical experiences they offer are unique and vital. Compared to the large ensembles that are, by nature, teacher-directed, the small groups provide students with opportunities for leadership, independence, and creativity. Decisions about repertoire, questions about interpretation, approaches to rehearsal, and even possibilities for performance venues may be addressed directly by the student musicians themselves.

The small ensemble setting allows students to inhabit their own personalized and democratic musical world, a world in which they draw on their nascent expertise to exercise creative control. This is in stark contrast to the large ensemble world in which they are required to adopt and adapt to pre-ordained standards of style and practice, a world that seems almost "colonial" in contrast (Allsup 2002, 353). These sorts of experiences may be particularly meaningful not only for the students involved but for the teaching profession itself as the opportunity for leadership within school programs has been found to exert a strong influence on the decision to become a music teacher.

Understanding the Instrumental Program

To describe the breadth of instrumental music in the schools only takes into account one plane of a rich, multidimensional reality. Perhaps more than any other aspect of school music, the instrumental program is a multilayered hierarchy. Dense symphonic scores, complex field maneuvers, and lengthy open solo sections reveal a complex web of musical, institutional, and personal relationships.

At the broadest level are the ensembles, relating to each other in terms of both prestige and centrality. At different schools, different groups may carry the

Instrumental ensembles feature many layers of student leadership.

identity of "premier" ensemble. In one school, the senior orchestra may be the public face of the instrumental program with its own collection of commercial recordings, annual tours, and a dedicated website. At another school the marching band may fill this role with "Home of the Marching Such-and-such" emblazoned just under the school's name on the sign at the entrance to the campus. This hierarchy of prestige may create tension when the majority of attention is accorded a group other than one of the large concert ensembles.

At the next level, we find a pecking order within each of the ensemble streams. A school's four jazz bands likely represent four distinct levels of seniority, achievement, or both. The Concert Band students are well aware that their group is not the Wind Ensemble. And where such organizations exist, it is rare that one would witness a parade in which the junior high marching band did not precede the high school marching band, usually by a considerable distance. Even in cases where there is only one school band or orchestra, students establish their own roles within the group by virtue of age (freshmen through seniors may take part in the same ensemble) and skill (every student can identify the best performers, no matter how much the teacher may downplay individual differences).

The existence of first, second, and third parts on many instruments (continuing to fourth and fifth parts for some jazz pieces) contributes to a general "sorting out" within the various sections. There is even added luster to being the "first" second player rather than the second. Hierarchical roles are also institutionalized in the form of band or orchestra officers, section leaders, and, in the case of the marching band, drum majors, a reflection of that ensemble's military origins. Depending on how the director wishes to structure them, these positions may have a great deal or very little to do with seniority or performance prowess, perhaps instead reflecting leadership skills or overall dedication to the ensemble.

So, in the instrumental program, everyone seems to have his or her own place, an amalgam of several identities. One young musician may be horn section leader in the symphonic band, mellophone rank leader in the marching band, fourth trumpet in the jazz band, and, as a reward for such commitment, music librarian. Alternatively, another student may only have played third clarinet in symphonic band for the duration of his high school years. This raises an interesting question, one that has been posited more than once to proponents of the traditional instrumental program—and one that deserves careful consideration. Why would one spend four years playing the third clarinet part? Should a student spend so much time in such a particular role? What benefit could that student possibly draw from his experience?

Perhaps the musical experience that students value is not one based on—or, at least, entirely based on—musical achievement. Consider that even after many years of participation in the band or the orchestra, students may not identify band or orchestra music as particularly interesting to them. Also consider that many students put their instruments away for good on high school graduation, even after exclaiming repeatedly that they love band or that orchestra is their favorite class. Perhaps some students place the highest value on the opportunity to *make* music rather than to *get better* at making music. Other students may find the social and personal identity that goes along with ensemble membership to be of the highest importance. For these students, ensemble membership may not be an experience that transcends time and place. It is an experience they have at a particular time and with particular people. They love band, but *this* band. Orchestra is their favorite class and they have taken it every time it has been offered, but now this class is over. Their value system may be quite different from that of a student who has chosen music as a profession, but it is no less valid. The quality of the broader ensemble experience requires every bit as much attention as the quality of the sounds that ensemble produces. That said, while it is important to understand why things are so, it is not necessary to assume there is no other option. It is still the responsibility of the instrumental music teacher to guide each student toward a deeper level of musical understanding, a higher level of musical achievement and a more confident posture of musical independence.

∴ BREAK POINT 9.3 Your Musical Identity

Who were you in your school music program? What identities did you take on? Compare these with those of your classmates. Do you find that, as a class, you are more similar or more different in terms of the roles you have played in your experiences thus far?

Teaching the Instrumental Class

While many of the instructional strategies employed by the instrumental teacher are similar to those used by their choral and elementary counterparts, there are several unique aspects to teaching orchestra and band. The aspiring band or orchestra teacher must quickly and accurately transpose between keys and clefs. She must read and interpret visually dense musical scores, some containing twenty or more staves on each page. She must possess a fundamental understanding of and achieve at least a minimal proficiency on virtually every instrument. She even must appear both commanding and natural when conducting with a baton. These skills support and enrich the instrumental classroom, but are still only tools to help shape the ultimate outcomes.

At its heart, the study of an instrument is about the development of fine motor skills and a high level of aural discrimination. Movements produce sound. Depending on the quality, placement, and function of the sound, decisions are made about subsequent movements and sounds. The permutations of this process are infinite, covering every level of challenge and every musical style. For new instrumental teachers and music educators with less experience in the instrumental area, this limitless variety of technical demands can be intimidating. Even a look through the most basic beginning method book suggests that instrumental instruction is a relentless march through an ever-expanding collection of skills, amassed line by line, page after page. Nevertheless, all these skills, regardless of the level of the performer, are based on the fundamentals of tone and precision.

Consider Figure 9.2. This may appear to be a very rudimentary performance task that one might expect to find on the early pages of a beginning trumpet, clarinet, or violin book. It would be easy to see this as a simple building block to be introduced, practiced, and quickly left behind on the way to more elaborate challenges. But within this small musical space can be found the fundamental components of outstanding performance. First, this task calls for 4 counts of a characteristic tone. Recall that a "characteristic" tone varies according to context—an instrument's ideal sound often depends on the type of music to be played. For beginners, a desirable tone is likely to conform to the standards of the concert tradition. A trumpet player on a marching field, a saxophonist in a jazz combo, or a fiddler in a bluegrass band may be working toward other sound concepts appropriate to their respective styles. Regardless of the performance style, tone production requires a combination of appropriate physical processes (embouchure, posture, finger placement, bow grip) and mechanical manipulation (reed placement, bow angle). Second, the correct placement of the tone in time necessitates precise onset and release of the sound. Within these two parameters can be added such stylistic refinements as the shape of the tone (phrasing, dynamics) and the style of the onset (articulation).

Figure 9.2 • A simple instrumental task.

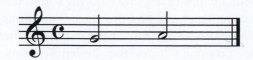

Figure 9.3 • A more complex instrumental task.

Now look at Figure 9.3. In its simplest form, this demonstrates the addition of technique, the movement of tone and precision across musical time. Ideally, a significant portion of instructional time is spent isolating and refining some combination of these three issues: tone and precision followed by technique. While commonly known as the "warm-up," the portion of the band or orchestra class devoted to fundamental performance skills equips students with the tools necessary for sophisticated musical expression. Few teachers have ever felt they spent too much time on warm-ups.

As in any music teaching context, successful instruction is based on careful selection of materials—in this case, the literature to be studied. Literature allows students to embed fundamental skills within a meaningful context. The music found in the band or orchestra folder will include simple pieces that provide repeated practice of basic ensemble skills, pieces that push students' technical skills to higher levels, pieces that introduce students to the core repertoire of the different ensemble traditions, pieces that stretch students' knowledge of musical form and structure, and pieces that expand students' experience of the musical world around them. When chosen well, literature presents challenges, the nature of each varying from piece to piece. And of course, literature should also be great fun to play. Students want to make music and little is more rewarding than making music well.

In addition to all the attention given to performance proficiency, the teaching of instrumental music is also about teaching musical literacy. The beginning student may have already spent five or more years in elementary music classes where he learned about clefs, time signatures, rhythms, and note names. Elementary students can be very sophisticated in both their musical understanding and their musical behavior. But all that knowledge can seem to vanish in an instant when he is handed a violin. For the band and orchestra teacher, teaching students how to transfer knowledge is as important as teaching new information and skills.

While the skill of accurately translating printed notation into sound is critically important for the band or orchestra student, it does not diminish the value of translating musical ideas into sound without the use of an intervening symbol system. For most students, the love of making music came from a lifetime of experimenting with, manipulating, and enjoying sound rather than notes and rests. Despite the strong emphasis given to music reading in the instrumental class—a student's first day with an instrument may often mean studying line 1 in the method book—it is equally critical that students develop an expressive mastery that does not rely on the printed page. Instrumental performance skills allow students access to a broad sonic palate with which they can construct their own melodic, harmonic, and rhythmic ideas as well as re-create those of others. Rote learning, imitation, and improvisation should feature prominently in the young instrumentalist's learning experience. Literacy skills allow the young musician to understand in a symbolic way ideas first formed in memory and imagination.

Among older students, literacy evolves into fluency by moving beyond the interpretation of note names and rhythm patterns. For these students, concert literature can be not only a vehicle for performance but also a means of exploring historical styles, cultural traditions, and variations of form, timbre, and harmonic language. It can be a model on which to base one's own musical creations and a target toward which one can aim evaluative and critical skills. To support the development of musically knowledgeable young people, performance-based courses cannot focus solely on the preparation of performances. After all, documents such as the National Standards describe music as a diverse and comprehensive learning experience. The Standards and other curricular guidelines like them should not be checked at the rehearsal room door.

Thus we see the structure of the instrumental class take shape: focused attention on the fundamental skills of tone, precision, and technique followed by application of these skills to challenging literature, all infused with opportunities for exploration of formal and contextual knowledge.

A Unique and Varied Place

In a number of nations throughout the world instrumental instruction holds a prominent and multifaceted place in the school music curriculum. Instrumental music in schools takes many forms, from a flute duet to a marching band, from a jazz combo to a symphony orchestra. By learning an instrument, a young person is able to make music in a new way; he is learning a unique set of skills in which a mechanical object is manipulated toward artistic and expressive ends. He is also joining a family of traditions that stretches far back into history and reaches every corner of the world.

By becoming an instrumentalist a young person adds a new dimension to his musical experience. But it also places him in a unique musical culture, one inhabited by generations of past and future band and orchestra members. Instrumental ensembles have been a major feature on the school landscape for over a century and their continued popularity, prevalence, and level of achievement suggest that the experiences they offer—musical, social, and cultural—retain a valuable function in the musical world of our society.

REFERENCES AND RESOURCES

Allsup, R. E. (2002). "Crossing Over: Mutual Learning and Democratic Action in Instrumental Music Education." Ed.D. thesis, Teachers College, Columbia University.

Birge, E. B. (1928). *History of Public School Music in the United States*. Boston: Oliver Ditson.

Casey, J. L. (1993). *Teaching Techniques and Insights for Instrumental Music Educators*. Chicago: GIA Publications. A compendium of thoughts and opinions offered by some of the most renowned teachers of instrumental music. Full of ideas, personalities, and conflicting points of view, this book is a stimulating collection of "best practice" tips organized by topic area.

Colwell, R. J., and T. Goolsby. (2002). *The Teaching of Instrumental Music*. 3rd ed. Upper Saddle River, NJ: Prentice Hall. A comprehensive resource covering every aspect of instrumental teaching including administration, rehearsal techniques, and instrument pedagogy. This is one of the very few books to focus on both band and orchestra in the same volume.

House, R. W. (1965). *Instrumental Music for Today's Schools*. Englewood Cliffs, NJ: Prentice Hall.

Humphreys, J. T. (1995). "Instrumental Music in American Education: In Service of Many Masters." *Journal of Band Research* 30 (2):39–70.

McKeage, K. M. (2004). "Gender and Participation in High School and College Instrumental Jazz Ensembles." *Journal of Research in Music Education* 52: 343–356.

Miles, R., ed. (1997). *Teaching Music through Performance in Band*. Chicago: GIA Publications. A multivolume series featuring essays on instrumental music teaching and detailed performance analyses of significant ensemble literature. All difficulty levels are included and separate volumes are available for beginning band, orchestra, and the teaching of marches.

Parncutt, R., and G. E. McPherson, eds. (2002). *The Science and Psychology of Music Performance: Creative Strategies for Teaching and Learning*. New York: Oxford University Press. Each chapter of this book presents a review of pertinent research literature on a selected aspect of performance and applies findings to the music teaching context. Included are chapters addressing performance anxiety, sight-reading, practice, and conducting.

Small, C. (1998). *Musicking: The Meanings of Performing and Listening.* Hanover, NH: University Press of New England. A careful examination of the broad and social nature of the music as demonstrated through the example of a symphony orchestra concert. Applicable across styles and traditions, Small's ideas provide a thought-provoking framework for understanding the musical ensemble experience.

Smith, C. M. (1997). "Access to String Instruction in American Public Schools." *Journal of Research in Music Education* 45:650–662.

chapter 10

All the Rest of the Music

High school student A: I won't be scheduling music next year.

High school student B: Why not? I thought you liked music.

High school student A: Well, yeah, I do, but not band.

High school student B: But there are three bands: cadet band, concert band, and wind ensemble. So you can take your choice. Or you can take choir.

High school student A: As if that's all there is in the world of music.

High school student B: Well, what do you want?

High school student A: Where do I begin? Nearly anything that's not school music.

Tradition and Change in School Music

In the United States and Canada of the middle of the nineteenth century, traditional "school music" education was once only group singing in elementary schools. Within several decades, secondary schools began to offer choirs and instrumental study, as well as bands and orchestras. These curricular offerings in music reflected the musical life of the community, and school music programs were historically aimed at developing the skills of children and adolescents so they could participate more fully in music making at their places of worship, in community ceremonies and celebrations, in holiday festivities, and in amateur and professional music organizations in their cities and towns. The training experiences in school ensembles became so successful that they took on lives of their own, and schools were graced with the music of students' performances at assemblies, sporting events, and graduations. Ensembles began to represent their schools at interscholastic festivals and competitions, and the music from the approved contest lists was performed by students to show their school spirit and musical excellence. These traditional music ensembles—the bands, choirs, and orchestras—were symbolic of their schools, just as the schools represented the values of the local communities.

Communities have changed, and the music that is valued locally has diversified. Outside schools, within families, in the media, and in a host of neighborhood venues, there is a wide spectrum of possibilities for the musical involvement of young people. They listen to (and some sing and play instruments for) music that is something other than the traditional school ensembles, from accordions to guitars, mariachi to salsa, gospel to alternative rock. Or they wish they did but have no way to learn how to do it themselves. Nor do they often have opportunities outside of school to study the historical and cultural styles of music, even though they have studied Western civilization or world history, or to learn the logic and theory of music as they have learned about logical structures and systems in mathematics and the sciences. Teachers can do much to open up the possibilities of musical study—all the rest of the music—to students in schools. Given that 10 percent of high school students typically enroll in school music classes, what would happen if there were more choices for the other 90 percent? Perhaps there could be more music in the life of the school, and in the lives of more of the students.

Performance courses, a wide variety of ensemble experiences, academic courses, and composition-related training should be made available to students, some of them as in-school elective arts (or humanities) choices within secondary schools. At least a few focal areas of study might be integrated within courses that are sometimes referred to as "general music," "classroom music," and more plainly "music." In the United States, for example, general music classes in middle schools and junior highs may rotate emphases every term or shift from one six-week period to another so as to offer students experiential units in the study of guitar, world music, composition, and popular music. Student interest in components of "general music" at all levels of secondary school has in some cases led to the development of all-year everyday classes on a single music topic or style. Of course, what works within the school-day curriculum can also be designed as after-school classes for children and adolescents (and maybe also for interested adults). Teachers who see the importance of broadening the course offerings to meet the wide array of student needs and interests might consider some of the explicit curricular offerings described below.

Performance Courses

Students are frequently interested in learning to play an instrument, but not always an instrument that is found in school bands and orchestras. Group lessons in guitar and piano are available in some programs; here individual students play together in class but take the techniques and repertoire out of the group and into their own individual experiences outside of school.

GUITAR CLASS

For several generations the guitar has held its own as an instrument of considerable social status. Students generally know someone—an uncle, a cousin, a neighbor, even their own mother—who plays guitar, and they associate the instrument with parties, summer camps, popular music, and singer-songwriter activity. Guitar classes attract students who might otherwise not be enrolled in music: the long-hairs; the aspirant rockers and poppers (popular music aficionados); the students who strive to make their own music, playing accompaniments for the songs they will sing; the young people who want to learn chording for sing-alongs and social reasons. They may arrive with little to no playing experience, or they may have learned some of the standard "riffs" of classic rock guitar pieces. They may also know an assortment of chords from playing with friends, around the campfire, or along with their favorite CDs. But young people are also looking for something more, including right-hand techniques for playing with a flat pick, or finger-style, or left-hand techniques that include chords, bar chords, and melodic solos played in different positions around the guitar neck.

Most beginning guitar classes are offered in high schools for one semester or for an entire academic year; in middle schools exploratory classes in guitar may run for as few as six or eight weeks. Classes may meet daily, which then allows regular and consistent practice for skill development. As many as twenty-five students (a reasonable cutoff point for class enrollment) arrive with their own personal acoustic and electric guitars, although inexpensive student-model guitars can be purchased by the school or rented from local music stores. Guitar classes aim at immediate hands-on experiences, with plans for providing fundamental techniques for chording, right-hand picking, and strumming patterns. Some theory is associated with group lessons, usually pertaining to the whole- and half-steps of a scale as they relate to the frets, intervals, and chord progressions. In school and studio settings, students learn to read musical notation and tablature, yet notation and other theoretical concepts are invariably related to performance practice. The class is filled out with opportunities to learn to play

Guitar-playing high school student.

basic blues, folk, and rock pieces, plus solo and rhythm techniques. Occasionally, students are introduced to a history of the guitar, and a few teachers bring in a cross-cultural study of guitar-like instruments (such as the Egyptian 'ud and the Japanese shamisen). Exercises and songs, including group and soloistic performance, are counterbalanced with opportunities for listening analytically to a variety of styles. Within an individual class period, students tune their guitars, play and sing several songs they know, learn a new technique (for example, barring I and V chords in F, or playing a G-major scale in one or two octaves), and practice the technique in a new song or exercise.

Teachers who play guitar adapt easily to teaching guitar classes, but even those who are new to the instrument can work up to a level of proficiency that will allow modeling of chords, scales, and basic melodies for a beginners' class. With a few lessons and some steady practice guided by a book, recording, or videotape, teachers who are new to guitar will gain a basic understanding of the instrument and ideas for teaching music through guitar performance. GAMA (Guitar Accessories Marketing Association) is a useful resource loaded with information useful to players, teachers, and their students (www.discover guitar.com). Teachers with greater playing experience will be able to model styles live, from swing and jazz guitar (with tunes like "Georgia on My Mind" and "Route 66") to the powerchords and melodic riffs of the music of Jimi Hendrix, Jimmy Page, and Green Day. The use of a drum set or drum machine adds beat to what otherwise might be dull chording exercises, and a musical instrument digital interface (MIDI) guitar and electronic keyboards add spice to the music that beginning guitar students can make.

❖ BREAK POINT 10.1 Guitars in Schools

Discuss the following questions that lead to a justification for the presence of guitar class in the curriculum. What might be the musical and social reasons for guitar classes in secondary school programs? Should guitar be taught by rote or by note? What style(s) of music should be taught? What would it cost to establish guitar instruction as a regular course offering?

KEYBOARD/PIANO CLASS

The piano remains the instrument of choice in millions of family homes in North America, Europe, Australia and New Zealand, Japan, Korea, and Taiwan and numerous other nations and regions. Most schools in first-world countries have pianos: the big grand piano in the auditorium, cafeteria, or assembly space, and a smaller grand, or upright, or console in the music room. Where there are no traditional pianos, there may be electronic keyboards and digital pianos, or even two-octave mini-pianos. The benefits of playing piano have long been recognized, and the outcomes of training can include a strengthening of eye-hand coordination and the development of fine motor skills, the enhancement of cognitive skills for sequencing and retaining information, and (as in the case of the other musical experiences) the reduction of depression and loneliness. Moreover, the act of piano playing is valued by many for its avocational benefits, its function in leisure, its personal rewards, its joys. Some children begin their study of piano in private lessons in the early elementary school years, and many continue for at least several years to develop a foundation for their musicianship even though they may move to another instrument or develop an interest in singing.

Many schools have invested in keyboard labs of twelve to twenty-five pianos for group piano instruction. Students may share a piano, particularly if the instruments are full-size, or they may take turns playing when there is not the exact match of students to pianos. A full class can also be divided into rotating groups for playing the piano, practicing music-writing exercises, and reading articles and books about piano, composers, and music in general.

In elementary schools, keyboard labs are a part of the broader set of musical activities, and a six-week or two-month unit of piano instruction may be set aside for students to learn the fundamentals of piano playing. Another common approach is to alternate group piano instruction with other music instruction, so that "if it's Tuesday, it must be piano time" while the second day of every two music classes is devoted to singing, listening lessons, or movement. Secondary schools are likely to offer piano as an arts elective, often daily for the entire year's enrollment; students receive training that leads to performance assessments and possibly an end-of-year piano recital.

The focus of piano classes in schools is typically the fundamentals of piano playing, including performance technique and notational literacy. Posture and other physical issues in playing (such as arm and wrist movement) are addressed in classes, as are how-to-practice schemes and the substance of complete musicianship. Instruction frequently begins with C-centered five-note stepwise melodies for the right hand; this is soon followed by left-hand patterns extending downward from middle C or open fifths and chords that are grounded in the octave C below. Single-hand pieces performed by the group are complemented by the teacher's harmonization, pre-planned computer sequence, rhythm track, or full orchestral track that comes with instructional materials. Exercises in note-reading, scale and pattern drills, rhythm, ear training, and creative work can be individualized through headphones, or worked on by pairs of students, completed in small-group collaboratives, or addressed in whole-group demonstrations and participatory activities. The essence of group piano instruction is peer group learning which, at any grade level, is active, motivating, and useful in stimulating the students' careful listening and constant appraisal of music made by themselves and others.

❖ BREAK POINT 10.2 A Place for Piano Study

Without keyboard instruction in schools, many students will never know the piano or its use as a tool for understanding music. Scout out a school where group piano instruction is offered. Talk with the teacher to find out how it fits into the curricular schedule, the needs and interests of students in the class, the instructional aims of the class, the materials, and the methods employed to steer students to piano skills and musical understanding.

Performance Ensembles

For many, music is meaningful when it is socially interactive, so bands, choirs, and orchestras are attractive to many young people. Today, group performance opportunities are diversifying beyond these standard ensembles to include a wide array of instrumental and vocal ensembles: "African" (and world) drumming, gospel choir, handbell choir, jazz (both instrumental and vocal), mariachi, marimbas, recorder consort, rock band, samba, steel drum band, and world vocal ensemble.

"AFRICAN" DRUMMING

Also called "drum circle" or "world drumming" (of which African percussion is key), the West African culture of the drum is popular among students in upper elementary and secondary schools. *Djembe* drums out of Ghana are central to these ensembles. Wide at the head and narrow at the base, standing about three feet from the floor, they are made commercially with sturdy synthetic material and are meant to be played by hands and fingers (and without mallets). The sounds of fifteen to twenty djembes can set a group of students into rhythmic motion. To the djembes are added double iron bells found in the West African countries of Ghana, Nigeria, and their neighbors; these connected bells, one larger and the other smaller, produce a lower- and higher-pitched sound when struck by a mallet. *Shekeres*, called by many names depending on their region of origin, are gourds covered with a beaded netting that is moved by hand to produce a scraped, rattling sound. While not precisely the drumming heard in West

Africa, the polyrhythms played on various higher- and lower-pitched drums are certainly African in flavor.

Other instruments can be added to the African instruments, including Latin-style conga drums, hand drums, pressure or "talking" drums (called *dundun* by the Yoruba of Nigeria), and even goblet drums (known variously as *dombek*, *darabukka*, and *derbeki*). In fact, drumming ensembles in schools often encompass Afro-Latin percussion ensembles of the sort found in Cuba and Puerto Rico, which play alone or form the rhythmic backbone of Latin jazz and salsa bands. Classroom instruments are sometimes substituted for the African instruments, as in the case of congas for djembes, cowbells for the double iron bell, and maracas for shekeres, turning the timbres toward an Afro-Latin flavor. Other instruments are brought into the mix as well, including *claves* (thick and resonant wood sticks) and *guiros* (ridged gourds often resembling painted fish). Students may be paired on the larger drums, regardless of the type or tradition, when teachers recognize participation are more critical than having a perfectly authentic ensemble of instruments.

African drumming ensembles are frequently based on the West African concept of a "rhythm complex," a multilayered set of rhythms that sound simultaneously in a polyrhythm that loops continuously, to which rhythms of ever-increasing complexity are added. The music is traditionally open-ended, so players can come in, stop, and re-enter as they wish. There is something

Student djembe drummer at work, fine-tuning his stroke.

hypnotic about the rhythmic ostinati, and hearing these repetitions, players often begin moving their heads and their bodies as well as their hands as they play. Often the drums give way to dance, and short songs or even melodic phrases can be sung in a further interweave of sound. Drummers may find their comfort level with just one pattern per piece, or they may change from one learned rhythm to the next at will or on the teacher's cue, or they may introduce improvised rhythms. Some teachers may prefer to allow students to find their own improvised rhythm initially, setting just the pulse to which various rhythms can be invented. Students may play with a recording (of Akan or Asanti drummers, for example), or listen to a recording and then attempt to play within the style. Percussion players will know about appropriate techniques to be modeled and shaped in playing the instruments, but music teachers will understand that the initial goal of getting students drumming can lead to the later development of performance technique.

As one of the more energized musical ensembles, African drumming can draw the attention of students who enjoy the rhythmic dimension of music making, the physical participation, and the oral/aural dimensions of the traditional means of transmission. Drumming groups develop a kind of social cohesion that is almost immediate and continuing. A whole year of experience in a drumming ensemble can bring a level of performance proficiency that gives pleasure to players as well as to audiences in school and outside of it.

⁘ BREAK POINT 10.3 The Communal Groove

> Before attempting to teach any musical genre, tradition, or style, even the rock-solid musician—skilled on one instrument (or voice) and with a well-developed ear—will need to study it. For those interested in African drumming, many music studios, schools, and stores, as well as community centers and arenas for adult education, feature workshops and longer-term classes in drumming. Particularly in university communities and large cities, teachers can find training in African drumming. Investigate the possibilities.

GOSPEL CHOIR

Thomas E. Dorsey is credited with the shaping of gospel music—and the choirs that perform it. Since the 1920s, it has become one of the most emotionally moving of all American music expressions. So revered is the genre that African-American-based gospel choirs are heard from Australia to Zimbabwe (and in Romania as well!). In recent years, gospel choirs—or choirs that perform gospel music—have appeared in secondary school curricula and after-school music programs. They are directed by experienced teachers who can model the singing and play the piano as it suits the style, or by a gospel musician from a congregation in the community who is contracted to teach the choir. These choirs are often in schools with significant African-American enrollments, but they have wide appeal, with an expressive style and repertoire that can be learned by all who are motivated to listen to the nuances and practice their parts to "lift their voices" in song. The singing of gospel music is energetic and spirited; performers often wear robes in their school colors and employ considerable movement as they sing. The choral sound is generally supported by a rhythm section that typically includes piano, drums, and electric bass.

The controversial issue of sacred music in schools has been raised and discussed as it pertains to gospel music (and other choral music traditions, too), but the standard position is that so long as the music is intended as a musical experience and not to proselytize and preach religious beliefs, the ensemble is appropriate to public school practice. To avoid controversy, sensitive teachers select music that refers more to freedom, power, community, love, and peace than songs with the most vivid of biblical and devotional texts (although that is not always the easiest of tasks). Some choirs hold their own with standards like "Amazing Grace," "Battle Hymn of the Republic," "Lean on Me," and "When the Saints Go Marching In"; others are drawn to the music of contemporary gospel choirs like that of Kirk Franklin. Gospel songs may be learned by note or by rote, although the oral/aural means is frequently more successful at cutting to the essence of the music as it swings its rhythm and slides from one pitch to another. The gospel choir may function at some schools as an extracurricular club activity or may be one component of a broader choral repertoire.

HANDBELL CHOIR

From the great traditions of Protestant churches comes the ensemble known as the handbell choir, which has made its way into some schools as a singular ensemble elective as well as a supplemental support to choral music. A full five octaves of bells, sixty-one bells in all, are possible, while some handbell choirs have as few as two octaves. Every player is responsible for one or possibly two bells in making the melodies and their harmonizations. Contributing a pitch or two to the whole guarantees the importance of every player, so all students are indispensable to the team. It is truly teamwork that makes the melody, and no one player can miss without leaving holes in an otherwise flowing melody.

The technique of bell-ringing in a handbell choir requires strength and coordination, so handbells are usually reserved for students in the upper elementary grades and beyond. The player's entire arm is involved in bringing the bell down and out in front of the body, and the wrist is important in tilting the bell slightly forward so that the clapper can fall forward to the side of the bell, which produces the ringing. Timing the preparation, the attack, and the follow-through that damps the tone before the player lifts the bell back up in a resting position can be physically challenging and requires as much attention to the production of the sound as to damping it. The lowest and largest bells require the greatest strength (the C3, two octaves below middle C, weighs thirteen pounds), which explains why full sets are reserved for players of high school age. Handbell choirs are found in private church-related schools to a greater extent than in public schools, but they are an option for the performance of secular and sacred music— the latter performed for its musical rather than religious intent.

JAZZ

Standard to secondary schools in the United States, the instrumental jazz ensemble has a history in schools that can be traced to the innovative stage bands of the 1950s. In fact, jazz bands were once called "stage bands" to distance them from jazz on the fringes of society that was not fit for schools. Times

High school jazzers in progress.

have drastically changed, and the jazz ensemble is often central to instrumental music programs, an elite small ensemble intended to provide the solid brass-and-wind sound (with rhythm section) that not only swings but also offers a venue for students who strive for original and creative improvisations in the styles of jazz greats like Miles Davis and John Coltrane. Jazz ensembles begin to shape as early as middle school, when young students with a year or more of study on an instrument are taught blues scales. They progress to playing a basic blues form together, which leads to the invention of melodies based on the blues scale for a twelve-bar phrase. They learn the importance of listening to jazz to pick up ideas and of playing written-out transcriptions of the improvised solos of jazz masters.

Teachers who direct jazz ensembles have typically played in them, too, sometimes for their entire high school career and often as part of their university program of study. Yet if they are less experienced, they know that it is never too late to learn. Some pick up an instrument to play in a community jazz group or enroll in summer classes in jazz, and some hire a jazz musician as a contract teacher within the program. Along with jazz styles of the swing-band era of Duke Ellington and others, there is growing interest in featuring Latin jazz, including salsa and mambo styles, within the repertoire of high school groups.

Vocal jazz has emerged in some regions as a complement to instrumental jazz ensembles and as a component of choral programs. The sophisticated rhythms and close cluster-harmonies challenge the ear and bend the voice in unique ways and are an expressive means of performance for singers who wish to develop a personal style in scat-singing. There is an initial financial commitment for microphones and amplifiers in establishing a vocal jazz ensemble (some of which is also necessary in instrumental jazz, for guitar, bass guitar, piano, and solo singer). Along with the vocal/choral and jazz expertise of teachers who direct this ensemble, there is also their need to be tuned to the training of a solid student rhythm section of piano, drums, and stand-up bass. Vocal jazz is distinguishable from show choir in its tendency to perform in concert style rather than with extensive movement routines, its improvised vocal solos, and its greater musical complexity. Like instrumental jazz, vocal jazz is directed by those who have performed it or who pursue training in workshops.

MARIACHI

Ensembles of mariachi musicians are springing up in schools whose communities have sizable populations of Mexicans and Mexican Americans. Schools in the Southwest but also in states far from the border are finding a place for mariachi music in their curricular offerings. Mariachi ensembles bring the cultural rhythms of Mexico into the school curriculum, and yet student players not from that heritage are drawn to the colorful timbres, the dancing rhythms, the harmonies, and the social life this music reflects and inspires. Mariachi ensembles typically include two to five violins, one or two trumpets, a *guitarron* (large acoustic bass guitar with a convex back), several *vihuela* (small five-stringed rhythm guitar with a convex back), and one or more six-stringed guitars. Teachers of string ensembles and orchestra are among those better prepared to work with the instruments, and yet all music teachers are capable of developing the contacts with mariachi musicians from the local community who can teach the techniques and repertoire. In this way, as their students learn to perform mariachi from experienced performers, the music teachers can learn along with them.

Some of the most successful high school mariachi bands emerge in environments where students have learned to play guitar, violin, and trumpet in elementary and middle school. They already have some facility on the instrument as they begin to work into the techniques of mariachi style on entering ninth or tenth grade. Expert mariachi players have observed that young guitar students who learn harmonic progressions in several keys (such as G, D, and F) at

High schoolers coordinating parts in a mariachi band.

an early age can then transfer them to vihuela and can even figure out the harmonic shifting of the guitarron's bass lines. It is also useful for young students to have studied some Spanish, or to have heard enough Spanish (conversational exchanges, numbers, colors, and such) to feel comfortable with the language of the songs. Students may already be familiar with some of the standard mariachi songs like "Cielito Lindo," "El Jarabe," and "La Negra," and may have even grown up singing the mournful tales of spurned love at home and in the family. Students may specialize in singing the mariachi songs, although instrumentalists are often called upon to sing as well as play.

Mariachi music is typically learned through the oral/aural process. However, for inexperienced players to gain performance techniques and a repertoire for public performance within a few months of study—and surely by year's end—learning by note is both effective and efficient.

Mariachi music requires attention to its different "feel," particularly the fluctuating hemiola effect of the duple and triple divisions of 6/8 meter; for first-timers, this can be complicated and challenging. Listening to the recordings of groups like Mariachi Cobre and Mariachi Los Camperos de Nati Cano as well as attending live performances of a local or touring mariachi ensemble can motivate and guide the performance of young players and singers.

❖ BREAK POINT 10.4 Mariachi Music Makers

> Get to know the music you wish to teach. In the case of mariachi, listen to the recordings of Mariachi Cobre and Mariachi Los Camperos de Nati Cano, watch a video (for example *!Viva el Mariachi! The History, the Culture, the Instruments of Mariachi Music,* www.visionquestent.com), talk to people at a local Mexican restaurant that features mariachi music, and find out if there are mariachi bands that perform in your area. Ideally, inquire about attending rehearsals and even joining in.

MARIMBAS

While chromatic marimbas have long been a part of secondary school bands and orchestras, and even specialized percussion ensembles, a relatively recent development has been the emergence of African-style marimba bands. Some elementary, middle, and high schools are now providing training in the performance of Shona-style marimba music. The Shona of Zimbabwe developed marimbas in the 1960s so schoolchildren could learn to play the traditional music of *mbiras* (sophisticated "thumb-pianos" with deep resonating gourds). Master musician Dumisani Maraire carried the concept to school and community groups in Seattle and across the Pacific Northwest. "Dumi" is referred to as the father of Zimbabwean music in America, as it was he who introduced marimba band music to teachers in Seattle and later up and down the west coast of North America in the 1980s. The genre spread through the work of his musical family, including Lora Chiora-Dye, and his protégées.

The traditional pedagogy of African-style marimbas is demonstration and imitation. Such instruction is not intended as a literacy-based program; aural learning is central to the process, and improvisation is key. Typically, marimbas are not played alone but with djembe-style drums, bass drums, seed pods, and iron bells or bars.

The wooden xylophones of Orff ensembles, as well as full-scale orchestral marimbas, are used to perform Shona-style marimba music, including its melodies in three- and four-part harmonies. Interest in the music has led a number of marimba makers to produce standing marimbas for classroom use, all with resonating columns to amplify their sound and many with collapsible parts that allow them to be transported and stored. Marimba workshops have sprouted up for prospective players of all ages, including teachers, who learn not only how to play but also how to make their own marimbas. The music is accessible to even first-time listeners due to its rhythmic drive, percussive articulations, and familiar I, IV, and V harmonies. Teachers claim that marimba training helps young players develop dexterity and coordination, aural skills, concentration, and knowledge of rhythm, melody, and harmony. The reactions of audiences, who often dance, clap, and sing to the marimba music, is ample reason for its enormous growth in schools.

RECORDER CONSORT

In the third or fourth grade of their elementary school music experience, children often learn to play the recorder. For many, group recorder instruction is a means to an end: learning to read music. It also helps to develop the coordinated tasks of breathing and finger dexterity that are necessary in playing instruments of the band and orchestra. Some students take it further, graduating from basic group lessons to performance in a recorder consort rich in the music of the European Renaissance, continuing from elementary school into middle and high school as well. The starting instrument is the soprano recorder, and alto is the second instrument learned in the full four-part ensemble that also includes tenor and bass. A soprano-alto-tenor-bass (SATB) consort is the ideal goal, but if for budgetary reasons the bass recorder is not affordable, the tenor can provide the bottom line of standard four-part pieces. (There are plenty of two-part soprano and alto arrangements as well.)

The music of recorder consorts include Renaissance galliards and pavanes, canons and double canons, fugues, minuets, chansons, gigues, basse danses, and country dances of all kinds. Along with music meant for recorder, some arrangements for woodwind quartets can be adapted for recorders, as well as music of some Andean, East Asian, and Native American cultures. There are opportunities for student performances of Renaissance recorder music, including early music festivals, Renaissance fairs, Revolutionary War reenactments, and winter holidays. Some teachers double and triple up on instruments or even amplify them so the music can be heard as accompaniment to dances of the period and culture. For students who get beyond "Polly Wolly Doodle" and "Ode to Joy" on their recorders, there is wide musical potential awaiting them in the recorder consort.

ROCK BAND

A number of secondary schools have successfully explored the development of a performance experience referred to as "popular music performance," "rock music performance," "garage band," or simply "rock band." Rather than a lis-

Rock band, intent and in action.

tening analysis or history of rock music and popular music, rock band is an opportunity for players of guitar, bass guitar, drums, and keyboard to play what they know, learn from one another, listen to forms and techniques of a variety of artists, and create songs and arrangements that work for them. Rock band often operates more like a studio class, the nature and pace of the activities frequently set by the level of student competence and experience, and the goals typically colored by students' interest in particular popular music styles (as well as the teacher's expertise).

Teachers who coach a performance class of this type, which may encompass a larger enrollment of students who break into smaller working bands, have often played rock music themselves and are likely still listening to artists and bands. They work from their instruments, playing riffs that students can imitate, and trading two, four, or even twelve bars with students who then imitate or invent, together or individually. Teachers invite students to work through earlier forms in laying the groundwork of current styles, including blues and rhythm and blues, and may then move them through a taste of country rock and folk rock to the music of alternative rock and jam bands. They develop the aural skills of their students, encourage their technical facility (sometimes with guest spots by local players), and offer commentary that helps to shape student performances and original songs. Still, the development of musicianship is emphasized and creative expression is honored; notation may be an additional learning expectation as a means of preserving the music that is made in a rock band class.

❖❖ BREAK POINT 10.5 Garage Band Phenomenon

You or someone you know may have played in a "garage band," an ensemble playing rock-style instruments that meets after school and on weekends to learn tunes, hang out, and dream about performing in public. Sometimes these bands may even make it to playing house parties, malls, and "battle of the bands" festivals. Discuss the repertoire for some of these bands, the ways players and singers learned it, and how some of the needs of young garage band musicians can be met in a school setting.

SAMBA

Exhilarating percussion music from Brazil is making its way into school music programs. Samba music is played on large bass drums called *surdos* and a range of smaller instruments such as *agogos* (bells), *tamborims* (small hand drums played with split sticks), *ganzas* (metal tubes filled with beads), and snare drums. The teacher, called *maestre*, directs the band through whistles to signal various breaks, solos, and even movement patterns made while playing in processions. Samba bands are particularly strong in schools and communities in the U.K.; they are found in elementary school programs as well as in secondary schools during the school day or in after-school clubs. Rooted in a song form and circle dance brought to Brazil by Bantu slaves, the polyrhythmic play of drums with metallic instruments energizes musicians to move as they play, and often to sing as well. Particularly during the time of Carnaval, the pre-Lenten holiday that usually lands sometime in February, samba bands create a frenzy of musical sound characteristic of the world's rowdiest party-time in Brazil.

For the uninitiated, samba bands may sound totally improvisatory in nature, but at work is a tight ensemble of musicians who must know their parts and keep them, despite the excitement and the dancing. As in a variety of African-inspired ensembles, there are layers of sound that build, one upon the other, from the steady and comparatively slow rhythm of the surdo to the fast shaking of ganzas and tapping of tamborims. For beginning groups, the parts are fixed and unchanging, taught through demonstration and imitation, with the rhythms played repeatedly like multiple ostinati. The variety comes with the maestre's direction for some instruments to stop so that others can be heard. Experienced players take off into improvisations within the style, adding flavor. Whole programs of samba and Brazilian-inspired music (including the *bossa nova*) are offered in some schools, complete with guitar performances of samba and Brazilian music for the choral singers. Teachers intrigued with developing a samba band often need go no farther than their local community to find a *sambanista* (samba player) to teach them or to serve as visiting artist-teacher in the school.

STEEL DRUM BAND

The steel drum band (or steelband) is at home in elementary and secondary schools, coming from the Caribbean island of Trinidad in the 1970s and spreading to many North American communities as a means of making lively music together. Early steel drums (or pans) on the island were percussive but without the resonant timbre or melodic versatility of the modern pan, nor could they produce harmonics from fundamental pitches that are present in school ensembles today. Four parts comprise the steel pan—the rim, the playing surface of inner, middle, and outer notes, the belly (underside) and skirt (resonator), and the steel pan sticks that are wrapped tightly with rubber so as to bounce on the pan in creating sound. The pan instrument now has a full chromatic range and is capable of playing nearly any music, including European art music.

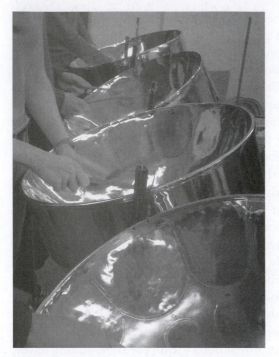

Hands on four pans of the steel drum ensemble.

There are three groupings of pans in a steelband: *front line* (melody pans, played by tenor and double tenor pans), *harmony line* (counter melody pans, played by double second pans and guitar), and *bass line* (chords, played by bass pans). These instruments offer the three-part texture of the music: the high-pitched lead of the tenor, the fixed-rhythms of mid-range instruments that provide the harmony, and the sparse repetitive "boom" at the bottom of the sound. Small steelbands consist of five or six players (occasionally, just a tenor and bass pan, with keyboard and drums), while steelbands in Trinidad featured in the parades of Carnaval may number one hundred or more players. There is an "engine room" of non-pitched percussion instruments, that in most ensembles consists of drumset, congas, large metal scrapers, and several ear-piercing irons struck with metal rods. The "braiding of the irons" is characteristic of steel drum bands, a polyrhythm of interlocking parts that creates much excitement and tension.

The foremost music of the steel drum ensemble is never far from the calypso tradition of Trinidad, that strophic form in which several verses are set to a repeated melody and whose texts (when sung) often deal with social issues and political controversies. Calypsos may incorporate sung calls and responses in some of their sections, and most have a recurring chorus section. As instrumental pieces without singers, there are elaborate variations to the calypso that, over continued repetition of the verse and chorus, pique the interest of dancers who respond to the beat and intensive rhythms of the music. Successful teachers have undergone training in how to perform the various instruments of the steel drum ensemble and are able to teach the parts to students by playing them, singing and chanting them, and clapping or moving to them when the notation does not capture the swing of the music. As improvisation is a feature of steel drums in Trinidad, classroom ensembles make for ideal settings where improvisation—and composition, arranging, and listening analysis—can be brought into the picture. Besides the obvious performance opportunities in school and in the community, there are steelband festivals that offer competitive adjudicated performances, concerts, and workshops.

❖ BREAK POINT 10.6 Steeling Yourself for the Pan Ensemble

In preparation for teaching steel drums, or as insertions for students at rehearsals, listen to recordings of the pan ensemble (by Lord Kitchener, the Mighty Sparrow, David Rudder) and view *One Hand Don't Clap*, a documentary film on calypso and steel drums (http://www.cinemaweb.com/rhapsody/). Even while there is plenty of notated music, the sounds and sights of the ensemble will offer the swing and spirit of the genre. While listening, tap the pulse of the kick drum, and then stand up and do as Trinidadians do: "chip" (a two-step forward shuffle) while clapping the off-beats or prominent rhythms.

WORLD VOCAL ENSEMBLE

High school choral teachers select some of the best of Western art music and popular choral arrangements for their mixed choirs, girls' (women's) and boys' (men's) choirs, and chamber groups. They may occasionally select music from other cultures, too, although sparingly, in order to keep the balance tipped in favor of the Western art styles that are promoted in festival lists of required songs. Some teachers develop a world vocal ensemble, in part to follow their own interest in music from other choral traditions and to respond to the positive reactions of students to the music of world cultures. The creation of a world vocal ensemble allows full effort to be given to learning music of cultures outside the standard festival pieces, the Western art music, and popular music arrangements. Selections in such an ensemble may include the polyphonic songs of Bulgaria, Georgia, and Russia; the homophonic song from southern Africa (South Africa, Malawi, Mozambique, Zimbabwe) and the southern Pacific (including the Maori and the Samoans); *joiks* from the Saami of Scandinavia; *sean-nos* from Ireland; mawlum from Laos; and vocal styles and choral arrangements from China, Japan, and Korea.

Modeled after innovative university ensembles, world vocal ensembles in high schools receive the support of administrators who view them as a way to help students understand other cultures through music. In the best-case scenarios, the music of the various cultures is performed in the original (native) language with the integrity of vocal technique and timbre very much in mind. Music is learned from a growing repertoire of printed scores but also by ear through listening to recordings. Video recordings are instructive, too, for understanding how the body moves to accommodate the sound and offer further expressive nuance of the style. Songs can be "danced," as students learn that singing in many cultures involves full-body movement, turns and twists of the torso, a shifting of the weight, and a variety of head, arm, and hand movements. When possible, traditional culture-bearers are brought in to the schools to model the singing (and often the associated movement and dance, when appropriate) and to share the stories behind the songs. In public performances of world vocal ensembles, it is helpful to include a number of songs from the same tradition so audiences get more than a single, fleeting taste that comes when programs offer too many styles. Rounding out the performances of the world vocal ensemble are featured solos or accompaniments on traditional instruments from the musical cultures.

Academic Courses

In addition to their ensembles and performance classes, secondary school music teachers can offer courses of an academic nature within music, the arts, and culture. Particularly at the high school level, students who seek their arts credit may be drawn to nonperformance classes in Western art music, world music, popular music, and music theory.

WESTERN ART MUSIC/WORLD MUSIC CULTURES

History and culture courses fit well into the high school social science curriculum, and those that stretch into the arts may be attractive to students with interests in interdisciplinary topics. Studies in Western art music and world music cultures allow students to pursue music from historical and contextual perspectives as they also study historical and cultural events, figures, and belief systems as they are musically manifested. The music teacher can present Western art music through experiences in listening, lecture-demonstration, group discussion, independent projects, and up-front and personal experiences with musicians in the field who perform or can otherwise share their knowledge of particular styles. Field trips to live performances of Western art music at the symphony hall and opera theater not only underscore the music in study but can provide memories that last a lifetime.

The study of world music cultures is successful with music teachers who can help students discover the roles of music in cultures both past and present, through various means. The involvement of students in various participatory experiences (singing Mexican corridos, clapping Indian talas, dancing Puerto Rican salsa) goes a long way to underscore issues concerning music's meaning in these cultures, even as listening analysis can impress upon students the different but equally logical structures of some of the world's musical expressions. University-level texts can be used with students, with extensions and reinforcements given by the teacher. Extensive listening experiences can be supplemented by video recordings, live performance, and participatory experiences.

POPULAR MUSIC

As a course all its own, popular music is taught as much by high school teachers of English and social studies as by music teachers. It may even be team-taught. Music teachers see the value in tracing a history of popular music from the nineteenth century onward as a means of understanding its musical forms and features, and as a complement to greater knowledge of the Western art music that was evolving at the same time. A musical approach to the study of popular music, even as an academic course, involves musical analysis of formal designs, harmonic functions, and melodic and rhythmic components in ways that include listening, demonstration and imitation, and participatory experiences in singing and even playing selected segments of the music. English teachers are drawn to the song lyrics, including the rhyming patterns and metric schemes, the use of consonance and assonance, and the imagery of the lyrics—components that may well intrigue music teachers, too. The lyrics are equally interesting to teachers of history, who look for songs whose messages express themes of youth and their social issues, as well as responses to recent historical events and stances (for example, rock and country-western songs written in reaction to 9/11 and Hurricane Katrina). Some of the texts utilized in university-level courses work well as high school texts that survey popular music.

❖ BREAK POINT 10.7 Reviewing the Concert

Students in classes of music history, literature, and culture benefit from attendance at live performances, especially when a concert review is a required assignment. Brainstorm criteria for a concert review by students: What would you want students to observe, note, and interpret as a result of attending a performance (or rehearsal) of a symphony, opera, chamber group, steel drum band, rock group, or mariachi ensemble? Would you require remarks both musical (repertoire, ensemble sound projection and balance, musicians' roles and functions) and extramusical (the venue itself, the program book, the audience reaction)?

ADVANCED PLACEMENT: MUSIC THEORY

The Advanced Placement Program, or just AP, is developed for highly motivated high school students who would like not only to gain theoretical knowledge but also to earn university credit for their effort. Many high schools offer AP courses in subjects from art history to chemistry to statistics to music theory. Students contemplating music as a major or minor area of study at a university, as well as those who just have an interest in music, may opt for a course in AP music theory. The not-for-profit College Board maintains the content of the course, supports teachers of the course, communicates with university personnel who define course acceptance policy, and administers the annual AP exams. Music teachers with interests in teaching AP music theory typically talk with their principal and colleagues, contact the College Board to determine the content and requirements of the course, and then make room in their schedule to teach it.

The goal of an AP music theory course is to develop the musicianship skills of students and their understanding of music's structures. They are expected to enter the course with performance skills on an instrument or in voice, and with the ability to read and write musical notation. Like a first-year theory course in a university, students are introduced to aspects of melody, harmony, texture, rhythm, form, musical analysis, composition, history, and style. Aural skills, sight-singing, and keyboard harmony may also be included as avenues for understanding music's structures. The AP music theory exam gauges the ability of students to recognize, understand, and describe materials and processes of music that are heard or presented in a score, and such skills as the harmonization of a melody with appropriate chords and the realization of figured-bass notation are likely to be tested as well as taught. Multiple-choice questions, which are computer scored, are combined with musical analysis and compositional exercises that are evaluated by a member of a university faculty.

COMPOSITION-RELATED TRAINING

While strands of creativity are woven through the elementary school music program, it is at the secondary school level that separate courses may be offered to young people in the development of their creative-expression skills for composition, improvisation, song-writing, and even creative work that utilizes a mix of arts, technology, and the media. Students are taught through hands-on experiential means to work with musical elements and structures, to investigate new and unfamiliar timbral possibilities, to align melody and rhythm with poetic verse, and to consider how musical invention might be blended and enhanced by dance, theater, film/video, and the visual arts. Sometimes with their own instruments, or vocally, and sometimes with the use of computers, electronic keyboards, and other technology, students learn to manipulate sonic materials to the point of creating, producing, and performing their individual musical expressions.

Composition studio, or just composition, is a time-intensive offering for both teachers and students. For students who read and write music, composition is a natural next step. Teachers may assign simple tasks to individual students or groups, such as composing a four-measure rhythm in 4/4 or a two-phrase AB melody in 6/8. Assignments may stipulate some musical parameters while leaving others to the discretion of the young composers but with expectations for the use of particular chords and their inversions, clusters, or other textural possibilities. Timbre may depend upon available instruments or the use of programs that provide a variety of instrumental and vocal possibilities. Similar to the way art students learn artistic styles by copying the models, students of composition might be asked to write music (even brief segments) in the style of a Bach chorale or fugue, a Beethoven sonatina, a Fauré chanson, or a piece similar to the music of Igor Stravinsky, Gyorgi Ligeti, Stephen Sondheim, Ali Farke Toure, Eric Clapton, or Tracy Chapman.

Improvisation studio is a curricular offering in some schools where, similar to composition, groups of students assemble with their instruments of choice to learn to create music with some spontaneity, within style guidelines or specific musical parameters. The aim of the experience is commonly group music making, and sound-sketches are as far as students go into notating what they play. Improvisation is not commonly found as a separate course, however, but is taught in performance classes in guitar and keyboard, and ensembles that range from African drumming to steel drum bands. Of course, improvisation is central to the content of a jazz ensemble, or vocal jazz, in which the stylistic intent is for an ensemble to frame the song with its introductory "head," or melody, and then to allow opportunities for individual musicians to express their interpretation and extension of the melody.

Song-writing courses may be taught by music teachers or by teachers of English who wish to guide students in a musical discovery of "poetry in motion" in songs. Team-teaching is a possibility, where music teachers may collaborate with teachers of English, social studies, foreign languages, and other courses in the humanities to present song models for study and analysis; address the subject, themes, lyric content, and form of classic "model" songs; inspire ideas; offer notational skills for preserving the songs; and provide the means for recording them.

After-School Music Possibilities

The school is the natural venue for music instruction in the after-school hours. In-house individual and group instruction can be attractive to students and their parents, who look for ways of enriching their children's experiences in the world beyond soccer, football, basketball, baseball, and swim lessons. Private or group piano instruction is an efficient way to teach basic keyboard skills and notational literacy, moving young people through the beginner books all the way to the intermediate level. Guitar classes are also appealing, as are some of the percussion ensemble courses. After-school choirs and instrumental ensembles are also possible. Teachers can offer after-school private lessons on band and orchestral instruments. For those who are too exhausted from a day of classes to teach after hours, independent music teachers (and university students) may be available to offer lessons at a reasonable fee (if your administration allows this). School music teachers may direct or at least help to set up the after-school music possibilities, knowing that it is in the best interest of the school program to have students shore up their skills in after-school music experiences and training.

Of course, music teachers may also teach and perform outside the school setting to supplement their income. They can offer lessons in piano, singing, or their favorite band and orchestral instruments in the homes of their students or in their own homes. Some music teachers direct community and church choirs, children's choirs, and youth choirs, or conduct youth symphonies and wind ensembles. They may enjoy working in early childhood music settings with very young children, and even infants and toddlers, sometimes through their own arrangements with local preschools or through such programs as Kinder-musik, Musikgarten, and Music Together. Others may look to lifelong learning in music programs, directing ensembles of senior citizens in chamber groups, choirs, and bands such as the New Horizons program. Along with their mar-ketable teaching and conducting skills, teachers may find many possibilities for after-school performance—often with remuneration on a professional scale.

Music for Everyone

A word of advice for teachers interested in the courses described in this chapter: proceed with caution so as to develop courses that fit the interests and needs of the school population. It is wise to learn the history and traditions that have served students well, and that appear to be of continuing interest to them and the broader community. Gauge the interest of students, colleague-teachers, administrators, and parents, and move gradually into developing courses that balance both traditional and contemporary needs. Work toward fashioning something that honors the past as well as the musical diversity that continues to emerge globally.

REFERENCES AND RESOURCES

Barnwell, Y., and G. Brandon. (1998). *Singing in the African American Tradition*. Woodstock, NY: Homespun Tapes. A choral and congregational songbook based in the oral tradition of learning-by-listening to the vocal parts and stylistic nuances featured on the accompanying CD, including "Steal Away," "I Feel Like Going On," "I'll Fly Away," "Soon I Will Be Done," and "Somagwaza."

Bay, M. (2005). *Complete Method for Modern Guitar*. Pacific, MO: Mel Bay Publications. First steps to playing guitar one string at a time, with gradual progress toward playing melody with harmony, right- and left-hand technique, including chording.

Dudley, S. (2004). *Carnival Music in Trinidad*. New York: Oxford University Press. CD and instructional web-manual by Victor Fung. This introduction to the context and style of steel drum, calypso, soca, and other musical forms of celebration offers an understanding of Trinidadian cultural expressions in music.

Fowler, C. (2005). *Music! Its Role and Importance in Our Lives*. New York: Glencoe/ Macmillan. Includes CDs and teachers' manuals. This student textbook is useful in secondary school courses in general music for its compilation of experiences and repertoire that provide an understanding of music for its many functions across time and place.

Goetze, M. (2002). *Global Voices in Song: An Interactive Multicultural Experience*. New Palestine, IN: Mj & associates. A multimedia collection of songs and dances from sixteen cultures, intended to be learned orally rather than in notated form, for use in elementary vocal and secondary choral settings.

Hampton, W. (1995). *Hot Marimbas*. Danbury, CT: World Music Press. Based on the musical style of the Shona people of Zimbabwe. This collection of layered melodies for marimbas and classroom xylophones offers vibrant danceable music for students in elementary and middle school settings. (See also *Mojo Marimbas* by the same author/publisher.)

Higgins, L. (1995). *Samba Drumming*. Norwich, UK: Norfolk Educational Press. A handbook for teachers for introducing samba batucada to elementary and secondary school students, with explicit techniques for playing caixa (snare drum), conga (drum), pandeiro (tambourine), ganza (shaker), reco-reco (scraper), tamborim (small hand-held drum), and agogo (double) bells.

Kerman, J., and G. Tomlinson, with V. Kerman. (2004). *Listen.* Boston: Bedford/St. Martin's. A historical survey of Western European art music, from ancient and medieval times to the present, with an introduction to musical elements and a final chapter on American music from the Age of Jazz forward.

Mach, E. (2004). *Contemporary Class Piano.* New York: Oxford University Press. A comprehensive introduction to the basics of keyboard performance for use in secondary schools, with notation, exercises, easy pieces and a selection of piano classics ranging from Rameau's "Tambourin" to Bartok's "Springtime Song."

Murphy, J. (2006). *Music in Brazil.* New York: Oxford University Press. An introduction to the myriad of musical styles in Brazil, with close attention to samba and popular music genres of the region, with CD and instructional web-manual of classroom applications by Bryan Burton.

Nieto, J., and B. Phillips. (2005). *Mariachi Philharmonic.* Van Nuys, CA: Alfred Publishing. Arrangements of traditional mariachi music for school mariachi band and string orchestra, with parts for violin, viola, cello-bass, trumpet, guitar, guittarron, vilhuela, piano, and harp. CD and teacher's manual also available.

Schmid, W. (1997). *World Music Drumming.* Milwaukee, WI: Hal Leonard. Seven study units for West African and Latin American drumming ensembles for use in elementary, middle, and high school settings.

Sheehy, D. (2005). *Mariachi Music in America.* New York: Oxford University Press. A review of the historical evolution of mariachi ensembles in Mexico and among Mexican Americans, complete with musical analysis and comparisons of styles, with CD and instructional web-manual by Ellen McCullough-Brabson.

Starr, L., and C. Waterman. (2003). *American Popular Music: From Minstrelsy to MTV.* New York: Oxford University Press. Themes and streams of music content and context are woven into a chronological and critical survey of music extending from brass bands and ragtime to alternative and rap music; CDs and listening guides direct attention to musical forms through the ages.

Wade, B. C. (2004). *Thinking Musically*. New York: Oxford University Press. A cross-cultural survey of music for its melodic, rhythmic, and textural dimensions, with discussion of music's meanings and uses in societies; a CD of fifty-nine tracks accompanies the book.

chapter 11

Diverse Learners and Learning Styles

A conversation between an elementary school mentor-teacher and student teacher:

Teacher: It's going to be important for you to think and act outside your comfort area. These kids will demand it.

Student teacher: Oh, you mean that even though I was trained as a choral teacher, I won't be doing much choral music in your elementary school?

Teacher: What I mean is that you're from an intact middle-class family, with privileges, and that you excelled in school all the way through. You're different from the average kid at this school, and so there's a learning curve ahead for you.

Student teacher: In what way?

Teacher: These kids come from single-parent families, and some are from jobless, even homeless families. Their parents are not the type to be going to PTA meetings: no time or no interest. The standardized test scores show that most of the kids in this school are struggling to read, and math scores are equally low. These kids learn, but differently, and we're trying to figure that out.

Student teacher: It's not been my experience . . .

Teacher: Exactly: your experience is very different from theirs. And yet these kids demand and deserve that we work hard to reach them where they are. You're going to need to step outside your zone and into theirs.

A conversation between a high school principal and an orchestra teacher:

High school principal: Your ensembles are stunning, truly award winning, and we're so pleased that you're here with us on our staff.

Orchestra teacher: Thanks. It's all about the kids, taking them as far as they can go. It's always been my dream to find ways for them to express themselves through music.

High school principal: I'm so pleased to hear you say that. A few parents were in to visit me yesterday, and they wanted to know how to get their special education kids into one of your ensembles. One of them has an autistic son, and two more have children with mild retardation.

Orchestra teacher: Gee, I'd like to help out. But I only teach strings and orchestra, 24/7.

High school principal: They know that, and that's what they want: a chance for their children to express themselves through music.

Many-Splendored Musical Children

The diversity of children and adolescents in schools is unparalleled in our time. They come from families of affluence and poverty, from blue-collar and white-collar families, and from families of the socioeconomic upper, middle, and lower classes. Their families may adhere to one of many religious belief systems, or may profess no religion at all. They are of an astounding variety of races and ethnicities, but may (or may not) identify strongly with a particular ethnic-cultural community. Some have recently arrived from other nations, while others can claim many generations of continuity in one region and even a single city. The lifestyles of their families vary, too, so that young people bring a range of values with them to the schools that enroll them. There are cultures marked by many factors, including age, gender, race and ethnicity, income level, and belief systems. There are also the cultures of exceptionalities, children with attention deficits, behavioral disorders, mental retardation, and learning disabilities. For five hours a day, five days a week, nine months a year, young people from these varied life and learning cultures come together under the same roof to be schooled and educated in the subjects that are deemed by society to be vital to their development as responsible members of their society. Diversity—with a capital D—concerns the many splendors of students' learning capacities and cultural backgrounds, which thus shape their learning styles, strengths, and needs.

Among the 53 million students who are enrolled in public and private schools in the United States alone, there is little doubt that they are "alike but different." Seven-year-olds, or sixth-graders, or high school juniors by and large share some similarities in the content of their schooling. How they are taught depends on school policy and teaching style, but how they learn depends on their individual abilities and needs. Their learning style depends on many factors, including their natural capacities, the modalities and processes that are favored by their families and communities, and their personal desire and motivation in choosing to learn some knowledge and skills over others. Students are individual learners, with personal learning styles and specific strengths and needs all their own. From a teacher's perspective, each one is unique and requires individual consideration even as they are grouped together in classes of twenty, thirty, or more for their learning encounters.

In nations of cultural pluralism, music makes its way into the wide-ranging educational plan that teachers design for young people in mathematics, the language arts, the social sciences, the sciences, and the arts. Regardless of who they are or where they have come from, children and youth have need for human artistic expression—and usually tremendous potential to feel it, respond to it, and make it themselves. Whether they live in mansions or tenement houses; in urban, suburban, or rural settings; in traditional and nontraditional families, they need music. Under every educational label, whether gifted or mentally retarded, or with sensory challenges (the hearing impaired and the visually impaired), learning disabilities, emotional disorders, or mental retardation, they can participate in musical experiences. It is the task of music teachers to include rather than to exclude young people from music-educational experiences, and to sort out and shore up their own sensitivities and strategies so as to give and to draw out music, regardless of who the children are or what their challenges may be. The diversity of learning styles among students may be one of the greatest challenges a music teacher can know. But the kind of schooling that a cultural democracy requires is the result of carefully crafted lessons and ensembles that reach all students in the wide spectrum of abilities, interests, and needs.

Diversity from a Multicultural Perspective

School populations have changed and are changing still, reflecting the explosion of racial and ethnic diversity within the populations in cities, suburbs, and even rural communities. Even those locales that are declining in population tend to be increasing in the diversity of the children and youth in their schools, many of them nonwhite. In many North American cities, the tables have turned: former minorities have become the majority population of some schools while the once-large and predominant Caucasian populations are drastically reducing in size. The continuing flood of immigrants from third-world cultures accounts for the greater diversity in first-world cultures, and the rate and flow of immigrants and refugees have continued unabated for at least a century. From every country in the world, people have come to the United States, Canada, the U.K., France, the Netherlands, and Australia (to name a few first-world countries undergoing demographic transformation) to seek out new lives for themselves

Children of a grand diversity.

and their families even while they hold on to some of their homeland traditions. In the United States alone, the flow of immigrants from Mexico, parts of Africa, Asia, and Latin America join the already diverse populations of longstanding Americans—for example, Native Americans and African Americans.

With the shifting ethnic and racial composite of populations has arisen the concept of multiculturalism, the processes of society and its schools to enable people from multiple cultures to live and learn together. In essence, multiculturalism is a movement aimed at the achievement of racial and ethnic equity in all of society, from education to employment opportunities. For fifty years (and in some cases for a century or more), teachers have been learning to honor cultural differences even while guiding students to attain a common core of knowledge deemed essential to all. With sensitivity and a drive toward developing competence for survival and success in the mainstream, teachers are allowing the cultural differences of young people to emerge at school without preventing their development of knowledge, skills, and values necessary for their contributions to the national and global arenas.

Terms like "multiethnic," "intercultural," "global," and "international," while having specific meanings, have been applied haphazardly to education and music education as synonymous with multicultural. They are not the same. Multiethnic was a term once used to distinguish ethnicity and race as separate from cultures such as gender and religion; multicultural is now commonly understood as having replaced this term. In some nations (South Africa, for example), intercultural is the preferred word in reference to the exchange between cultures to enable the development of mutual understanding. Global or international education extends the curriculum to an international scope, as students learn of people and cultures from across the world, while multicultural education commonly concerns ethnic-cultural groups that live in the community of the school—both traditional minority groups and recent immigrants. Regardless of the terms in use, it is of central importance in education today to recognize that even as home and family values vary, all young people merit and can excel through the educational opportunities presented to them.

✥ BREAK POINT 11.1 Varied Meanings

Investigate some of the behaviors and values that children bring to school as a result of their growing up in particular cultural communities—by asking them, and talking with other teachers. Seek out their foodways (weekday meal fare, table settings, dinner venue), clothing and hairstyles (with differentiations among children, youth, and adults, and between genders), festivals (their function, celebrative or commemorative components, and the presence of the arts, including music). Children are at least partly what they eat, wear, and celebrate, and knowing something of their family values helps to shape music lessons and sessions with sensitivity.

Diversity in Music Education Practice

In the field of music education, two approaches to diversity are frequently encountered: (a) multicultural music education, the intensive study of one or more cultures outside the mainstream, with attention to music as an expression of cultural beliefs and values, and (b) world music education (or "world musics in education," even "global musics in education"), the study of musical components as they are treated in various musical styles across the world. In either approach music teachers find themselves concerned with the repertoire performed by their ensembles and studied in their classes. In both approaches, the emphasis has tended to be on the music as sound, behavior, and idea, with less attention to the strengths and needs of students whose learning styles are shaped by their cultural communities. Obviously, cultural diversity in music education can be interpreted in more ways than one: as music selections from a broad variety of cultures for all students, regardless of cultural background, and as pedagogical experiences that fit the diversity of learning styles of students so that any and all music may be experienced and learned. It seems reasonable that a balanced view can be developed of the importance of diverse musical expressions as well as the strategies for reaching populations of diverse learners and their learning styles.

All students deserve to be musically nurtured, embraced for the musical experiences they know, and motivated to achieve musically at high levels. Since they all have the potential to sing, dance, play, read, write, and create music, and to listen with a keen ear and clear head, it is the challenge of teachers to figure how best to reach them, tap their strengths, and fill their needs. Yet there is frequently a cultural divide between teachers and students: coming from experiences that are distinguished from those of their students, teachers often feel ill-equipped to teach those whose experiences they do not fully understand. They have read the reports of the poor academic achievement of students of ethnic minorities and low socioeconomic communities, and yet they recognize this as a systemic failure and not a true reflection of their students' ability. Teachers are working to bridge the cultural gaps between themselves and their students, and they are seeking to understand and integrate the prior knowledge and cultural and linguistic heritage of their students into the content and delivery of their classes and ensembles. They know that nothing short of an educational paradigm shift to a culturally inclusive pedagogy will ensure the success of their students in music, the arts, math, the humanities, the sciences, and the social sciences. No child is incapable of musical and academic development if teachers are willing to find the points of entry and channels of stimulating this development.

❖ BREAK POINT 11.2 Cultural and Musical Diversity

Explore cultural diversity in music education as it is operating in two elementary, or middle, or high schools within different demographic settings. Describe the composite of the student populations. Check out the music learning styles of students and the pedagogical strategies that are used in bringing all students into music-educational experiences. Talk with the teachers, observe the classes, and make notes of strategies in play, to bring to class discussion.

Music teachers need to develop the musical and cultural competence to teach music effectively to their multicultural student populations. To leave no child behind, they must practice inclusivity, embracing students regardless of learning style and the prior experiences that frame their worldview, enticing them into curricular offerings and instructional-style experiences that balance their strengths with their needs. Culturally competent music teachers are responding to cultural and linguistic differences, and communicating verbally and nonverbally with students from different backgrounds. Just as their students learn to switch codes between home and school, and between minority and mainstream cultures, music teachers with cultural competence make headway in communicating verbally and nonverbally with students of every race and ethnicity. They are untiring in their acceptance of students for their cultural learning, even as they pursue every avenue to meet students' learning needs so that they may acquire the knowledge and skills that take them beyond "potential" to genuine achievement.

Beyond the mandates for equitable and inclusive music education across race and ethnicity, cultural diversity plays itself out in many ways. Uncertain teachers get grounded as they not only learn to perform and understand many musical expressions but as they discover the meaning behind the music, and the importance of knowing music makers within the local school community. They learn to juggle their programs and their lesson plans, making room for the music that their students value in their cultural communities, balancing music from the festival lists with music that has not made these lists: blues, mariachi, *mawlum,* and *merengue.* What their ensembles cannot play can be experienced in listening to live music or to recordings of their music, and through dialogues with visiting artists. Music teachers are making time to teach any music in ways that reach students: orally/aurally, visually, and kinesthetically. Not only are many of the musical genres of the world's cultures meant to be learned without notation, but many learners learn without notes, along with notes, or only eventually with notes—once the symbols have meaning that is heard and felt. Repetition, reinforcement, and variation are techniques that do well for everything from phrases to full pieces to bring all students along in their musical growth.

❖ BREAK POINT 11.3 Two Scenarios for Three Students

Read and reflect on the cases of Rahwa (*Music as Language*) and Jamal and Jorge (*Music Studio*), three diverse learners from among multicultural populations in their schools. Discuss the circumstances of the students and the effectiveness of music-educational strategies. What would you do if you were in such circumstances? What would you not do?

Music as Language

Rahwa, age six, arrived this year from a village in Somalia to James Madison Elementary School. She speaks no English nor does her mother or two little brothers, and her father is just beginning to learn English as part of his job training. Her first-grade teacher understands that an effective plan is to provide for Rahwa's immersion experience in school culture, where she may sit alongside her classmates as they count, color, read beginner books, and learn cursive writing. Rahwa also spends two hours every morning in an English as a Second Language (ESL) classroom, joining children from China, Ethiopia, Guatemala, Mexico, and Russia in exercises intended to build their language skills and conceptual knowledge across subject areas and in the world beyond school. She goes with her first-grade classmates to music class, where the music teacher uses singing games for vocal development and to prepare children for music reading. The music teacher, Ms. Rhodes, noticed that Rahwa frequently follows behind the others in learning the games, but that she is singing and dancing well by the third or fourth time around. Rahwa took well to "Bow Wow Wow," "Jump Up My Ladies," and "Sorida," smiled a lot, but was otherwise quiet. Not until Ms. Rhodes asked her to "tell the class which phrases were the same and which ones were different" did she learn what the children shouted at her, that "Rahwa doesn't know English." The next steps were clear to her: She would find out more about Rahwa from the classroom teacher, continue to build plenty of repetition into her lessons, encourage and reinforce her learning with nods and smiles, and keep instructions simple. Maybe the songs would speed her acquisition of English, Ms. Rhodes thought. It dawned on her, too, that down the road a bit, perhaps Rahwa would share a song in *her* language from *her* homeland country.

Music Studio

Jamal and Jorge are enrolled in an urban high school where one of the graduation requirements is two units of study in the arts. Jamal, age fifteen, plays piano for his Sunday morning gospel choir at First A.M.E. Church, and Jorge, age sixteen, plays congas and timbales in his uncle's weekend salsa band. They like music, although neither one of them reads notes, and yet they would prefer to study music rather than a class in painting or clay pottery. As they are friends, they decide to go together to the band teacher, Mr. Tillman, to discuss their schedules for the following year. As it turns out, Mr. Tillman has a very full schedule: freshman band, concert band, keyboard class, wind ensemble, jazz band, and study hall; altogether, a full-time position (even though he feels like he's working overtime in his after-school rehearsals). Still, a brilliant idea strikes him as he speaks with Jamal and Jorge: Why not go to the administration to request that an additional music period be added to his schedule as catch-all to students who wish to perform, study, create music beyond the music classes he offers? He does so, preparing a formal request complete with mission statement, educational objectives, and a weekly outline of activities across the academic year. Their wish is granted: Jamal, Jorge, and others are invited in to a Music Studio course where almost anything musical can happen, where performance is mixed with creative composition, recording activity, and self- and peer-critiques. The eclectic group consists of one pianist, seven guitarists with and without amps, three drummers (one on drum set and two on congas), a violin, two flutes, a saxophone, a trumpet, a clarinet, a bass guitar, and three singers. Mr. Tillman is able to bring several students with rich musical experiences outside school into school music classes, and he persuades the talented Jamal to double his arts credits by joining his jazz band along with the music studio course the following year. Meanwhile, both Jamal and Jorge are learning to read music as a skill to help them preserve the music they are creating. The intensity of Mr. Tillman's schedule increases, and yet his efforts are noted by the principal, who wonders aloud, "With this kind of action, we may need to hire a colleague for you."

Music-making oblivious of cultural differences.

The presence in schools of young people of various races and ethnicities can challenge music teachers to think and act outside the limits of their own personal experiences, but such diversity is replete with benefits for teachers as well as their students. Diversifying the musical content of curricular programs is an important step that teachers take in reducing ethnocentrism in their classrooms, as it demonstrates to all within earshot the many musical expressions that, while different, are equally logical and beautiful. Critical to the diversity of learners and their learning styles, however, is for music teachers to adapt their communication and delivery systems to students of a wide spectrum of ethnic-cultural, socioeconomic, and linguistic backgrounds. The approach to multicultural populations is one of an "arms-around" recruitment and continuing support from start to finish, so that all children and youth might be brought to their fullest musical realization. It is then that music teachers become part of the team of educators with interest in the social reconstruction of education for the sake of a more equitable society.

A Diversity of Exceptional Learners

There was a time when individuals referred to as "handicapped" lived at the margins of U.S. and Canadian society, beyond the realm of those considered of average (or "normal") intellectual, emotional, or physical abilities. They were classified and labeled as mentally retarded, emotionally disturbed, and physically disabled, and their needs rather than their strengths were assessed to immediately mark them as unfit for the everyday life of the rest of society at work and in school. The handicapped were kept at home or sent away to institutions where they joined others with similar conditions, and they were neither seen nor heard from by the mainstream of society. Not until the middle of the last century was legislation directed toward more progressive health care for all people, and universal access to public education, at which point the special needs of exceptional children began to be met. In 1975, the United States passed the Education for Handicapped Children Act, Public Law 94-142, which led to a free and appropriate education for all children within the least restrictive environment. This law mandated an Individualized Educational Plan, or IEP, for every special needs child. A second law, Individuals with Disabilities Education Act (IDEA), Public Law 101-476, went into effect in 1990 to address the needs of children with autism, traumatic brain injury, and attention deficit disorders (ADD), and to aid in the school-to-job adjustments that young people with special needs must make. Inclusionary practices within schools—and society at large—are a huge leap away from centuries of isolation, and diverse learners today are not only accepted but even celebrated for the varied contributions they are capable of making to the life of the community.

While most young people may find some challenges in the course of their learning, these challenges tend to be more subtle than extreme. Diverse in their learning styles, many students are able to overcome their challenges without special support, while others require the help of special services, special education teachers, or at least ancillary learning aids. Yet it is consistently proven by exceptional learners themselves, those with greater-than-average needs, that they are able to compensate for a challenge in one area by excelling in another. A child may lack verbal fluency but be highly capable of developing rich interpersonal relationships. Another child may not be able to draw a stick figure, but his understanding of algebraic concepts may be unusually swift and sure. Still another may not be able to walk without help, or may find mechanical movements of handwriting and toothbrushing difficult to coordinate, but she may sing like an angel. For all children, the strengths are there to be found even as arrangements are made for challenges to be met.

❖ BREAK POINT 11.4 The Spectrum of Exceptionalities

Discuss the wide range of abilities and needs within the population, based on personal experiences (recollections of the struggles of yourself, family members, friends, and classmates). Research descriptions of exceptional learners and societal laws intended to provide for their education and development. Discuss curricular accommodations to support the belief in educating all children and youth to the maximal extent possible.

Exceptional learners are children and adolescents with special needs who comprise 9.5 percent of the school population. Nearly half of this group are diagnosed with specific learning disabilities, while approximately 20 percent have speech and language impairments, 11 percent are mentally retarded, and 9 percent have emotional or behavioral disorders. There is also a population of gifted children with exceptional across-the-board intelligence, and talented children who, through both nature and nurturing home environments, have unusual capacities for dancing, drawing, playing musical instruments, singing, and writing poetry. Special services are made available to support the learning and development of students whose intellectual functioning capacity runs several standard deviations from the norm (in either direction), or whose various perceptual dysfunctions, or emotional or physical conditions are extreme enough to warrant such support. The task of special student services in schools is to provide the instructional support that will allow young people to achieve their maximal potential. Exceptional students need to be guided down avenues of learning and development—sometimes through modifications of standard school subjects or adapted instructional strategies—that stretch them to the point of acquiring the necessary skills and knowledge to bring them complete or partial independence. They may discover en route that they are more abled than disabled (at least in some areas), and with this remarkable discovery comes improvement of their self-image.

Music and Education for Exceptional Learners

A large percentage of exceptional learners, including those in regular and self-contained classrooms, are mainstreamed into music classes in elementary schools. Increasingly, enlightened secondary school teachers are also finding places for exceptional learners in their ensembles, from bands, choirs, and orchestras to African drumming and steel drum bands. Music is viewed as a positive experience for children and youth at large, due to its ability to tap nonverbal ways of knowing; to provide auditory, visual, and kinesthetic stimulation; to allow personal gratification as well as the collaboration of social groups. Musical experiences can reach deep levels of emotional affect and aesthetic experience, and can offer a means of communication and a sense of belonging to a musical group. Music that can be learned orally and without notation can bring many into music making who might otherwise stumble and fail. Music is readily justified as essential to the educational programs of all learners, and exceptional learners may find considerable fulfillment in their successes at making and responding to music.

Music teachers must prepare for the unique abilities and needs of their diverse learners. Mainstreaming of the past, and the concept of inclusion that requires teachers to be fully inclusive of all students in their classes, is not a haphazard gesture that "dumps" students without consideration of their needs and the goals of programs, classes, and ensembles. The provision of a least restrictive environment for learning refers to the integration of special needs students into regular classrooms, yet it requires consistent attention by music teachers to monitor who is learning what, how well they are learning, and what adaptations of lessons and activities need to be made to ensure their growth. Teachers must maintain checks on their music classes as to needs for special equipment and resources as well as the support of counselors and special education teachers so that students may know success rather than frustration in their musical development. Individualized Education Plans (IEP) are available to music teachers for reviewing students' strengths, skills, and talents, as well as their weaknesses and limitations. IEPs also provide information on the present functioning levels, instructional objectives, and special services for students across academic and social areas. In some cases, music teachers may be involved in creating these plans. On the other hand, they may wish to create their own contracts with students who, through the approval and support of their parents and teachers, may come a long way as a result of focusing on particular musical skills and social behaviors.

The classifications of exceptional learners are intended only for understanding who they are so that they might be best served by all teachers at all levels, including those who teach music. The disabilities of these diverse learners are classed and labeled, and a description of traits, educational adaptations, and strategies relevant to their musical education are briefly noted in Figure 11.1. This is a bare-bones introduction to the complexities of the human condition, something that continues to engage specialists in the health sciences, psychology, sociology, and social work. Teachers in special education and across all subjects, including music, are searching for best strategies for learning and development of their young people.

Teaching music to exceptional children and youth, along with the diversity of other learners in classes and ensembles, requires thorough knowledge of the music; it is an absolute given that teachers have a deep familiarity and comfort with songs and selection. Only then can they give their attention to the immediate behaviors of students in the music-educational experience, including the ease with which some sing, play, listen intently, move appropriately, or create, and the struggles which others may have to focus and achieve in ways that are satisfactory to them, their teacher, and their classmates. The musical education of a mixed group of diverse learners requires flexibility of teachers and their instructional processes, and an understanding of how to adapt the pace and clarity of instructions. Learners may require simplification or a very gradual sequence of moving from simple to more complex tasks; the adaptation of classroom settings, materials, and instruments; or processes that allow multiple modes of activity and response, or cooperative learning in pairs and groups. The reward is in the way music loses its sense of exclusivity, as if it should be reserved for only the "talented," and becomes the property of the community of learners—a process shared by all.

Class/ Label	Description of Disability	Educational Adaptations	Music Educational Strategies
Mental Retardation	Below average intelligence: Mild: IQ 50–55 to 70–75 Moderate: IQ 35–40 to 50–55 Severe: IQ 20–25 to 35–40 Profound: IQ less than 20–25 (May vary depending upon social, practical, conceptual intelligence.)	Focus on important information. Offer patterns to learn and retain. Organize for ideas and abstractions. Extend low spoken pitch, small range.	Expect performance on one musical task at a time (for example, singing but not moving, or moving but not playing). Perform repeated patterns only, or a song chorus but not verses. Teach music by rote rather than by note. Exercise students' voices to expand their range upward. Encourage them to match pitches with accurate singers. Recommend private instrumental lessons to allow one-on-one focus. Suggest percussion instruments, or simple repetitive patterns on brass, winds, and strings.
Learning Disabilities	Significant difficulties in the acquisition and use of language, listening, speaking, reading, writing, reasoning, or mathematical abilities.	Allow simultaneous or sequential sensory stimulation (see, hear, touch, move; case-specific). Slow down instructions. Separate components to be learned. Proceed in small steps.	Learn difficult musical parts separately. Separate rhythms from pitches in reading exercises. Teach music first by rote, then add notation to read. Outline components of skill to be learned (for example, "First, we will listen to the recording, then we will sing the melody, followed by my playing and then your playing of it on your instruments").

Figure 11.1 • **Descriptions and adaptations for exceptional children.** (continued)

Class/ Label	Description of Disability	Educational Adaptations	Music Educational Strategies
Attention Deficit-Hyperactivity Disorder	Difficulties in paying attention; hyperactive and impulsive; lack of ability to inhibit behaviors and to organize self.	Keep well-organized classroom. Use nonverbal signals as reminders of appropriate behaviors. Mix low- and high-interest tasks. Work through different modalities (auditory, visual, tactile/kinesthetic).	Approach music through hearing it, seeing it iconically, and kinesthetically moving to it. Maintain children's active involvement. Limit the length of time on one musical piece or activity.
Emotional/ Behavior Disorder	Aggressive and acting out behaviors or withdrawn and anxious behaviors; extreme, chronic, and socially unacceptable.	Clarify expectations and be consistent in reinforcing them. Offer choices but not mandates. Use rewards and reinforcements. Provide for the practice of new skills and familiar material.	Provide careful and consistent instructions on musical activities. Reinforce successful attempts at music making. Allow democratic process of choosing music and musical activities. Build in opportunities to sing and play familiar and learned music.
Hearing Impairment	From mild to profound difficulties in perceiving conversation, so that information is received from careful listening, amplification, speech-reading, and/or sign language.	Speak face-to-face. Speak clearly, not too fast, and not too loud. If using microphone, be sensitive to distortions.	Provide visual aids, including notation, in lessons. Place instruments close to students so as to feel vibrations (of drums, piano, marimbas, guitar). Offer opportunities to play above instruments, and others according to interest. Rely on live music making rather than recordings. Offer movement activities with a strong beat. Add signing for all children in singing groups and choirs.

Figure 11.1 (continued)

Class/ Label	Description of Disability	Educational Adaptations	Music Educational Strategies
Visual Impairment	From mild to profound difficulties that range from blurred vision, poor peripheral vision, and nearsightedness to seeing lights and shadows, or nothing.	Enlarge symbols. Use auditory cues and stimulation. Develop manipulatives to enforce concepts.	Develop listening skills to a high level of refinement. Trace or highlight notation in colors. Use computers to enlarge notations and music graphs. Recommend instrumental study with performance by ear and by note (including Braille notation).
Physical Impairment	Orthopedic impairment (skeletal or muscular disabilities) or neurological impairment (nervous system disabilities); cerebral palsy is one condition that affects breathing and movement of the limbs.	Adapt implements so that they are graspable. Create space and sight lines favorable for wheelchairs.	Use singing to increase breath capacity. Adapt classroom instruments (velcro strips to hold mallets in place; large flat sticks as plectrums/picks). Arrange for wheelchairs to dance in patterned movements.
Communication Disorders	Difficulties in speech and language development, beyond mild impediments and stuttering to information processing; autism and Asperger's Syndrome are included	Reinforce steady eye contact. Utilize speech imitation. Provide group and partner activities.	Sing to develop language, fluency, phrasing. Utilize vocal and instrumental imitation. Offer call-and-response song and instrumental play.
Gifted/ Talented	Advanced general ability (gifted) or ability in a specific area (talented).	Encourage independent projects.	Offer opportunities for creative composition and improvisation.

Class/ Label	Description of Disability	Educational Adaptations	Music Educational Strategies
		Offer leadership opportunities. Allow interdisciplinary extensions of subjects.	Challenge students to employ technology for composition, arrangements, learning music theory, and music history/culture. Encourage solo performances. Provide private lessons or tutorials. Allow students to conduct songs, sections, and full pieces.

Figure 11.1 *(continued)*

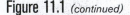 BREAK POINT 11.5 All-Inclusive Music Education

In the following sections, read and reflect upon the situations of Ms. Emery (*Open and Receptive Teaching*) and Mr. Barton (*Many Responses*) in the inclusion of exceptional learners in their ensembles. Discuss these questions: What seems to be working? How might you use a different approach in similar situations?

Open and Receptive Teaching

Ms. Emery has long dreamed of raising the standard of a middle school band program, challenging students to work their way into skills they are capable of developing, if only they had the kind of rigorous training that a supportive administration and community could allow in both school and after-school scheduling of classes and rehearsals. Now is her chance, as she has moved from a small suburban school where music could barely get a toehold in the curriculum to Longview Middle School with its considerable reputation in festivals and competitions across the state and region. As she arrives, her principal explains a new mandate within the district: that all secondary school music ensembles practice inclusion in the intake of students, regardless of their previous level of achievement or aptitude. At first, Ms. Emery is taken aback, since she has not previously taught exceptional learners (at least, not to her knowledge). Her initial encounter is in her first period class, the sixth-grade band, in which there are sixty-six students, including a considerable number who are "chatty," unfocused, and "antsy"—seemingly unable to sit still. One boy consistently twitters away on his trumpet past the cutoffs, and another two enjoy noodling away on their alto saxes in the front row while she speaks. There's a steady stream of commotion from the percussion section, and a trombonist who enjoys shooting spit out of the instrument to the boy below him. Ms. Emery is sure that this is the entire school population of special education students—until four more students arrive (with a state-required instructional aide) to announce that they, too, are joining the class—even though they have never played an instrument before.

Not about to be defeated before she begins, Ms. Emery does her homework: She scans student records for clues to student ability, talks with school counselors about past histories of "offending" students, and checks with special education teachers for further information about student strengths and needs. She speaks to parents about her program goals and goals for individual students, and shares with them her expectations that students without previous experience join before-school group lessons (for which she hires instrumentalists from the community to teach). She declares on e-mail, in parent newsletters, and at parent meetings that the program is open and receptive to all learners, as long as they work to the best of their ability. In class, she sets up the framework for appropriate behavior and enforces the consequences for inappropriate behavior, and finds herself working with struggling students who are still finding their way musically and behaviorally. She offers a few of them "one more chance," depending on their particular learning profile. Her plan works: the first period sixth-grade band quiets down, gets their focus, learns a repertoire of easy-to-moderate levels of difficulty (with some modified parts she arranges for rank-beginners). For those who pass their performance tests and play musically, she takes them to festival. This Longview Middle School band gets a "2," but the experience also stirs the pride of the young players and gives them concrete direction for honing their collective skills in the year to come.

Many Responses

On Tuesday mornings, three children are wheeled into Mr. Barton's third-grade music class, each with an instructional aide. They join a class just beginning a lesson in reading various sixteenth-note patterns, mostly seated in a half-circle on carpet squares he has strategically placed. He reminds Jimmy and Bryan to sit up straight on their squares and keep their hands to themselves, and then steps over to give a handshake of welcome to Anthony, Robert, and Tarana. Anthony smiles his response, Robert calls out a gurgling "Good morning, Mr. Barton," and Tarana nods her head from side to side, never making eye contact. The aides draw up chairs next to the three children in the wheelchairs as Mr. Barton steps back up to the front of the room. Mr. Barton is chanting "kookaburra" as he walks, patting the individual syllables on his knees. He leads the class in singing "Kookaburra," which they had learned in an earlier class, encouraging them to pat the "kookaburra" pattern of four sixteenth notes into their laps each time they sing that rhythm. Most of the children respond moderately well to this task, although many of them stop singing while they are patting. Jimmy and Bryan are pounding out sixteenths throughout the song, shifting from their laps to slapping sixteenths on the floor, snickering and then giving way to uproarious laughter that has them both on their backs, kicking up their heels. Meanwhile, Robert is patting one hand unevenly into his other hand, while Anthony and Tarana are receiving the stimulation of their aides' own tapping on their knees, shoulders, and hands.

Mr. Barton announces to the class that they will follow a sequence of (a) singing only, (b) rhythmically chanting the words, (c) patting only on the rhythms while silently singing, and (d) singing and patting through the song. He walks in between the little bodies, smiling in approval when children are following the pattern, gesturing for others to watch him as he models the sequence at their side, and patting the hands of the children who are challenged by the physical effort of keeping the rhythm pattern, or who do not yet perceive the sequence, or who are finding it difficult to focus their attention. After many revolutions, Mr. Barton announces: "OK, we're about ready to play instruments." Jimmy and Bryan shout out loud, "Yes!" and run to the table of instruments. Mr. Barton waves them back to their places, and then distributes rhythm instruments to the students—wood blocks, claves, agogo iron bells, hand drums, and two djembe drums. He gives woodblocks to Anthony, Robert, and Tarana, placing the block in one hand and the mallet in the other, curling the children's fingers around it and nodding to the aides to help the children. He assigns both Everett and Allyson to the prized djembe drums "for their excellent coordination skills of singing and patting at the same time" (which is no small feat for them, due to their diagnosed attention deficits), and gives the agogo iron bells, another favorite instrument, to Shawn (a child with developmental delays) for "following the sequence so well."

In the end, all children have instruments except Jimmy and Bryan. "I'm going to let you sit this one out, Jimmy over here and Bryan over there, so that you can think about your behavior," he says, while pointing to the class rules posted at the front of the room. He makes a mental note to check with their classroom teacher as to possible explanations. The sequence begins, and with each go-round, the children sound more (and more) in line with each other—including, with help, Anthony, Robert, and Tarana. They perform louder and softer on cue, and faster and slower, following Mr. Barton's conducting gestures. There are smiles from all the children, as they sing, chant, and play in ensemble. (A later word with the classroom teacher helps Mr. Barton to understand that Jimmy and Bryan were capable of excellent academic work but both were "hyper" and "mischievous," and prone to pressing the limits of classroom rules—and the teacher's patience. Some time later, due to Mr. Barton's own suggestion, the boys are tested and each shows a consistent pattern of hyperactivity, impulsivity, and attention deficits—all of which can be modified by a prescribed behavioral contract.)

Unity within Diversity

There is no doubt about it: music teachers have a curriculum to teach and a lineup of knowledge and skills to develop in their students. They are expected to make strides in meeting the national standards in music and the music benchmarks of the school district relevant to particular grade levels and secondary ensemble classes. Still, even as they are teaching the subject of music, they are also teaching children—and there is nothing so variable as the human species. The best-laid plans scatter in the wind when students are not going with the flow because they cannot, or because they need time and special prompts, accommodations, and strategies. It is the responsibility of music teachers to understand that there is a wide spectrum of young people in their classes, and that each one comes with a set of strengths and needs that are based upon considerations that are both personal and sociocultural in nature. In the end, the curricular aims of a music program are there to be met as well as they can, and with sensitivity and skills, teachers can ferret out avenues and angles for reaching into the lives of all children and draw them forward in their musical accomplishments.

REFERENCES AND RESOURCES

Atterbury, B. (1990). *Mainstreaming in Exceptional Learners in Music.* Englewood Cliffs, NJ: Prentice-Hall. A compendium of descriptions of special populations of schoolchildren, and the music instructional modifications and lesson plan adaptations that can be designed and delivered to children and youth to tap into and add to their musical strengths.

Banks, J. A., and C. M. Banks. (2004). *Handbook of Research in Multicultural Education.* New York: Macmillan. A collection of essays on concepts and theories of multiculturalism as they affect teaching student populations of diverse racial, ethnic, and social class groups.

Campbell, P. S. (2004). *Teaching Music Globally*. New York: Oxford University Press. A handbook for teachers who seek to establish a comprehensive musical understanding for students living in a global era, with a large selection of exercises and activities for discovering rhythm, pitch, and form in various world music traditions.

Hallahan, D. P., and J. M. Kauffman (2000). *Exceptional Learners: Introduction to Special Education*. Boston: Allyn & Bacon. A volume dedicated to the study of the abilities and needs of exceptional children, and current instructional practices and special services to ensure the realization of their full human potential.

Volk, T. M. (1998). *Music, Education, and Multiculturalism*. New York: Oxford University Press. A historical account of cultural pluralism in the United States and internationally and its influences on method and content of school music programs.

chapter 12

Classroom Management and Motivation

Matt, a clarinetist: I don't feel like getting my instrument out today. I need to do my math homework.

Mr. Alon, the band teacher: I understand. You do what you need to do.

Matt: I know.

Sarah, a trumpet player: I don't feel like getting my instrument out today. I need to do my math homework.

Ms. Timm, the band teacher: Sarah, get your instrument out or I'll make you stay and practice an extra hour.

Sarah: Yeah? F— you.

Erica, a violinist: I don't feel like getting my instrument out today. I need to do my math homework.

Ms. Kelly, the orchestra teacher: Erica, get your instrument out and afterward we can talk about how you can plan your schedule so that your work is done before orchestra class.

Erica: Well . . . all right.

A False Dichotomy

Picture a music classroom. The teacher might be leading a group of elementary children in song, guiding secondary school students through a composition exercise, or rehearsing a new piece with a performing ensemble. Does this teacher believe that, through his teaching, he will help these students actually learn a new song, explore means of creative expression or become more proficient vocalists or instrumentalists? Is he confident that these students will acquire and refine new skills through his guidance and expertise? Not only is the answer to these questions most likely a resounding "yes!" but it is probably true that this very confidence in his potential abilities as a musician and teacher propelled him into a music education program. He can easily see himself as a successful and effective music teacher.

Now picture that same music classroom with a second-grader who is running around the room instead of singing, a secondary school student who is reading a magazine instead of working on her composition, or a violist who is hitting the student next to him with his bow. Does the same teacher believe that he can help these students learn to sit still, attend to the lesson, or keep their bow to themselves? Perhaps he is less sure about himself in these situations. He may have more trouble seeing himself as an effective classroom manager than as an effective music teacher.

Why? Music teachers do not hesitate to believe that they can impart musical knowledge. They are, after all, experts who have reached a high level of musical achievement. But aren't they also equally adept with social knowledge? At this point in their lives haven't they also reached a very high level of achievement in such areas as attentiveness, work ethic, and interpersonal communication? Indeed, one would find it difficult to succeed as a professional educator without such skills.

In classroom activity, it is not uncommon for a teacher to draw a sharp line between "the music" and other matters like poor behavior. The former is a noble, positive, and rich part of the educational enterprise. The latter is distracting, negative, and antithetical to learning. In the case of music, teachers use the powers of observation to make things better. In the case of bad behavior, use of these same powers can catch students acting in ways teachers wish they wouldn't. One might even draw so vivid a distinction between music and classroom management that it would seem to take two entirely different sets of skills to address them. But in reality, the very expertise that allows a person to improve the sound of a choir is the same expertise that can allow her to improve the focus, attentiveness and self-control of students. Establishing and maintaining a smooth-running classroom—much like shaping a superior musical performance—is a matter of teaching and learning.

Students—and all people, really—are learning machines. They constantly take in information about the world around them. They observe the effect they have on their environment (including other individuals in it) and the way that effect, in turn, affects them. They are also clever enough to observe and learn from others' actions and the ensuing consequences. In the context of school, it is a teacher's role to structure an environment where what students learn is consistent with the values held by the society at large. Ideals such as honesty, respect, and responsibility are taught in much the same way as artistry and musicianship.

In its most stark form, classroom management revolves around three questions: (1) What should students be expected to do? (2) What should happen when they do it? (3) What should happen if they don't do it?

Great Expectations

When you think of the best music classrooms you can imagine, they are probably characterized by the presence of cooperative, attentive, and enthusiastic students. These students are not asking *not* to get their instruments out, like Matt, Sarah, and Erica are at the beginning of this chapter. That is the class aspiring music teachers want, isn't it? They want the class where they can concentrate on the music, one that needs little attention to discipline issues. How can you get a class like that? Actually, the question to ask is not how teachers *get* such classes, but how teachers help groups of students *become* such classes. It all begins with a plan.

The best music classes can typically be traced back to good planning. What will the students learn? How will the teacher present the new information? How will the students demonstrate their learning? In terms of classroom management, the same is true. Well-managed classrooms can also be traced to good planning. What is expected of the students? How will the teacher convey these expectations? How will the students demonstrate that they have met them? In fact, meeting classroom management expectations is a prerequisite for successful musical learning. Students will not learn the song, write the composition, or perform the part until they learn to act in ways that support the musical goals. Matt, Erica, and Sarah will be ready with their instruments only if they *understand* the expectation that participation is an essential part of class as *demonstrated* by such behaviors as bringing the instrument to school, keeping it in good working order, and—in this case—completing other work at a time other than the music period. (Notice that expectations can just as easily outline what students *should* do as what they *should not*.)

Issues relating to classroom management, then, require attention early in the school year. Consider Figure 12.1, representing any given period of instruction. This figure illustrates that attention to social behaviors (represented by the darker shading) often outweighs attention to musical behaviors at first. Before elementary students can learn a song in music class, they must learn how to enter the classroom and attend to the music teacher. Before a high school orchestra can learn a new concerto, they must learn where to find new sheet music and how the rehearsal order is conveyed. None of these skills is particularly artistic or even musical, but all are essential to supporting a productive music class.

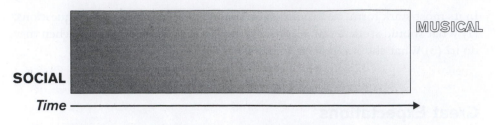

Figure 12.1 • Balancing attention to social and musical behavior across time.

Early on, musical matters (represented here by the lighter shading) may account for only a small percentage of the teacher's energy, though they should never be completely absent. Over time, as students learn what is appropriate behavior in the music room, attention to musical matters will become predominant, though never to the complete exclusion of management issues. Note, though, that attention is not to be confused with time. Repeated short bursts of attention to inappropriate behavior can seem to occupy an entire class period even though not much actual time is lost. Management issues may or may not seriously affect the quantity of time a class spends making music but they certainly can have a significant effect on the quality.

❖ BREAK POINT 12.1 Learning Social Behavior

Identify at least 7 specific nonmusical behaviors that students would need to know to be successful members of your music class. Which of these behaviors do you think students would know in advance? Which of these behaviors do you think you would need to teach?

By establishing clear expectations and demonstrating consistent responses to students' behavior, a teacher sets a solid "operating background" against which musical activities can take place. Note that exactly what these expectations and responses are is not specified here. A great deal of "bad" behavior is only bad in certain situations. One choir teacher may *expect* students to remain silent throughout the class period, constantly focusing on the conductor and raising a hand if someone wishes to initiate a contribution. When student contributions are made, his *response* is positive, taking them seriously, discussing them at length and even often incorporating them into the rehearsal. Another classroom music teacher may want students to interact constantly, chatting among themselves as long as it pertains to the topic at hand. To attract the teacher's attention students may walk over to the teacher at any time and ask whatever question they wish, providing it is a question that could not be answered using any of the books, computers, and recordings strewn about the room. Again, the expectation is clear and, when met, the response is positive.

Both these teachers have made decisions about the environment they wish to foster and will use similar fundamental teaching strategies to set it in place, even though the outcomes will look and sound very different. In each of the two cases, the teachers have a clear plan and the patience and tenacity to implement it. If hand-raising is a behavior valued by the choir teacher, then he must resist the impulse to recognize a student who shouts out, no matter how intelligent or witty the student's comment may be. Similarly, he must recognize hand-raisers even if a student contribution doesn't quite fit into the lesson presently under way. As for the classroom music teacher, if she really wants students to ask only questions that are unanswerable using other available resources, then she must refrain from responding to students who come to her too quickly, no matter how polite, sincere, and earnest they are. She must also be ready to respond appropriately and positively to students who approach her after an exhaustive yet fruitless search for information.

Recall that students are always learning by watching the effects of their actions. Teachers, then, spend a considerable amount of energy monitoring their responses to student behavior. The development of a classroom management plan is not so much a function of time but of repeated instances of student behavior and teacher response. When responses to appropriate behavior are *consistently* positive, the likelihood of such behavior occurring more frequently increases. Look again at the exchange between Erica and Ms. Kelly at the beginning of this chapter. Ms. Kelly responded both positively and specifically by offering a solution that headed off Erica's inappropriate behavior (not getting her instrument) and, ultimately, might help Erica to improve her own time management. Mr. Alon also responded positively to Matt, but in such a way that will probably result in more instances of Matt not taking part in class.

Alternatively, negative responses would tend to decrease instances of a particular behavior. The problem is that reducing an inappropriate behavior does nothing to help a student learn what an appropriate behavior would be. Negative responses can also lead a student to be embarrassed, defensive, or hostile, fostering even more inappropriate behavior (consider the exchange between Sarah and Ms. Timm). A teacher's negative response is a powerful tool that, as with many such tools, should be used carefully, sparingly, and only if all other options have been unsuccessful.

While it is desirable for a student to be sensitive to a teacher's response (and *vice versa*), one may wish to avoid situations in which a student's behavior becomes *dependent* on the teacher's response. For example, does a student keep her eyes on the teacher just because she likes it when the teacher looks back and smiles? Or does she do it because she has found that by watching the teacher, she can follow the music much better, sound better singing her part, and ultimately enjoy choir more than before? Is one of these reasons better than another if the outcome is the same in both cases? This becomes a question of motivation.

Why Can't You Behave? A Look at Motivation

One of the most common complaints voiced about problem students is that they are "not motivated." In fact, students are *always* motivated. A motivated student is sometimes mistakenly identified as one whose behavior conforms to a teacher's value system while an unmotivated student is one whose behavior is contrary to that value system. Consider Kate, a student who eagerly participates in class, regularly practices her part at home, and consistently attends to the teacher's instruction. You may think of Kate as motivated. But Rachel, who sits quietly and idly in the corner of the band room, rarely even touching her instrument, is equally motivated. In the first case, Kate's behavior may be motivated by her love of music, her desire to do well in classes, or her wish to receive the teacher's approval. Rachel, on the other hand, may be motivated by a desire to avoid embarrassment because she doesn't read notation as well as her stand partner or because her instrument isn't working and she doesn't know what to do about it. Or perhaps her stand partner makes rude comments about her playing. Motivation is actually the driving force *behind* the behavior we observe rather than the behavior itself. If a student was truly unmotivated, she would do absolutely nothing (and even this she would do involuntarily rather than because of fatigue, shyness, or fear).

Misusing the notion of motivation has its consequences. Identifying a student as "unmotivated" allows a teacher to explain inappropriate behavior in terms of an intractable, even clinical condition. If a student is "unmotivated," so the logic might go, then there is nothing that can be done. That's the way he is and nothing anyone does will change it. To that extent, a teacher can feel relieved of the responsibility of trying to redirect a student's behavior and subsequently give up a portion of the power with which she is charged as an educator.

If, on the other hand, the teacher takes an active role in discovering the motivation behind a student's actions, then she begins to take on the challenge of altering the motivation structure for that student and opening up the possibility of a change in behavior. Will Rachel, introduced above, ever change her behavior if her teacher merely labels her as unmotivated? Maybe she really wants to be an active member of the class, but her motivation to avoid embarrassment or her stand partner's comments is stronger than her desire to participate. By discovering the reason for Rachel's disengagement, the teacher can then take steps to change the motivation structure. If her inactivity is due to note-reading problems, perhaps the teacher can provide some extra note-reading help during the lunch period. If she isn't participating because her instrument is broken, giving her information about the local repair shop may be all that is needed. If the problem is with her stand partner, separating the two may be the solution (though that may not fix the other student's rudeness—that will require another strategy). Fear is reduced and Rachel's desire to be a contributing class member becomes the stronger motivating force, much to the relief of the teacher, Rachel's classmates, and, most probably, Rachel herself. Understanding motivation helps teachers formulate decisions, take action, make appropriate responses, and restore the classroom environment.

INTRINSIC AND EXTRINSIC MOTIVATION

Few things are truly intrinsically motivating, things that we are compelled to do naturally without any instruction whatsoever. Eating, for example, is an activity undertaken because our bodies demand it. Often we may choose to eat because sharing a meal with friends is enjoyable or because certain mealtimes have become customary but, above all, we eat to sustain life. Other things may be perceived to be equally motivating. A person may claim to be "unable to live" without at least one cup of coffee in the morning, a favorite television program, correspondence with a dear friend, or certain social rituals. For many, music may fall under this category. In truth, people have developed such powerful and positive responses to these stimuli that they seem life sustaining when, of course, they are actually not. They have become imperative for *quality* of life and individuals may go to great lengths to ensure that their accessibility remains intact.

Regardless of whether an individual seeks something because it keeps her alive or because it is something she desires, these things are considered to a greater or lesser extent *intrinsically* motivating because (1) she is seeking the thing itself for its own sake and (2) she is doing so of her own choice. *Extrinsic* motivation, on the other hand, operates when (1) something is sought because other motivators have been associated with it and (2) someone else has imposed the motivation structure. A student practices his scales so he can get a gold star on the weekly playing quiz. Another student steals reeds from the teacher's desk to prove her loyalty to a particular group of classmates. In these cases, neither practicing nor stealing is of interest to the students. They are motivated to engage in these behaviors to achieve recognition and acceptance, respectively. The motivation structure has been established by the instructor and the group of friends, not by the students themselves. If the extrinsic factor was removed, the behavior would probably cease.

There is plenty of gray area between the intrinsic and extrinsic extremes. Imagine a student who plays the recorder with gusto because he enjoys the sound of it. You would say that, for this student, recorder playing is intrinsically motivating. However, in the music classroom, the teacher may have established a structure whereby students are allowed to play the recorder only after they have taken out their instruments and sat down in a quiet and orderly fashion. The contingency by which the student will be able to play the recorder has been extrinsically imposed. Because humans live, work, and play with other humans, it is often just such a mix of internal and external factors that operates to shape behavior.

✤ BREAK POINT 12.2 The Driving Force

> Think about Matt, Sarah, and Erica, introduced at the beginning of the chapter. What might be motivating their behavior? How might you, as a teacher, be able to affect this motivation structure? In what ways do your proposed solutions reflect intrinsic or extrinsic forms of motivation?

THE IDEAL MOTIVATOR

Obviously, motivation is a powerful force in life. It follows then that motivators must be handled with great care. In music education, one of the primary goals is to establish and maintain music as a motivator in people's lives (though, remember that many students enter school already holding music among their favorite things). People's interactions with music should be so powerful and positive that they will choose to engage in such interactions again and again throughout life. Students should value music for its own sake and should seek it by their own choice—intrinsically, in other words. To this end, three essential ideas should guide the manner in which music itself can, for better or worse, become part of the classroom management structure.

MUSIC AS A POSITIVE EXPERIENCE

For those who have made music their professional calling, it is hard to imagine that music can be anything but a positive experience. Sure, there have been some tricky quizzes, nerve-wracking performances, and grueling rehearsals in the past, but the positive power of music *itself* has always shone through.

Young people love music. In fact, maximizing musical activity and engagement is one of the best strategies for minimizing inappropriate classroom behavior. But school represents an ongoing series of new musical experiences.

Elementary children's encounter with music in an organized classroom setting may be entirely new to them. Making music in a formal ensemble setting is novel to the late elementary instrumental or choral student. Performing as a soloist and receiving evaluation from strangers is a first for the older performance student. Each of these new experiences asks students to redefine music and, in each case, presents students with the opportunity to reevaluate their relationship with music. Is music, in this new and unfamiliar form, still motivating?

Teachers attend to such fragile times of transition by structuring small-scale successes early and often. Lessons are designed to equip students with fundamental skills and knowledge on which they can build more sophisticated—and more risky—experiences. To do this, management decisions are made with musical success in mind. Behavioral expectations are set forth not for their own value ("I just like it when the children are quiet") but because these behaviors will help facilitate the kinds of rewarding musical encounters at hand ("When everyone is quiet, we will all be able to hear the recording clearly"). Even early in an experience when social behaviors are still being established and may command the better part of a teacher's attention, meaningful musical encounters can still infuse the classroom to help students ease into a new musical environment and maintain music's place as a powerful motivating force.

MUSIC AS A CHALLENGING EXPERIENCE

As positive as music is, it is still difficult. It is unreasonable to expect that no musical encounters will ever push a person to the brink of frustration, exhaustion, or discomfort. Some argue that one of the values of music is its very ability to stretch one's intellectual and physical capacities as a human being. It is the responsibility of educators to encourage students toward higher levels of achievement, pushing them to master challenges that perhaps the students themselves didn't think they could surmount. This path toward ultimate success can result in any number of failures along the way, few of which will be construed as positive experiences.

Mediating these challenging experiences is also the task of an educator. Students may need help learning that the frustration they are feeling in practicing a new song is due to one or two very particular difficulties (a challenging rhythm or pitch pattern perhaps) rather than to some fundamental unpleasantness of music itself. Teachers help students see that problems are specific and can be fixed ("Let's work on pushing the second valve instead of the first") rather than broad and intractable ("You're just not very musical, are you?"). Adults who recall supremely unpleasant past experiences in music classes often are remembering just such sweeping indictments.

In the end, challenges themselves can become motivating to young musicians. When students learn that the musical problems they are facing can be remedied, then feelings of helplessness and inadequacy can be avoided. Otherwise, such feelings can lead students to direct their behavior toward less positive and less productive ends that, in turn, can lead to disruptions in the classroom or, worst of all, a student's abandonment of music altogether.

MUSIC AS A PUNISHING EXPERIENCE

Is music a punishment? Remember Sarah and her band director, Ms. Timm, from the beginning of this chapter? Ms. Timm chose to threaten Sarah with an extra hour of practice if she did not conform to the classroom expectations. Keeping in mind that students are always learning, what does this teach Sarah? She will now learn that practicing is an unpleasant experience, one to be avoided if at all possible. No doubt Ms. Timm would never have intended to teach such a thing; nevertheless, she did.

Similarly unintentional consequences—and similarly misguided learning—may result from such responses as these:

"If you people don't start paying more attention, we're going to have an extra rehearsal."

"Joey, I don't think you practiced your part. Will you please play alone for everyone?"

"Olivia, are you talking to Elaine again? Sing the song by yourself."

In these instances, students are learning that rehearsal time, playing alone, and singing solos are negative things. The motivation to avoid certain otherwise positive musical situations thus can become stronger than the motivation to practice as a group or play and sing alone. Music can become a punishment. The problem is that music can be very effective as a punishment, but this use closes doors for students' future musical experiences. Seemingly effective solutions to bothersome classroom situations can, if not carefully thought out, lead to ultimately undesirable or even destructive ends. The ability to think ahead and see the entire chain of such cause-and-effect relationships is what makes teaching such a powerful art.

Power and the Teacher

Teachers possess a tremendous amount of power. Students see the teacher as the individual who disburses grades, homework, seating assignments, chair placements, awards, praise, punishment, calls to parents, letters of reference, and, of course, knowledge. At any given time, a student may perceive any one of these things as absolutely consequential to his success and happiness. Taken together, these responsibilities constitute a veritable arsenal of contingencies that set a teacher apart as one of the most imposing individuals in a young person's life. Having spent the better part of their lives so far as students, new music teachers may find the prospect of so much power overwhelming. Being particularly sensitive to the strengths and the needs of students, they may even find the prospect of such power distasteful. In relation to classroom discipline, being comfortable with the power that comes with teaching is one of the biggest challenges educators face.

Power takes many forms; discipline is not the same as punishment. It may be tempting to think of a disciplined class or ensemble as one that is ruled by a strict, iron hand. But a truly disciplined group is one in which members understand shared goals, know the expectations placed on them, and understand and accept a predictable set of contingencies. Such a group grows not through sheer force of will but through consistency and clarity, the fundamental components of any approach to classroom management. The *manner* in which these are applied can vary, from a teacher who is quiet and reserved to one who is loud and aggressive. But the general principles remain and it is in the application of these principles that teachers' power resides.

The very act of walking into a classroom on the first day of school establishes a power relationship that students will immediately begin to explore. How do we, the students, address this person? How will he or she, this teacher, respond to our questions? Can we joke with him? Does she get angry easily? How much homework will he give? Will he check it? Are her tests difficult? Can we sit where we please? What happens if I swear in class? When will class really begin? Who will determine when it ends? Students will seek answers to these and many, many other questions by observing the words and—more important—the actions of the teacher. Whether the teacher's actions are intentional or offhanded, whether they occur during the "formal" class time, during the passing period, or after school is of little consequence. Students are *always* learning; therefore teachers *always* must be aware of the weight their behavior can carry.

Sometimes teachers assert power through overt action. For example, one teacher may announce and post rules that require students to do this or that. Student behavior is subsequently met by teacher approval or disapproval. The teacher chooses the music, sets the tempo, paces the lesson, and evaluates the outcomes. At other times, the exercise of power appears more indirect, as with a teacher who chooses to let students make many of the decisions. In this class, rules as well as guidelines for addressing appropriate and inappropriate behavior emerge from class discussion and possibly even a class vote. Students may choose some of the music they sing, play, or hear. Classroom procedures become a more student-driven enterprise; and when they are carried out in the right manner, either of these classrooms can be a happy, positive, productive place. But in both cases, the class environment is grounded in decisions made by the teacher, either the decision to be the sole administrator of classroom behavior or the decision to delegate a portion of management responsibility to the students. Both are exercises of power.

Recall the three teachers introduced at the beginning of this chapter: each has dealt with power in a different way. Mr. Alon has let Matt choose whether he will do his math homework or participate in band. If Mr. Alon feels that Matt's decision will be acceptable no matter what, then his response may be appropriate. But if he actually feels that Matt should get out his instrument, then his response is incorrect. He has attempted to abdicate his position of power—perhaps fearing to seem heavy-handed or unkind—and has potentially succeeded only in teaching Matt a new way to avoid the consequence of irresponsibility. Ms. Timm has responded with a grand display of power by threatening Sarah with punishment. Sarah, in turn, has responded with a display of her own. She has potentially turned this interaction into a power struggle that the teacher, at least in the short term, cannot win since Sarah has decided to take a path—escalating verbal abuse—down which she knows the teacher cannot follow. Ms. Kelly has made it clear to Erica that nonparticipation is not an option while still acknowledging the importance of getting the math homework done. Her response was firm but not threatening. Erica realizes that Ms. Kelly has listened to exactly what she said and will follow up later. If it turns out that the need to do math homework was not the true motivation behind Erica's comment, Ms. Kelly will discover this and address it after class.

Of the three teachers, Ms. Kelly has demonstrated the firmest grasp of discipline (as opposed to sheer force) while still exhibiting the most positive (as opposed to weak or evasive) response. To put it another way, kindness is not the opposite of discipline. Power is not so much a display of strength as of control. Sometimes, though, control can be hard to maintain especially when a teacher takes discipline problems to heart.

Taking It Personally

When a student demonstrates inappropriate musical behavior (playing an F# instead of an F, for instance) it is easy for a teacher to identify this as, most likely, a minor skill deficit and to introduce swift and specific remediation. It is unlikely that the teacher would view such an incident as a personal affront. Even referring to the appearance of an erroneous note as an "incident" seems exaggerated. Social transgressions, however, are much more difficult to address in such a cool, detached manner. One takes these incidents—and they often *are* thought of as "incidents"—personally, particularly when they are directed at the teacher or in clear and deliberate contravention of classroom expectations.

If a teacher responds personally and emotionally to inappropriate behavior, there is a danger of overstepping the boundaries to which educators are confined by propriety and by law. Despite the temptation to exert their power as adults and as agents of the educational system, teachers must maintain composure and respond in a thoughtful and professional manner. A measured response can help diffuse a volatile situation and impart a sense of reassurance that other students will appreciate and respect.

At the same time, teachers must accept the fact that in the heat of the moment, a student can always go further than the teacher. A student can physically lash out or hurl verbal abuse. Under no circumstances can a teacher respond likewise. In fact, it is an educator's professional charge to attempt to "talk students down" if they are showing signs of losing control. Just as they are attempting to overwhelm a situation with force, volume, or emotion, the teacher must focus on removing any "fuel" that might promote further conflagration. It is the teacher's responsibility to keep all students—including the unruly student—safe.

Admittedly, these loud or violent outbursts are the sorts of classroom management problems that get the most attention. But it is very unlikely that such incidents will occur frequently. Much more common are the small events that take place day to day. These, too, can carry a personal component. When a student who usually exhibits exemplary behavior begins acting badly it is entirely reasonable to feel a sense of disappointment. If a student who has been a "project" demonstrates a lapse in judgment, teachers may feel a tinge of doubt in their efforts or abilities as teachers. They are undoubtedly biased; they want to see and try to see the best in their students. When students fall short, it can hurt a bit. But such feelings are and must remain separate from the response a teacher chooses to make. Similarly, students who have managed to evoke a firm or negative response from a teacher may take it personally, too. For some students, a harsh response from a teacher may leave them feeling embarrassed or humiliated. It may even serve to reinforce their own belief that they are inadequate or to help them rationalize perceptions of failure. Students often need to be reminded that "bad behavior" is quite different from just being "bad."

In the end, children and adolescents are still children and adolescents. Despite any displays of bravado or apathy, they still put great stock in how their actions are viewed by adults. Having the conviction and objectivity to address inappropriate behavior is, in many cases, the first and most critical step in solving the problem.

Making Management Decisions

Professional educators encounter a constant variety of views on classroom management. They hear the opinions and "best practice" recommendations of their colleagues. They encounter schoolwide or districtwide efforts to establish innovative management systems. They read books and articles examining current ideas and issues regarding student behavior. And they receive a healthy complement of fliers, brochures, and advertisements announcing the latest surefire method of running a classroom, possibly explained over a series of videos, lectures, or workshops.

At times, these provide useful ideas; at other times, they prove to be sources of confusion or frustration. The ultimate decisions concerning how to manage a school classroom take a good deal of thought and study. Teachers must consider the ideas they encounter and evaluate how intellectually and professionally sound these are, how much they agree with the fundamental premises presented, and how well such suggestions fit within their own teaching style. While it is not possible here to review all the prevalent management theories and systems, each features its own unique interpretation of the following questions. Your interpretation of these questions will go a long way toward determining the way your classroom will run.

STUDENT-DIRECTED OR TEACHER-DIRECTED?

Teachers ultimately make all classroom decisions, thus all classrooms are teacher-directed at the most basic level. Similarly, all classrooms are student-centered, and all decisions are made with an eye toward creating the most stimulating, challenging, and rewarding learning experiences possible. What is at issue here is the teacher's decision regarding how active a role students will take in determining and maintaining the classroom procedures.

In the most teacher-centered environment, teachers determine rules and expectations. They also determine the consequences for student behavior, both appropriate and inappropriate. Those who decide on this approach may feel that their high level of expertise both in subject matter and in the educational process can best guide the class toward the highest level of achievement. They may also feel that expecting students to make such decisions places extra responsibility and pressure on them that is not appropriate. Students—particularly younger students—may feel awkward making management choices that affect their peers.

In a more student-centered classroom, students may be actively engaged in deciding the rules of the class. They may even be charged with setting up a system of rewards for appropriate behavior or interventions for transgressions.

Teachers who oversee such classrooms may feel that by giving students the responsibility of setting expectations, they become more invested in the every-day running of the class. Students can have the experience of setting and maintaining their own limits rather than having them imposed from outside. They can also evaluate whether their decisions were beneficial or if they were less than successful.

ADDITIVE OR SUBTRACTIVE?

Is classroom management about punishing students who demonstrate inappropriate behavior or is it about building students' repertoire of appropriate behavior? Musical behavior is typically evaluated according to how much students learn—how far students get in the method book, how many new songs they learn, how many scales they can play. Musical achievement is a measure of success; it is ever expanding, constantly moving in an upward direction. Social behavior may be viewed from the opposite perspective—how many times students are caught talking, how often they are late with homework, how aggressive they are with their peers. Discipline can be a measure of failure, an index of how far a student has fallen from the ideal.

Some management models are built on the premise that removal of something—privileges, points, grades, comfort—is the preferred means to effect behavioral change. Such an approach is subtractive, taking away something a student desires in order to evoke a positive response. This principle of deterrence is not limited to the classroom, of course. The possibility of losing something of value affects the way people behave in many situations, from competitive sports to driving and even to international relations. In contrast, other models are more additive in nature. Teachers seek out students' appropriate actions and respond in ways conducive to increasing such behavior. Inappropriate behavior is often ignored or redirected toward appropriate behavior. Punishment, in such models, is viewed as a last resort and may even be discouraged entirely.

PROACTIVE OR REACTIVE?

The most typical question asked about classroom discipline is, "What should I do if a student does such and such?" This question suggests that classroom management is about reaction—if a student does X, the teacher does Y. While it is true that much of what teachers do is respond to student activity, it is also true that student activity is usually initiated by actions planned and implemented by the teacher.

Reactive models of classroom management involve an initial establishment of basic guidelines and expectations. The teacher's role is then to carry out the academic lesson plan, attending to discipline issues only if inappropriate behavior is observed. When this occurs, there may be a prescribed or predetermined set of steps that the teacher will follow as a consequence of the student's actions. A variation on this includes peer mediation models in which students rather than teachers respond to rule infractions. Such models are particularly conducive to systematic implementation throughout an entire school building.

Proactive models, in contrast, are designed with the intention of heading off inappropriate behavior before it happens. As no assumptions are made about what students already know and can do, appropriate behaviors are carefully taught from the outset. In some cases, students develop independent decision-making skills that may help them avoid situations that would lead to misbehavior. In other cases, students interact with each other in ways intended to keep classroom expectations at the forefront of attention or to diffuse unpleasant situations before they escalate. Proactive models stress student independence and problem solving while de-emphasizing punishment.

METHODOLOGICAL OR PHILOSOPHICAL?

How precise should a management model be? Is it a set of clear, easy-to-use procedures designed to promote smooth classroom operation? Or is it a broad set of principles that teachers will need to apply in their own particular ways? Philosophical models stress basic views of human motivation, social interaction, and educational psychology. Their underlying frameworks might be quite complex and difficult to call up quickly when a student is beating on the tympani with her clarinet. However, philosophical models provide a rich source of ideas that, with effort well invested, a teacher can use to develop a grounded approach to a particular teaching situation. Some philosophical models may be criticized for not providing enough information about their specific implementation but may be more easily adapted to different students or circumstances.

Methodological models, alternatively, are very specific, designed more for implementation than reflection. They are typically laid out in a sequence of detailed steps that allow the teacher—and sometimes the student—to monitor the progress of the intervention. Some methodological models may be criticized for being too simplistic or effective only in very specific situations, but they may be very helpful in providing firm guidance in situations that may become unwieldy or emotional.

The best management models offer both the possibility of application to real-life situations (otherwise they risk wallowing endlessly in philosophical abstraction) and a sound basis in the science of human learning (otherwise they may be little more than gimmicks). The most enduring perspectives on classroom management tend to have a healthy portion of both methodology and philosophy, even if originally oriented toward one direction or the other.

As they read the sections above, aspiring teachers may have recognized themselves—or the teachers they see themselves becoming—in some of the descriptions. None of these are either/or issues. Some teachers may choose to lean a little toward one direction or another. Some vary their approach across time or context. Many are continually reconsidering and refining their approach to classroom management. Regardless, successful teachers are as they are because of decisions they make. Their responses to student behavior are based on rich experience, extensive prior thought, and strong beliefs. The result is a consistent and logical approach to student behavior.

❖ BREAK POINT 12.3 You, the Classroom Manager

Consider the four dichotomies introduced above: student-directed/teacher-directed; additive/subtractive; proactive/reactive; methodological/philosophical. Where do you see yourself in regard to each? Do you see your decisions varying depending on the type of class you are teaching or the age of the students? Describe classrooms you have observed that you feel are clear illustrations of decisions made in each of these areas.

Managing the Classroom and Beyond

People are by nature learners. Their behaviors, values, and views of the world are largely determined by their interaction with the other people who inhabit it. The principles in this chapter have been presented as an exploration of how the behavior of teachers can affect the behavior of students. But issues of appropriate and inappropriate behavior, as well as the ways people may respond to either, are not restricted to the classroom or to the young people one finds there. Understanding motivation, taking honest account of power relationships, and formulating clear and consistent expectations are fundamental to every positive and productive encounter we have with others including parents, colleagues, and administrators.

After all this, it still may seem that the ideal teaching situation is one in which students are thoroughly self-regulating and music making is the only matter in need of attention. This will never be the case. As much as music pervades the lives of students, life—with all the highs, lows, doubt, uncertainty, joy, optimism, and exuberance one associates with youth and childhood—will also pervade their music-making experiences. Striking a balance between social and musical challenges occurs not only in the music classroom but in the real world as well.

It may be that the challenge of helping students to become responsible, intrinsically motivated adults actually allows teachers to exhibit their most refined teaching skills. The pleasure that comes from hearing a group of young people sing, create their own compositions, or play instruments actually *can* be equaled by the pleasure of watching a student correctly choose between attention and distraction, cooperation and selfishness, honesty and deceit. Neither learning nor teaching stops when the music ends.

REFERENCES AND RESOURCES

Kohn, A. (1993). *Punished by Rewards: The Trouble with Gold Stars, Incentive Plans, A's, Praise and Other Bribes.* New York: Houghton Mifflin. An incisive examination of extrinsic and intrinsic motivation, in which the author calls into question a number of well-known strategies for shaping student behavior.

Madsen, C. K., and C. H. Madsen, Jr. (1998). *Teaching/Discipline: A Positive Approach for Educational Development.* 4th ed. Raleigh, NC: Contemporary Publishing Company. These authors, one of whom is a music educator, provide a series of thoughtful essays along with related activities about behavior, learning, and life. This edition features an extensive chapter on behavioral strategies.

Valente, W. D., and C. M. Valente. (2001). *Law in the Schools.* 5th ed. Upper Saddle River, NJ: Merrill Prentice-Hall. This book provides a concise review of legal precedents relating to public education. Of particular relevance to classroom management, the authors include chapters on teacher and student rights addressing such issues as grading, expression, and punishment.

Wolfgang, C. H. (2005). *Solving Discipline and Classroom Management Problems: Methods and Models for Today's Teachers.* 6th ed. Hoboken, NJ: John Wiley. A comprehensive text that reviews the leading contemporary classroom management models including detailed procedures for dealing with violent students. Extensive references and critiques are provided for each model.

chapter 13

Assessment

Mrs. R: Ms. King?

Ms. K: Yes.

Mrs. R: I'm Mrs. Robinson, Claire's mother. I just wanted to talk with you about her grade in band.

Ms. K: Oh yes, Claire got a B minus this term, but I'm sure she can bring that grade up with hard work.

Mrs. R: Well, I was just wondering why she got a B minus. She loves band and seems to be practicing regularly. What was it that lowered her grade?

Ms. K: Claire just didn't seem to be progressing as well on her concert music this term and she was late a couple of days to rehearsal.

Mrs. R: Do you have the results of her playing tests? She didn't show them to me and I'd like to know how to help her improve.

Ms. K: Well I didn't give a *test*; it was just from hearing her in rehearsal.

Mrs. R: Did you give her specific things to work on so that she could improve?

Ms. K: I give feedback to all the clarinets in every rehearsal on how they are doing.

Mrs. R: You mean the whole section got a B minus?

Ms. K: Well, no.

Mrs. R: Ms. King, how can I help Claire improve if she doesn't have specific information on how she's doing or on how she can become a better instrumentalist?

Assessment is an extremely important issue for music teachers. This is not just because they should be able to justify their grades, but because it is critical that they have concrete evidence of how each individual student in their classes is progressing. Assessment can be a particular challenge in the music classroom because of large numbers of students, the performance-based nature of instruction, and the multiple levels of achievement within the same class. In the last ten years, music assessment has become particularly significant as the National

Standards and other state standards for music have been implemented. Music teachers who excel at group assessment (e.g., hearing and fixing ensemble problems in rehearsal) often find themselves less prepared to deal with the demands of individual assessment. This, in turn, can create a great deal of stress and discomfort when it comes time to grade students on their individual achievement. What are the purposes of assessment and how can music teachers best implement effective assessment in their classroom?

Assessment serves a number of important purposes in music education. It provides ongoing feedback to help students learn, it identifies clearly how much students have learned in relation to a preexisting goal, and it helps teachers determine whether an instructional approach is effective. A good assessment instrument should provide something of a blueprint for success. That is, it should describe the knowledge or behaviors most important to learning a particular musical skill or concept.

Types of Assessment

There are several different types of assessment, each of which provides different information for the student and the teacher. While individual school districts may have different names for these types of assessment, they should all be present in some form. *Diagnostic* assessment can help music teachers decide the level and extent of instruction students will need. A common form of diagnostic assessment in secondary school music programs is the audition. While auditions are typically used only to determine group membership, they often assess musical skills that are relevant to the teacher's instructional goals such as tone, technical skill, and music-reading ability. If teachers were to score students' performances on the various components of the audition, they would have an excellent starting point for determining the appropriate level of their instruction. *Formative* assessment is designed to give a student the feedback necessary to develop a particular competence. Music teachers continuously engage in assessment of this type informally throughout every lesson or rehearsal, as they give feedback to an individual or to an entire section to improve their performance. By providing more structured opportunities for formative assessment, music teachers can provide students with a set of individualized strategies to help them achieve the desired goal. *Summative* assessment provides feedback on the presence or absence of a particular skill or understanding. This is often done near the end of the learning process, using playing tests to see if individuals have learned their parts, performance tests to see if skills such as beat keeping have been mastered, or written tests on the content learned in a unit.

All of these assessments can provide information that eventually leads to *evaluation*; judging a student's musical achievement in relation to a standard or expectation. Evaluation is usually represented by putting a particular value, such as a grade, on student achievement. One way to understand assessment versus evaluation is to consider the familiar process of a music contest or festival. In a music contest, participants often receive two kinds of information: (1) comments from the judges that *assess* how well they performed in such areas as tone, intonation, and phrasing, and (2) a numerical rating or *evaluation* of how well they did in relation to the standard for their age level or school classification. While many participants focus more on the rating they receive, it is clearly the least informative part of the contest feedback. It is the assessment via written comments that gives music students and their teachers the information they need to continue to improve.

While contest comments and ratings do provide one measure of progress, it is only at the level of the ensemble—not the individual. Feedback at the group level is not sufficient for assessing the progress of the individual student, because there is a lack of transfer between what ensembles as a whole can do and the level of individual learning in the music classroom.

❖ BREAK POINT 13.1 Examining Assessment Models in Your Own Education

Examine the ways in which you are being assessed in your music education classes and in other classes at your university. Do the assessments reinforce the stated goals for the course? Which assessment models are being used (diagnostic, formative, summative) and how often are you given feedback?

Implementing Effective Assessment in the Music Classroom

One of the most challenging aspects of assessment is designing a system that measures progress on the particular knowledge and skills the music teacher feels are most important. Setting up an assessment system is similar in many ways to designing a good lesson plan; in fact, the two are intertwined. A four-step process helps teachers ensure that their goals and assessments are aligned with each other and are clearly defined (Figure 13.1). First teachers must identify the learning goals—that is, what they want the students to know and be able to do. A good starting point for such decisions is the National Standards for Music

Education (see Chapter 4) as well as state- and district-level standards. The National Standards provide a general framework for the knowledge domains to be covered and some of the skills the profession deems most important, from singing and playing instruments to understanding music historically and culturally. Eventually the music teacher must bring the goals down to a more specific classroom level. For example, under standard 6 for students in grade K–4 is the achievement standard "identify simple musical forms when presented aurally." A music teacher might identify this as a classroom-level learning goal by saying "second graders will identify the A & B sections of *El Floron*" (a children's singing game from Puerto Rico).

The second step is to translate those learning goals into learning outcomes. Learning outcomes essentially describe what successful achievement of the goal would look like. Outcomes are usually written in language that allows the music teacher to observe achievement. For example, the learning goal of identifying A and B sections in a second-grade lesson might be translated into the following outcome, "The students will be able to change to the appropriate beat-keeping pattern to match the A & B sections of *El Floron*." This puts the achievement of the goal into a form the teacher is able to observe and assess. Both learning goals and their outcomes are essential to curriculum development and lesson planning. Once an outcome has been determined, the next step is to develop an instructional strategy to achieve that outcome. This strategy is usually represented as the sequence of the lesson and includes the materials and activities involved.

The final step in effective assessment involves recording the student's performance on the learning outcomes at an individual level and providing feedback. The outcome specifies what the students will do to demonstrate learning,

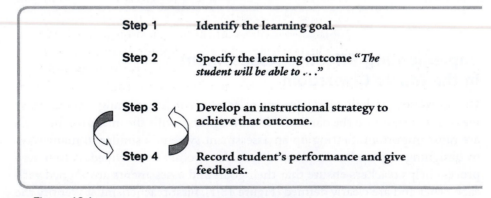

Step 1   **Identify the learning goal.**

Step 2   **Specify the learning outcome "*The student will be able to . . .*"**

Step 3   **Develop an instructional strategy to achieve that outcome.**

Step 4   **Record student's performance and give feedback.**

Figure 13.1 • **Four steps for effective assessment.**

but the music teacher will need to assess individuals within the group during the performance of the song to see whether the students have mastered the standard. This final step in assessment includes an opportunity to observe the outcome, a system for recording or scoring the performance and feedback to students on their performance. Notice that steps three and four are recursive. As teachers assess student performance and give feedback, they are also assessing the effectiveness of their instruction and making modifications that can help more students to achieve the desired outcome. A number of assessment models have been developed over the years that can help teachers to quickly and efficiently assess student performance in their classrooms.

Models for Music Assessment

While assessment demands are often different for elementary and secondary school music settings, they have in common the need to assess large numbers of students. Consequently, any assessment system must be efficient so that it can be implemented frequently and consistently to monitor student learning. While tests and homework assignments are the normal forms of assessment in most classes and subjects, they do not always serve the performance-based needs of the music classroom. Following are several models for recording student performance and giving feedback.

At the elementary school level, the assessment of musical knowledge and skills is increasingly tied to grade-level standards. A straightforward approach to individual assessment is to identify the desired standard for learning at each grade level. Then the teacher can record at each observation whether the student is Approaching Standard [**O**], At Standard [√], or Exceeding Standard [**+**] for a particular outcome. If this assessment model is combined with descriptions of the behaviors for each level of understanding, it offers some feedback about the eventual goal. The teacher in the second-grade lesson on *El Floron* has only to put a mark for each student as he or she sings the song and taps the beat. Figure 13.2 illustrates how this marking system could be used as a summative assessment of student progress on the National Standards in a marking period.

For assessing complex skills like playing an instrument or reading music, a *checklist* can be used to outline the component skills required for successful achievement of particular outcomes. Figure 13.3 illustrates a checklist for a beginning band student's playing exam. The score on the playing exam is simply the sum of the number of checks.

Grade 2 Quarterly Music Report

____ Singing—Can sing songs accurately with the class and sings at solo opportunities.

____ Playing an Instrument—Can play two-note Bordun, keep a steady beat, and shows proper mallet technique.

____ Improvising—Can create answers on the question song and add names of animals on the animal song.

____ Creating Music—Shows sense of repetition and contrast in his or her own songs.

____ Reading Music—Can echo one-measure solfege and rhythm patterns and show pitch direction with movement.

____ Listening—Can identify changes in form through movement and demonstrate strong and weak beats.

____ Evaluating—Can hear and correct his or her own musical performance.

____ Music and Other Arts—Can identify common elements of pictures, stories, and songs.

____ History and Culture—Can identify characteristics and repertoire from music of other cultures/times.

Assessment Key: O = Approaching Standard √ = At Standard
 + = Exceeding Standard NA = Not assessed this period

Figure 13.2 • **A grade 2 assessment of student progress in music.**

Performance Test

1. Demonstrated good posture and breath support. _____

2. Tone was full and consistent throughout range. _____

3. Pitches were accurate and in tune. _____

4. Rhythms were accurate and in tempo. _____

5. Performed with expressive phrasing, articulation, _____
   and dynamics.

TOTAL SCORE_____

Comments:

Figure 13.3 • **Checklist assessment for instrumental performance achievement.**

Performance Test

	Never		Sometimes		Always
1. Demonstrated good posture and breath support.	1	2	3	4	5
2. Tone was full and consistent throughout range.	1	2	3	4	5
3. Pitches were accurate and in tune.	1	2	3	4	5
4. Rhythms were accurate and in tempo.	1	2	3	4	5
5. Performed with expressive phrasing, articulation, and dynamics.	1	2	3	4	5

TOTAL SCORE _____

Comments:

Figure 13.4 • Rating scale assessment for instrumental performance achievement.

If teachers wish to provide a little more complete information as to how accomplished the student is in the components of a complex skill, they might choose to use a *rating scale* assessment instead of a checklist. Figure 13.4 offers an assessment of the same performance skill, but now each element of performance can be rated from 1 to 5, in this case indicating the relative frequency with which each component of the skill was demonstrated during performance. This allows the teacher to show the students how they are progressing before they reach the standard.

To be effective as formative assessment both the checklist and rating scale models would presumably be combined with feedback on where and how the student needs to improve. In an assessment model known as a *rubric*, each rating comes with a description so that students can see where they are on a particular scale, and also where they need to go to be successful. Figure 13.5 is a rubric for a sight-singing assessment that describes the desired outcomes in each area.

Individual Sight-Singing Evaluation

1	2	3	4	5
Missed starting pitch, no clear sense of key.	Correct starting pitch, key center changed throughout.	Good sense of key, awareness of tonic throughout.	Strong tonal center, most pitches correct, a few intervals were incorrect.	Pitches were accurate throughout.

PITCH _____

1	2	3	4	5
Inconsistent beat from the beginning. Stopping and/or starting over repeatedly.	Started in a tempo, but lost sense of steady beat. Stopping or slowing on certain patterns.	Kept sense of steady beat but with fluctuating tempo, several rhythmic patterns incorrect.	Steady tempo, missed a few rhythmic patterns in the line.	Steady tempo and accurate rhythms throughout.

RHYTHM _____

1	2	3	4	5
Sung with inconsistent tone and no clear sense of phrasing or general dynamic level.	Sung with good tone, but with little attention to phrasing or dynamics.	Sung with good tone and accurate phrasing. Did not reflect accurate dynamic level or dynamic changes.	Sung expressively with accurate phrasing and general dynamic level. Lack of dynamic shading and nuance.	Sung expressively with good tone, clear phrasing and accurate dynamic level and dynamic shading.

EXPRESSION _____

TOTAL SCORE _____

Comments:

Figure 13.5 • A rubric for assessing sight-singing performance.

❖ BREAK POINT 13.2 Designing a Skill-based Assessment

Design a performance-based assessment with observable, measurable criteria for one musical skill you feel is important to assess. Connect your assessment to the appropriate National Standard.

Alternative Assessment Options

Not all approaches to assessment require the teacher to make judgments about the student. A number of alternative assessment options provide students with opportunities to demonstrate and reflect upon what they have learned. *Portfolio* assessment, sometimes referred to as *authentic* assessment, is an accumulated record of the student's musical accomplishments. While painters' portfolios are full of canvases, musicians' portfolios might include tapes of playing tests, recordings of songs they have composed, or a list of songs or skills mastered. This type of assessment is termed authentic because it can often be the most natural way to represent the outcomes of instruction. Rather than tests or single points of assessment, they can represent the progress of a student's work over time and reveal more of the processes involved in learning through particular tasks.

Music teachers frequently employ some form of *self-assessment* with their students. While students may not have the ability to assess themselves objectively, self-assessment is useful in providing opportunities for students to sharpen their listening skills and to develop their understanding of the criteria involved in a musical performance. Many of the same forms used in teacher-based assessments can be applied to student self-assessment. *Journals* and *practice logs* (recording the quality and amount of student practice) can also help students reflect on their accomplishments and set goals for future success. As young musicians progress and become more self-directed, these approaches can help to transfer the responsibility of learning to them.

Assessment in the Ensemble

The assessment models described above can all be employed effectively in the ensemble class. One of the challenges of doing assessment in the ensemble, in addition to class sizes of fifty or more, is the presence of multiple levels of musical achievement. Teachers cannot use a one-size-fits-all approach to assessment or they will have outcomes that are well below some students' skills and too far above others. Teachers need to use a combination of diagnostic and multilevel assessments geared to meet a variety of student needs. Figure 13.6 shows a summary checklist of possible requirements for a Level 1 Musician in a high school band or choir class (this model could be adapted for any type of ensemble). With this kind of system, performance assessments like those illustrated in Figures 13.3 and 13.4 can be applied to examples of different difficulty levels depending on the student's musical achievement. In this way, every student in the ensemble can, through testing, find his or her own achievement level and then progress from there. Students can control their progress by deciding when they are ready to test on a particular skill. Teachers often set aside some time in class once a week or after school for individual testing. Some skills can even be peer evaluated or use the section leaders. Using this multilevel approach to assessment, grades can be tied to students' progress within each level rather than to a particular level of achievement. Music teachers who employ such multilevel assessments often come up with more creative names for the levels, and even offer certificates, awards, and school letters for the completion of each level.

Musicianship Level 1: Choir

_____ Can demonstrate appropriate singing posture and proper breathing.

_____ Can sing an arpeggio (1-3-5-3-1) on all five vowels with relaxed and focused tone and solid breath support.

_____ Can perform any rhythm from the Level 1 rhythm-reading sheet.

_____ Can sing any melody from the Level 1 sight-singing sheet on solfège.

_____ Can sing his or her voice part accurately and expressively for any song of the director's choosing from the current repertoire.

_____ Researched the composer, style, and historical/cultural background of one piece from the repertoire.

_____ Completed one written evaluation of the choir's performance or rehearsal.

Musicianship Level 1: Band

_____ Can demonstrate appropriate posture, instrument position, and breathing.

_____ Can play any major scale in two octaves with relaxed and focused tone and solid breath support.

_____ Can perform any rhythm from the Level 1 rhythm-reading sheet.

_____ Can play any melody from the Level 1 sight-reading sheet.

_____ Can play his or her part accurately and expressively for any song of the director's choosing from the current repertoire.

_____ Researched the composer, style, and historical/cultural background of one piece from the repertoire.

_____ Completed one written evaluation of the band's performance or rehearsal.

Figure 13.6 • Checklists for musicianship Level 1 in choral and instrumental ensembles.

Assessment and Grading

How, then, can these music assessments be tied to a grade? Grading, like assessment, is a process of identifying the most important aspects of instruction. Students' grades in music should be based on their achievement of the goals and objectives the teacher has identified as central to the class. If the two primary skills taught in choir are vocal performance and sight-singing, then students' grades should not be based on attendance and concert reports. Increasingly, states and school districts are insisting that grades be based solely on a student's performance of a set of benchmarks or outcomes, not on elements like attendance or participation. To connect assessment to grading, the music teacher needs to weigh the various elements of the curriculum according to the time spent and the perceived importance of the skill. Grades then are based on *progress* in these areas rather than an absolute standard of achievement. Figure 13.2 illustrated a standards-based assessment for elementary school. Figure 13.7 shows a sample grading plan for a middle school drumming ensemble. In this example, rather than participation as a generic component, specific elements of the desired knowledge and skills related to rehearsal preparation and ensemble participation can be specified.

Another important consideration in grading the music class is the role of concerts and other activities that take place outside the school day. While concerts are typically the culminating activity of ensemble instruction, they often occur outside of class time. Consequently, participation in such events cannot be included in the grade without careful planning and parental support. The grading plan must balance the importance of group experiences with a clear record of individual progress. A system of assessment that is tied to grading and to content is essential if music teachers are concerned with the education of the individual student.

❖ BREAK POINT 13.3 Designing a Grading Plan for a Music Class

Create a grading plan for a class of your choice. What combination and weighting of skills, activities, and content would make up the criteria for determining students' grades in music?

In the opening scenario of Ms. King's band class, Claire's instrumental performance had not progressed as she expected it to. Had Ms. King implemented

Drumming Ensemble Grade Sheet

Practice Skills   20   _____
  ✛ The student comes to rehearsal prepared, turns in practice logs,
     and demonstrates consistent improvement over time.

Rehearsal Skills   15   _____
  ✛ The student is on time, with his or her instrument ready,
     and is actively engaged musically and personally in the rehearsal.

Improvisation Skills   15   _____
  ✛ The student has successfully participated in at least one
     improvisation opportunity at his or her level in the marking
     period.

Individual Performance Skills   20   _____
  ✛ The student has completed at least one rhythm sight-reading
     test and one technique test at their level in the marking period.

Concert and Rehearsal Evaluation   10   _____
  ✛ The student has completed at least one performance
     self-assessment form in the marking period.

Group Performance Skills   20   _____
  ✛ The student has successfully demonstrated his or her
     learning as a member of the ensemble through scheduled
     performances during the marking period.

                                                          TOTAL   _____

100–90	89–80	79–70	69–60	<60
A	B	C	D	F

Figure 13.7 • Sample grading plan for a middle school drumming ensemble.

an assessment plan in her classroom, the discussion with Claire's mother could have been an opportunity for sharing those concerns in a concrete and thorough way:

Mrs. R: Ms. King?

Ms. K: Yes.

Mrs. R: I'm Mrs. Robinson, Claire's mother. I just wanted to talk with you about her grade in band.

Ms. K: Oh yes, Claire got a B minus this term, but I'm sure she can bring that grade up with hard work.

Mrs. R: Well, I was just wondering why she got a B minus. She loves band and seems to be practicing regularly. What was it that lowered her grade?

Ms. K: Claire did a fine job with her practice time, but practice logs are only 20 percent of her grade. Her playing tests did not show much progress from last term and she only checked off two of her skills for her musicianship test. She was also late to rehearsal three days this term.

Mrs. R: I'd like to know how to help her improve. What can I do?

Ms. K: The playing tests include feedback on the areas where she did well and the areas that need improvement. You might center some of her practice time directly on those skills. Claire can always schedule time to work with me or with her section leader prior to a playing test. I would also encourage her to work on checking off at least two more skills on her musicianship level; she's close to finishing Level 2. Claire has many opportunities to raise her grade before the next marking period.

Mrs. R: Thank you, Ms. King.

One of the benefits of going through the process of assessment outlined here is that an effective assessment system helps a teacher determine how to best use class time. Without clear goals, there may not be a strong connection between the skills teachers say they value and how they actually spend time in rehearsal or class. Another important benefit of assessment is the opportunity to educate parents and colleagues about the important content of our discipline. If music teachers at all levels cannot articulate what students can learn from their instruction, and identify the progress of that learning, then music classes truly do not belong in the curriculum.

REFERENCES AND RESOURCES

MENC. (2001). *Spotlight on Assessment in Music Education*. Reston, VA: MENC, the National Association for Music Education. Part of the "Spotlight" series, this publication is a compilation of short articles on assessment from the state journals and offers many practical models for assessment.

The complete text of the National Standards for Music can be found at www.menc.org/publication/books/standards.htm. This online resource provides the text of the standards and offers assessment strategies for each standard listed.

NOTE: In addition to published resources, there are numerous web-based sources for music assessment ideas from state and national curriculum guides to the sites of individual teachers. One example of such a resource can be found at artswork.asu.edu/arts/teachers/assessment/resources.htm

chapter 14

Technology

An online chat:

diva: when r u going to do ur songwriting asst?
mallethead: just finished, wanna hear it?
diva: yeah!
mallethead: brb

mallethead wants to send file: C:\Documents and Settings\jazztopia.mp3
diva received: C:\jazztopia.mp3

diva: awesome! where did u get that drum trac?
mallethead: i mixed one off this website with another one i made.
diva: can i borrow a piece of it?
mallethead: sure.
diva: thnx. :)

Music technology options are constantly changing and evolving as new software, hardware, and sound equipment are developed to upgrade or replace existing resources. There are, however, guidelines for using music technology in the classroom that remain relatively consistent and can help teachers make decisions about the uses of technology in their classrooms. Most people associate the term "technology" with computers, and computers have become an increasingly important part of music education and the music industry at large. Advances in music computing have created new ways to make music and new ways to understand the art of music. Computer technology has actually created distinct ways for students to experience and interact with the music they hear or create. Computers are, however, only one facet of the technology that is available for the music classroom. There are also sound systems, digital audio and video recording equipment, digital keyboards, electric instruments, and CD/DVD resources for teaching.

Planning for Music Technology

As with assessment, technology decisions start with what the students need to know and are able to do. Once those decisions have been made, teachers can determine whether technology is the best way to reach their goals. For example, technology can be a very powerful tool for practicing aural skills and music fundamentals, for improvisation practice, for composing/recording music, for mixing and remixing existing music, combining music and video, or even for practicing solos with a virtual accompanist.

There are many ways that the music teacher can use technology behind the scenes in music arranging, charting for marching band, sequencing accompaniments, laying out lesson plans, and printing out exercises. There are also many ways for individual students to use technology, each requiring only a few computer stations located in the classroom or in nearby practice rooms. These include self-directed aural skills and music fundamentals practice, composing and sequencing software, recording and editing equipment, and accompaniment tracks.

Some schools are able to have space for a music computer lab where students can work on either group or individual projects in composition, arranging, digital recording, and musicianship training involving a variety of written and aural skills. While this is sometimes the most common vision of music technology, it is also the most expensive in terms of space and equipment. Unless a teacher implements a series of technology-centered music courses, a music computer lab may not be the best investment. Much can be accomplished with one complete teacher station and a few student stations.

Technology for the Teacher

Every music teacher in every setting should have the technology available to play back recorded music in CD, MP3, or other high-quality digital format. Most elementary and secondary basal textbooks and beginning instrumental method books now come with CDs and/or DVDs, and music publishers are augmenting their materials with web-based sound resources that can be downloaded. In addition to sound equipment, teachers at every level should have a computer with the following software and capabilities:

- ❖ Word processing—for lesson preparation, written communication with parents, and creating forms and flyers.

❖ E-mail—for efficient communication with students, parents, and boosters.

❖ Database—for record keeping for grades, equipment, music, and any other clerical aspect of the program. There is specialized software for a number of these uses or if teachers are proficient with a program like Excel, they can create many of the forms they need.

❖ Music notation (with or without musical instrument digital interface [MIDI] sequencing)—for creating notated exercises, arrangements, and editions of music for the classroom. Most of these programs have some form of playback that can also be used to help students with part work.

❖ Web-based resources—for authoring and accessing web pages. Such web-based resources can allow students to access crucial information around the clock, to submit homework electronically, and to share information and audio materials with each other.

❖ BREAK POINT 14.1 Making Technology Choices

Identify one way you would use technology to help you teach. What is one way you might use technology to benefit your students' musical learning?

In addition, other technological resources are available to augment the music program. Many music teachers benefit from having access to digital audio and video recording equipment and editing software that allows them to record student performances and encourages students to create and record their own music. There are software programs that will provide background tracks for improvisation and hardware that can accompany student solos freeing the teacher to work directly with the students. Many teachers have also employed web-authoring software to create a web page that provides classroom materials and program details so that students and parents always have access to important information. These pages can be restricted so that the information (especially photo and video information of children) remains confidential. Students can also post and download audio files of each other's work and submit ideas and critiques to the group electronically. These virtual communities can be very vibrant and extend student learning well beyond the class period, but teachers must be conscious to monitor content and access. Other specialized software for tasks like charting marching band shows or even scheduling rooms and accompanists for music contests can help to simplify these complex processes.

Technology for the Student

Providing students access to music technology can enrich their learning and provide opportunities for individual exploration that are not always available during the limited amount of class time. Several resources allow students to explore music composition, music fundamentals, improvisation, and instrumental practice on an individual basis with little or no background on the student's part or input on the teacher's part. All of these resources are more effective if the teacher can provide some basic instruction and guidance as to their use and a clear structure for how they will fit in the larger curriculum.

COMPOSITION

Computer programs are available from kindergarten through professional level that allow students to explore, record, and modify their musical ideas in a number of different ways. Figure 14.1 is a screen from a popular music exploration program for young children that offers opportunities for them to compose as

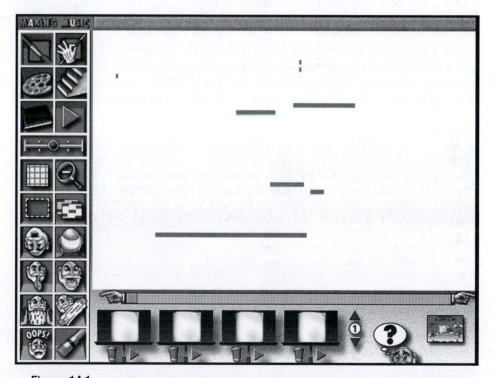

Figure 14.1 • The music canvas where children can paint their own composition in *Making Music (v.1.0.3)*. Each line is a different color representing different instrument sounds.

well as develop basic aural skills. Some composition programs require a Musical Instrument Digital Interface or MIDI to input and play back musical ideas, but more recent programs are more self-contained using the increasingly sophisticated sound resources of the computer. The teacher must find ways to integrate this kind of musical exploration into the broader curriculum. If there is a music computing lab with digital recording and MIDI capability, then entire courses on composition and sound production are possible. For the teacher who has only a couple of computer stations, it is important to provide sufficient opportunities for individual exploration while maintaining the flow of the larger class. In elementary school music classrooms, computers can serve as part of a larger set of learning centers with other centers using musical instruments, tape recorders, or other music materials for children's exploration. One solution in ensemble classes is to provide class time on a particular day, or as a part of a longer class period in block scheduling, that can be used for small-group work. This breakout time can include section work, solos and small ensembles, and composition projects.

Like composition, improvisation can also be developed using computer resources. Teachers interested in improvisation can choose to sequence their own virtual rhythm sections for basic blues progressions, use a play-a-long CD, or use a program like *Band in a Box* (Figure 14.2). The computer environment offers many advantages like an almost limitless variety of instrumentation and harmonic changes, texture control, tempo control, recording capability (through MIDI), and various notation options. One disadvantage is that the

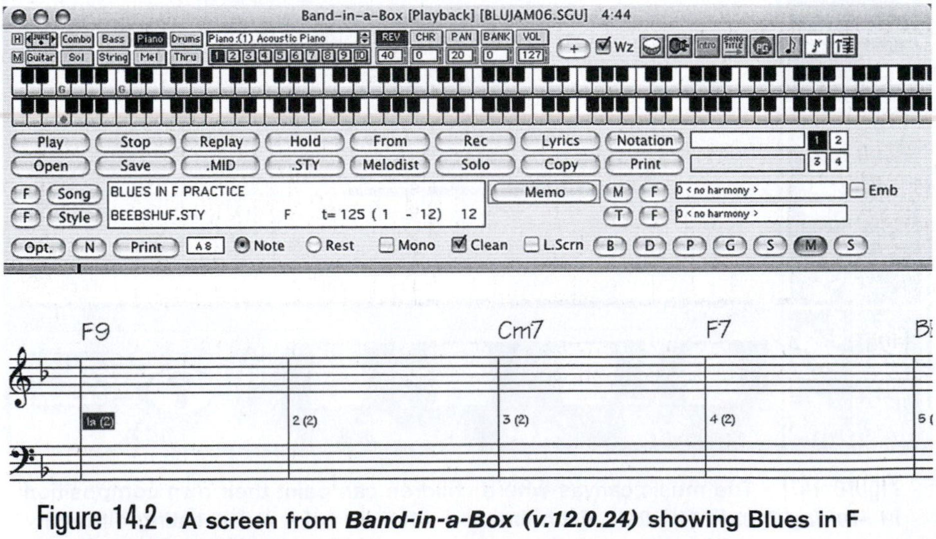

Figure 14.2 • A screen from *Band-in-a-Box (v.12.0.24)* showing Blues in F practice with notation provided.

computer-derived background tracks are often not as musical as prerecorded tracks of live musicians, though the most recent versions of the program seem to have addressed this problem much better.

MUSICIANSHIP

While fundamentals and aural skills can be taught very effectively in a classroom context, there are often several levels of understanding within a single class. Having the option of individual study can benefit students at any level who wish to be challenged and to direct their own learning. While some computer programs are very prescriptive in their sequence and design, most allow students to choose the level at which they work. Having some system for checking in with students on their progress can help to avoid frustration as these programs do not always give enough feedback for the student to progress without additional help. Figure 14.3 shows a screen from a popular aural skills program that offers a number of levels of practice and tracks students' progress.

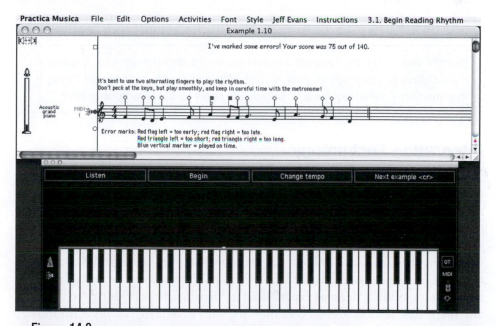

Figure 14.3 • A rhythm reading exercise at Level 1 difficulty in *Practica Musica (v.4.5.6)* with feedback on the student's performance.

INDIVIDUAL PRACTICE

There are software and hardware resources for students' individual practice of either their concert music or improvisational skills. One of the most basic ways of providing practice opportunities is for the teacher to isolate the parts of a piece. If the music for the marimba ensemble, choir, or orchestra was created using a notation or sequencing program, each part can be printed out and played back separately. Students can then practice either by playing along with their part, or by turning off their part and playing with the other parts. This approach to practice has advantages over prerecorded accompaniments as it provides student control over the tempo and texture. The student may want to play only with the percussion or sing his or her part against the bass line. The disadvantage of this approach is the time the teacher needs to enter all of the music, although people who are proficient at notation or sequencing can often create parts very quickly. For practicing in a more complete context, a program like *SmartMusic*™ offers students a virtual accompanist that will actually follow their tempo and give some feedback on the accuracy of their performance. *Smart-Music* repertoire includes exercises from the major instrumental method books, accompaniments for some of the major vocal and instrumental solos, and the option of teacher-created exercises imported from *Finale*.

❖ BREAK POINT 14.2 Employing Student-centered Technology

Identify two ways to integrate student-centered technology into a general music class or ensemble of your choice. What skills are best taught through this medium? What equipment would you need to achieve your goals?

Integrating Technology

These examples represent only a fraction of the technology options available to the music teacher. Teachers must decide how far to go in integrating technology into the music classroom. Each new technology component requires them to spend time learning to use it effectively and even more time to teach it to students. Most teachers have some students who are adept with technology. They may allow these students to learn the new computer programs and devices, and then have the students teach the teachers how to best use them. Most high school students today are at least as experienced as their teachers in using technology, and many have already begun experimenting with web-based resources for music. They may have even recorded, mixed, and edited their own recordings.

Most music technology can be used either in individual computer stations located in or near the music room or in a more extensive computer lab setting. One important consideration in offering music in a lab setting is that some of the equipment required may not be a standard part of the existing school computer labs. For example, if the teacher wants MIDI capability, some kind of controller like a piano keyboard is required. This means that separate space and expense for the music lab is required, which makes music labs less practical unless there are courses that would use them extensively. Recently, programs for music fundamentals and even some composition and editing software have come to rely on the increasingly sophisticated sound resources of the computer itself without the need for external controllers. This allows music to be integrated into the general computer lab with only the addition of headphones. Another option is to integrate the computer lab into courses that already involve using piano keyboards.

PIANO LABS

Some elementary and secondary schools have dedicated piano labs that allow teachers to provide beginning piano instruction to large groups of students. The basic technology for such a lab involves electronic keyboards with headphones that are networked together with a teacher station so that the teacher can communicate with students individually or in groups while remaining at the teacher station. This arrangement allows for both group and individual playing in a variety of configurations. Piano classes are very popular in secondary schools and can be an excellent way to serve students who are not interested in the traditional ensemble offerings. Some elementary classrooms also make extensive use of electronic keyboards as a way of teaching general music although the primary goal is usually overall musical development, not piano skills.

Because keyboards labs require a larger space and already contain instruments that are MIDI compatible, they are an excellent way to initiate a music computing lab. By adding a desk with a computer and MIDI to each keyboard station, the piano lab is easily converted into a computer lab and can be used for both. Having MIDI capabilities in your keyboard lab also allows beginner students to play simple pieces with virtual ensembles. This can enrich and enliven the traditional beginning piano class and help motivate students to practice and perform.

❖ BREAK POINT 14.3 Designing a Technology-centered Course

Based on all the models discussed thus far, describe a course you might teach that would be centered on technology. What would the focus of such a course be? What musical knowledge and skills could be taught? What types of hardware and software might be needed?

Technology is becoming thoroughly integrated into everyone's daily life, and music technology is no exception. Music teachers need at least a foundational understanding of the major types of software available for music instruction and sound processing. Music education students should seek at least one course in music technology as a part of their undergraduate training. Technology can provide a wealth of resources for the music class, but the benefits must always be weighed against the costs, both in money and in time. Hardware and software options change rapidly, sometimes rendering older equipment ineffective, so one has to consider the costs to maintain and upgrade a lab as well as to get one started. The simpler the technology setup, the less effort will be needed to maintain and update it. Fortunately, with even a basic computer setup, music teachers can realize many of the benefits of music technology in their classrooms.

REFERENCES AND RESOURCES

Software

Evans, J. (2005). *Practica Musica (v.4.5.6)*. Kirkland, WA: Ars Nova Software. This popular aural skills program is available in both Macintosh and Windows platforms. For more information see www.ars-nova.com/practica.html.

Gannon, P. (2005). *Band-in-a-Box (v.12.0.24)*. Victoria, BC: P G Music Inc. This program is available in both Macintosh and Windows platforms. For more information see www.pgmusic.com/products_bb.htm.

The *SmartMusic* practice system is a product of MakeMusic! Inc. Eden Prairie, MN. For more information see www.smartmusic.com/default.aspx.

Subotnick, M. (1995). *Making Music (v.1.0.3)*. New York: Viva Media. Newer versions of this program and others are available for both Windows and Macintosh platforms. The author also offers online exploration at www.creatingmusic.com.

Books

Reese, S., K. McCord, K. C. Walls, and MENC. (2001). *Strategies for Teaching: Technology, MENC's Strategies for Teaching Series*. Reston, VA: MENC, the National Association for Music Education. Part of the MENC *Strategies for Teaching* series, this book focuses on meeting the National Standards through technology. The editors have compiled practical ideas that range from integrating technology in ensembles and elementary general music to teaching technology-centered classes.

Rudolph, T. E. (2004). *Teaching Music with Technology*. 2nd ed. Chicago: GIA Publications. Written by a practicing music teacher, this book covers a wide range of topics from MIDI and electronic keyboards to the Internet and copyright law. The new edition includes a companion CD-ROM with assignments, projects, and lesson plans to use with students, and links to websites that offer free software, demo programs, and up-to-date technical information.

Williams, D. B., and P. R. Webster. (2006). *Experiencing Music Technology*. 3rd ed. New York: Thomson/Schirmer. Now in a third edition, this book with companion DVD-ROM is the most comprehensive and up-to-date source of technology options in music education. It helps teachers to make intelligent technology decisions and provides opportunities to learn the basics of different types of software.

chapter 15

Out in the Field: Look-Listen-Learn

University student A: Have you been out to Blackwell High School yet?

University student B: You mean Teresa Guerrero's program? Yeah. What an ace!

University student A: You bet. She's got it all: the pacing, the high energy, the variety of approaches, the student rapport. She's good and she seems to be having fun, too.

University student B: She's also got a sense of humor, and the kids love her. And have you heard her play?

University student A: Trumpet? Or piano? She's amazing at both.

University student B: Yeah. I'd like to have her skills, every last one of them.

University student A: I'm planning more visits out to Blackwell. I figure maybe some of what I see and hear in Teresa Guerrero's classes might rub off on me.

Defining the Field

Beyond the relative comfort of a university campus where music students—prospective teachers—refine their musical skills, read and reflect on pedagogical theory, and design and deliver sample segments of lessons and rehearsals, there is "the field." Among teachers, the field is the school, be it elementary or secondary school; public or private school; the individual classes of music, math, science, or history within school; and even the halls, cafeterias, playgrounds, and play fields of the school compound. The field is the real world of workaday teachers in their daily interactions with children and youth in the instructional process. Look and listen to the activity in the field and you can learn much about teachers and students, what they say, what they do, and what they mean. The techniques and process of musically educating young people in schools are played out in everyday activity.

Anthropologists and teachers share some common understanding of "field," and it is the fieldwork—the work that occurs in the field—that defines them professionally, gives them purpose, makes theory mean something real and useful. The hallmark of fieldwork within the social sciences is observation, the process of taking note of and attending to what can be seen and heard in a given place. The words and actions of individuals in the field, the events that occur there, and the general images of scenes and settings that contribute to how the events unfold—these are observable in the communities studied by anthropologists and in the learning spaces where teachers work. By looking and listening objectively to what happens, noting who the actors are, and observing the circumstances of the action, astute observers can develop a deep understanding of their field of interest.

"Field experience" is the standard term for the fieldwork of prospective teachers. These experiences are opportunities for music students to find out what transpires in schools in the name of music, teaching, and learning, particularly within music classes and ensemble rehearsals. The techniques of instruction, the interactive processes by which teachers teach and students learn, and the individual segments of music classes and rehearsals (and the transitions between them) are matters to be carefully noted for the details that make education effective. With theories of learning and instruction in hand, and with minds open to new and meaningful understandings, musicians who will teach find that field experiences can show them the realities of music education in motion. They learn through direct observation that music teachers are not only able to perform, create, and analyze music intellectually, but that they have acquired the skills to communicate music to children and adolescents. Field experiences are excursions into the school lives of young people and their teachers, opportunities for prospective teachers to learn what works in meaningful music encounters. They can lead to careful reflection and practice of those behaviors and skills that are vital to effective music education.

The links between theory-based university courses in music education and the actual instructional practices of elementary and secondary schools are already there, yet they await discovery by those who aspire to teach. Theories support practice, just as practice illustrates theory: each is necessary to a deep understanding of the process and products of music education. First impressions of the physical space of a school site and the students enrolled there give way to the careful scrutiny of the behaviors of teachers and students in action and interaction, so as to provide an understanding of the essence of instruction, learning, and development. The lasting impressions of what makes for effective music education are an amalgam of what can be observed, interpreted, and eventually selected for use by astute and thoughtful teachers.

Maneuvers of the Field Experience

Field experiences require astute observations to detect "what works" in music education practice, as well as why it works so well (or less well). Looking and listening, observers can take in the physical setting of the school and classroom, the character of the student population, and the particular behaviors of effective (and also not-so-effective) music instruction as delivered by teachers and received by students. Field experiences can be arranged for one school site, with frequent observations allowing for opportunities to track the evolving nature of music learning over time—be it the development in an elementary school music class of children's understanding of 6/8 meter in a selection of songs and their accompaniment on classroom instruments, or the rehearsal of a high school choir of a Bach chorale (or a Copland song) from its first sight-reading to its full-fledged pre-performance rehearsal. Observations in the field can also span numerous school sites, in which particular characteristics—the layout of elementary school classrooms, the content of warm-up exercises in string ensembles, the use of positive reinforcement in band rehearsals, the pedagogical strategies for developing jazz improvisation skills—can be compared and contrasted. Both intensive (at a single school site) and extensive (in multiple school sites) observations can be highly informational for understanding the practice of music education in all of its complexity.

❖ BREAK POINT 15.1 Child Alert!

Observe just one child (or youth) at a time, carefully, for his or her actions and reactions within a music class. Choose a child who appears very much like you, and consider the way the music, the teacher, and other students shape the child's overt and demonstrated learning behaviors. Later, select a child very much unlike you, observing his (or her) actions and reactions within the course of music instruction.

The information collected in these field experiences—observations, examination of materials (scores, textbooks, recordings, lesson plans), and conversations or even formal interviews with teachers—should be documented. Since parental permission is typically required for audio- or videotaping children under the age of eighteen, the most common and nonintrusive documentation continues to be note-taking. Keeping a journal, filling out an observation form, and writing notes of interviews are common recording methods. These means of documentation are briefly discussed below.

THE JOURNAL

A field experience notebook is useful for jotting down the substance of what can be seen and heard with regard to teacher and student behaviors. At the school site, notes can be made as to the use of major chunks of class time, which are frequently delineated through the musical selections targeted for experience. The teacher's verbal and nonverbal behaviors can be noted, be they musical, pedagogical, "human interest," or directed toward motivation, reinforcement, and behavior management. Later, the jottings can be filled in, described in a more expansive way, and reflected on to puzzle out reasons for and reactions to particular events.

THE OBSERVATION FORM

Various straightforward observation forms can be prepared to capture some of the key traits of teachers and their teaching strategies. Figure 15.1 offers an observation form that can be adjusted according to targeted interests; each item is detailed in this chapter.

THE INTERVIEW

In a field visit, a conversation with the teacher can be as quick as a greeting and an expression of appreciation for the opportunity to visit the classroom. At other times conversations with the teacher can stretch to the length of an interview, an opportunity to respectfully ask questions concerning the philosophy and practice of music education. In a fifteen-minute interview conducted at lunch, during a free period, or before or after school, the teacher can provide much insight and essential information on the professional tasks of teaching well. Live, in-person interviews need to be arranged in advance of the visit; interviews can also be conducted by telephone or electronically. Suitable questions include the following: When did you decide to become a music teacher? How long have you been teaching? Who has inspired your teaching? How are you rewarded (or challenged) by your professional choice to teach music? Do you teach music, or children, or both? What are the greatest strengths of your musical and teaching personas? How do administrators, teaching staff, parents, and community members support your work? What is your five-year plan for students in your program? How do you continue to grow professionally? What do you know now that you wish you had known as you prepared for a teaching position? The substance of a teacher's responses can be integrated into a report of information as well as reflective commentary by the interviewer.

Date:_____ Time:_____ School Site:_____

Teacher:_____ Class:_____

Description of the School (building(s), grounds, student population):

The Music Classroom (physical setting):

Music Selections Heard/Performed in Class:

Activities Heard/Seen in Class:

Teaching Behaviors:

- What is the first thing a teacher does at the start of class?
- How does the teacher incorporate listening?
- How does the teacher build performance skills?
- How does the teacher facilitate critical thinking?
- How does the teacher manage conflict in the classroom?
- What classroom management strategies are most apparent?
- How does the teacher come to closure at the end of class?

Figure 15.1 • Music education observation/evaluation form.

First Impressions

There is no mistaking a school and its grounds. You can almost feel the energy several blocks away. Your sense of arrival on the campus is verifiable through the school-crossing signs that are posted in the nearby neighborhood. In the early mornings and mid-afternoons, the crossing guards are posted at elementary school sites, and the school buses are lined up in the parking lots and on the public streets just beyond. When you arrive on campus you see students walking, running, grouped together, talking. You can hear schools too: the laughter, the shouting, school bells, and the low rumble of high schoolers in their secondhand cars. You are entering a place that you may once have thought was forever in the past. Welcome to the world inhabited by young people, their teachers, and their daytime community of committed caretakers.

School buildings vary, as do their campus grounds. Some—mostly elementary schools—are single buildings; others—often secondary schools—are a settlement of multiple buildings. These secondary school buildings or areas in the buildings are marked by particular functions: classrooms, the gym, the cafeteria, and even the performing arts auditorium. Play equipment, from swings and

The playground, a place where musical expressions happen.

slides to tetherball courts, is at the center of outdoor play at elementary schools, while bus drop-off zones and parking lots are central to much socializing among students in middle and high schools. All paths lead to the main entrance, with the main office just inside, where the principal is housed, and where all guests sign in and note their destination and function within the school. This is where the maze of school hallways and classrooms begins, and the place to pick up a campus map to steer visitors to where they need to go.

The halls fill and empty with the sounding of bells and buzzers: they are active places to be at school arrival and departure times, and during the changing of classes. Peer down the corridors and peek into classrooms, and the sights are a colorful and varied rhythm: a flurry of activity here, a stream of energy there, even repose (as in the case of a class of first-graders with their heads on their desks, resting as directed by their teacher). Again, the sounds are notable. While the "outdoor voices" are gone, there are high-pitched voices reading and repeating letters, numbers, and words; the sounds of teachers talking and "chalking" (those who still use chalkboards); the rustling of papers and clicking of computer keyboards; the buzz of industry as students work in their collaborative groups; occasional laughter, even song; and the background music of various media presentations.

❖ BREAK POINT 15.2 First Impressions of a School

> What do you see and hear as you approach a school, survey its grounds, enter its building, and walk its halls? Write a description of your sensory experiences of the school. Compare it to the experiences of your colleagues. Compare your impresions of two or more schools.

The Domain of School Music

There is no standard physical space for music in school, but the music room (or rooms) tends to stand apart from the rest of the school for good reason: its sounds permeate the walls and halls. While often pleasing to hear, music is easily distracting to students who are expected to focus on academic work, and thus music is typically housed away from the offices and the academic classrooms. In elementary schools, the music classroom is often located at the end of the building, in the basement, or sometimes in "portables," the "temporary" structures that stand disconnected from the school building at the edge of the playground. Secondary school music programs are likely to be housed in a suite of spaces, also at one end of the building, or a separate wing, or occasionally in a building devoted to music, drama, and dance.

Note just how busy elementary school music rooms seem to be. Even without the presence of children who fuss and fidget, turn and twist, the rooms are an array of xylophones, drums, small rhythm instruments, guitars, books, and recordings. There is almost always a piano in the elementary classroom, and a teacher's desk and computer work station. Sometimes there are guitars, autoharps, and buckets of recorders sitting in water near a sink, sterilizing. Child-sized chairs may be arranged in horseshoe-shape so that there is plenty of room to move into singing games, eurhythmic experiences, and folk dances. A set of choral risers may be pushed against the wall for singing or sitting on, and there may be a keyboard lab lined up along another wall. A sound system is set up on the piano or on a moveable cart, often with a VCR/DVD system adjacent to it. The standard overhead transparency projector or LCD is typically close at hand. The walls are filled with photos of great performers and composers, instruments and ensembles, and notational symbols. Posted somewhere for all to see is a set of three to five rules for music classroom behavior. There may be a lineup of classes nearby with stars to indicate days and weeks of these appropriate behaviors, one class after another, and a second star-chart may be hanging to display children's mastery of musical skills or songs learned. The music room is a colorful extension of other classrooms in elementary schools, but the extent of music equipment that fills it literally shouts out "activity."

Secondary school music spaces can range from humble to overwhelming and deserve careful consideration by the keen observer. There are often several large rooms for band, choral, and orchestra classes, many of them with tiered rows that rise and curve from the center space that is marked by a podium, a large music stand, and a piano. There are frequently acoustic-tiled practice rooms with and without pianos, several offices for teachers, instrument lockers (or instrument rooms—especially for percussion instruments, basses, guitars, amps, and other sound and recording equipment), and rooms for marching band uniforms, choir robes, and other necessary paraphernalia. Some music suites have piano labs, music libraries, and even small concert spaces in addition to a performing arts auditorium. School banners hang from ceilings and on walls, and posters of performing artists fill spaces as well. Schedules are posted on the bulletin board announcing rehearsals and festivals, and black-, green-, and whiteboards show rhythmic phrases, chordal progressions, and lineups of repertoire to be rehearsed. The standard media equipment is there, too, including CD, VCR, and DVD players, and various means of displaying material. And, as a distinguishing mark of secondary school music programs, there are music stands and chairs everywhere.

Some music classrooms are more conducive to learning than others. Well-lit, well-ventilated, well-organized spaces are more effective places in which to perform, listen, and move. Lights may be recessed within or hang from ceilings and may be necessary even in rooms lined with windows. They can be controlled for effect, such as darkening rooms to focus attention on screen presentations and listening lessons, or light-flicking by teachers in an attempt to settle down lively children. Room temperatures can be kept at moderate levels, and some rooms have built-in heating and air-conditioning capacities. The flow of fresh air from open windows can sweeten the atmosphere as well as awaken students to higher levels of concentration. Critical to many learners are physical spaces whose furniture, equipment, and other materials are organized and uncluttered. Colors can also have an impact on learning; muted colors on walls and ceilings can calm students, while neon-bright colors tend to have an energizing effect. Teachers make many of the decisions that enhance the learning environment and over the years can be influential in everything from the floor coverings and wall colors to the design of new and improved facilities.

✜ BREAK POINT 15.3 The "Feel" of a School

Look around you as you settle into an elementary music classroom or walk through a secondary school music complex. What does the music domain feel like? Why? Note the design of spaces that are more and less conducive to learning. Observe what teachers do to fill their spaces, to get around disadvantages (like ambient noise), to compensate for small spaces, low lighting, and minimal equipment. What would you want in a music classroom or rehearsal space? Talk with teachers about what they are doing to adapt and even appeal for improved places where music is taught and learned.

Music Teachers in Action

Regardless of where they work and under what conditions, the ace music teachers are effective because of who they are musically and humanly, and as pedagogically astute practitioners of their art. They have the power to persuade, to model, to inform, to facilitate the learning of their students, and to change their lives. This they do daily and over time, through the music that is made and heard in their classes, and through the quality of their interactions with their students. The values of teachers are embedded in their words and actions, and their students learn as a result of their fine-tuned, conscious behaviors. Every glance, nod, and wave of the hands conveys meaning, as do their words and the expressive tones and gestures that communicate them.

Walk into a classroom, and certain music teachers appear more effective than others. They are the ones who treat the music lesson-session as the precious little time it is, moving efficiently through the lesson or rehearsal to be able to achieve the goals they set for their students. They press hard but with humor to provide young people with the sequential learning events, the exercises, and the beautiful and sublime experiences of great music. A sixteen-bar melody for recorders and voices, a South African freedom song in four choral parts, a composition assignment for studio group, Berlioz' *Candide* for orchestra (or transcription for symphonic band), a Charlie Parker tune for jazz band—any of these and countless other experiences work well in the hands of teachers who are so well prepared that one action seems to flow to the next. Well-seasoned music teachers have managed not to bump along in unnatural chunks of lesson bits and rehearsal bytes, and their students percolate in a rhythm for learning that is neither too fast to frustrate them nor too slow to bore them to tears. These teachers know the music so they can concentrate on the pedagogy, and they know their pedagogical techniques so they can go deeply into the music. Further, they know both music and pedagogy so well that they can be playful and build rapport and positive working relationships with their students.

Teachers in action possess qualities that come with a strong and steady professional preparation, and these qualities are further strengthened through the on-the-job honing of them as they practice what they have learned through formal coursework. These traits are activated as teachers present the music itself to the students, as they offer them the skills and the knowledge it takes to become deeply musical. They are also in motion as teachers convey their feelings about the music, and as they elicit the feelings of their students. A wide assortment of qualities are operating as teachers bring an understanding of not only music, but of the people, principles, and practices of society that envelop the music.

Just what traits qualify teachers as effective? As the saying goes, "the devil is in the details." These details of key traits are described below: musicianship, pedagogical knowledge, rapport with students, communication style, delivery system, professionalism, and classroom management skills. Descriptions of individual traits are followed with questions in Break Points 15.4 to 15.10 to direct the eyes and ears of astute observers.

MUSICIANSHIP

Musicianship includes the skills of vocal and/or instrumental performance, conducting, sight-reading and aural skills, and arranging and improvisation abilities. Music teachers show musicianship on their primary instruments when they perform with good tone quality, intonation, and (in the case of singers, brass, and wind players) breath support. Their musicianship allows them to model correct posture and to utilize appropriate techniques of bowing, embouchure, tonguing, and finger and hand positions that produce the rich tone and technical qualities that are called for by the music. They perform with attention to the nuances of articulation, dynamics, and phrases. While they may be less technically proficient on other instruments, some of the most effective music teachers can nonetheless play a number of them with musical sensitivity. Further, most who play an instrument can also sing with accuracy, just as those who sing can play one or more instruments. The musicianship of teachers is at work whether they are modeling phrases or parts, or simply sharing a song or musical piece with their students, when they do so with accuracy, technique, and feeling.

As conductors, strong music teachers learn to utilize clear beat patterns and clear gestures for cues, phrasing, and expressive elements. They understand the importance of gaining and maintaining eye contact in their conducting, and they know the score, having spent time analyzing it, often singing and playing parts of the music individually or by realizing them at the piano. They can sight-read and sight-sing with ease, and detect errors with immediacy. When working with students with limited skills, they can adjust parts or rearrange them with satisfactory musical results. Good teachers need improvisation skills to demonstrate techniques, patterns, and phrases within musical styles or to help students become improvisers. As they work with different ensembles—jazz, West African and world drumming, guitar, and gospel—they can demonstrate solo expressions and lead students in the discovery of their own improvisatory ways. Music teachers with solid knowledge in music theory and history can use this to greatly enrich their teaching.

❖ BREAK POINT 15.4 The Musicianship of Music Teachers

As you visit the classrooms of music teachers, note the specific ways they demonstrate musicianship. How do they demonstrate their performance skills? Do they sing in instrumental classes, or play instruments in vocal classes? To what extent and effect? What conducting skills are effective? Do they show their skills as arrangers and improvisers? In what ways does their musical knowledge (of theory, history, and culture) help them? Reflect on the areas of your own musicianship that need to be strengthened for you to become the teacher that you want to be.

PEDAGOGICAL KNOWLEDGE

In the field of music, pedagogy refers to the practice of systematic instructional techniques, methods, and processes. A pedagogy may be named or unnamed, and collectively known or personally defined. An example of a "named pedagogy" is the one associated with composer and educator Zoltán Kodály and his Hungarian colleagues, including its sequential process, techniques, and even a standard repertoire of songs and choral works. "Kodály" is the pedagogy of choice of some elementary and secondary teachers, especially those with interests in the development of the singing voice and notational literacy. Like any pedagogy, it encompasses skill-building experiences, is attentive to diverse learning modes, and is sensitive to the developmental ages and stages of learners. An example of an "unnamed pedagogy" is the set of techniques employed by an instrumental teacher who has forged her own means for taking first-year string players from the entry point of understanding the fundamental playing position to the performance of two-octave melodies across the four strings; not Suzuki, nor Rolland, nor one of dozens of methods books, but rather her own experience has led her to establish a teaching-learning process that works for her students.

Teachers with a handle on pedagogy are able to shape the processes by which their students learn musical skills associated with singing, instrumental play, listening, creating, and responding to music through movement. They understand the techniques that are appropriate for students of particular developmental and experience levels, and know when and how to adapt and shape these techniques. They recognize that the instructional character of their lessons and rehearsals must above all have musical integrity and must be keyed to the skill level and interest of their students.

❖ BREAK POINT 15.5 Teachers in Action

Arrange to observe a teacher in action, and schedule some interview time. What are the pedagogical preferences of this teacher? Does his or her instructional style reflect a particular pedagogy, or is it an amalgam of multiple techniques and approaches that have fused into a workable system? Does the pedagogy succeed in achieving musical goals? How does it address the needs of diverse learners? Compare what you have observed to the teacher's response to these questions.

RAPPORT

Some music teachers are naturally adept at developing positive and supportive relationships with their students, while others find the building of rapport to be one of their professional challenges. It is not that they dislike children or adolescents but rather that they may not have yet learned to express warmth in the midst of their lessons, to allow their sense of humor to shine out, and to respond to the facial expressions, gestures, and comments of their students. Some may feel like "fish out of water" with young children, uncertain of what to say or how to say it, while others may appear awkward and shy with older students whose casual talk and body language may hold meanings they cannot interpret. Rapport builds from an understanding by the teacher of students, as well as student trust in their teacher. The quality of rapport can take time to fully develop.

Teachers with outgoing, other-directed personalities and high levels of sociability are at ease with their students, and this allows them to temper and balance the serious business of learning with playful repartee and light-hearted commentary. Some teachers are naturally quieter and less outgoing, and find it more demanding to bring a light-heartedness into serious study. Still, quiet teachers can be very successful, too, depending on their skills and knowledge of music and its pedagogy, and the human empathy and warmth that they instill in their teaching. Those who struggle in building rapport with their students can make progress simply by knowing their lessons so thoroughly that they can step back from the lesson goal long enough to pick up on student interests, responses, and needs. They can learn to relax in teaching-learning situations by being their positive selves: smiling when appropriate, showing enthusiasm in what they say and do, being willing to try new music and new approaches to it for the sake of their students. Teachers who achieve rapport with their students encourage their questions, comments, and full participation in class activity. They are inclusive of all students in the class, respecting them for their strengths, reinforcing them for their achievements, and giving time and attention to all who need it.

❖ BREAK POINT 15.6 Building Rapport

In your observations, look for signs of strong positive rapport in the relationships of teachers with students. What behaviors do teachers exhibit that indicate the achievement of rapport? How do they show enthusiasm and the acceptance of student feelings? What are the responses of their students? Consider what you have done to build relationships with friends; how different is it to develop friendly and respectful relationships with young students?

COMMUNICATION

Some of the most effective teachers talk less and make more time for students to perform, create, and listen to music. Still, when teachers do talk—and of course they must—they communicate effectively and meaningfully. Their voices are expressive, with inflections that include high and low tones spoken more loudly or more softly (sometimes even whispered), at faster and slower tempi—all of this to aid communication, underscore particular points, and maintain student interest. They are not monotone in their speech, which can come across to students as deadpan, distinterested, and monotonous. Teachers who communicate well understand that the engagement of their students depends on their expressive speech, the animation of their faces, and even the energy conveyed in the position and posture of their bodies.

Effective communication is in full operation in the classroom when teachers offer clear and understandable instructions, and use appropriate gestures with their hands to reinforce ideas. Teachers who are able to employ questioning as a learning technique (as opposed to a "telling technique") and who use age-appropriate language and images are communicating effectively. The proximity to their students helps them to convey their genuine interest in student learning, and so they move away from the front of the class or ensemble with some frequency—away from the podium, piano, desk, stool, and into the student group. Critical to their communication is the continuous eye contact they make with their students, so that there is a genuine link between them.

✥ BREAK POINT 15.7 Communicating with Clarity

Select a teacher whose classes you might visit at least once, to observe the communication skills she/he employs. Make notes of the following techniques: vocal inflection, use of gestures, questioning technique, frequently used verbal directives and comments, proximity of the teacher to the students, and eye contact. Over the course of a class, what were some of the most effective moments of verbal and nonverbal communication? Describe these moments, including as well the responses of students to these behaviors.

DELIVERY

The way the lesson or rehearsal proceeds has very much to do with the teacher's delivery style. There is a flow of musical activity, and of the give-and-take exchange between teachers and students, in classes where delivery is smooth. Teachers with a smooth delivery style are energetic and confident, come prepared with the necessary materials and equipment for their classes, know their subject and lesson aim and sequence well, and demonstrate a certain momentum that drives students to achieve clear-cut objectives. They also understand that learning does not emanate from them, and that they must facilitate learning through their advance planning and motivational cues. The most effective teachers know quickly when students are puzzled and then proceed through a logical instructional step-by-step sequence to clarify the issue. Transitions between songs and selections are quick, too, so that no time is wasted in making the most of every class. In short, delivery has everything to do with pace and flow of instruction.

Teachers with solid delivery systems understand that formal opening and closing procedures can frame and sum up their students' learning. Thus, they tend to begin and end their classes with music, and to announce class goals (at the beginning) and achievement (at the close). One thing may lead rapidly to the next as instruction begins. For example, an elementary music teacher might be playing piano (or violin, trumpet, or drum) as children enter the music classroom, stop to welcome the children to a class where they will study sixteenth-note patterns, and then sing a song that illustrates these patterns. A high school band teacher might be playing a recording of a piece the band is to study as students take their places in the rehearsal hall. As the bell rings for class to begin, students are ready with instruments in hand to begin warm-up exercises, followed by the teacher's quick announcements as to the content of the rehearsal ahead. Likewise, experienced teachers drive their students toward a successful musical close—for example, they may have students perform familiar music, which they will play well, followed by positive comments or a quick "what-did-we-learn?" dialogue. In these ways, the teacher's smooth delivery follows a clean (and musical) setup and a concise summing up of learning.

❖ BREAK POINT 15.8 A Teacher's Style

When you visit a class or rehearsal, be sure to check for the teacher's style and pace of delivery. Is the teacher able to move the students fluidly from one musical activity to another? Is the flow of events concise yet creative? How many clear-cut events are there within the period of your observation? What are the occasions when the teacher identifies errors, and what is the sequence by which students are led to greater skill development? How do they start and stop their classes? Record your observations, and compare them across several teachers.

PROFESSIONALISM

Teaching is a profession, and professional teachers look and act the part of individuals committed to the art and science of their work. Their professionalism shows in the way they dress, the language they use to communicate everything from instructional directions to reinforcement, their punctuality, their adherence to school rules, and their confidentiality. Music teachers do not need to dress in elaborate or expensive clothing to demonstrate their professionalism, but in fact, should dress simply, sensibly, and in ways that do not distract their students. They should wear comfortable clothes that are neither too *haute-couture* nor too casual, so that they can bend, lean, stoop, move furniture—and in the case of elementary school teachers, model movement of all sorts. Professionalism requires that teachers are well-groomed, neat, and clean.

Professional teachers use a vocabulary that is rich with musical terms and descriptive language; they avoid street talk, slang, and an overabundance of colloquialisms (which may not be understood by some of their students). Teachers are punctual in starting and ending classes, and prompt in meeting all scheduled appointments with parents, other teachers, and students. They know the regulations of the district and school for faculty and students, and they ensure that these are followed. When issues of a sensitive nature crop up, such as family troubles or the breakup of a romantic relationship, the professional teacher is discreet in not spreading information that does not concern others. Teachers continue their own education, seeking out new ideas in music and education that will benefit their students and the overall program. They join professional societies, read professional literature, and participate in professional meetings, workshops, and clinics to keep updated and continue their education as musicians and teachers.

At the head of the class in a professional manner.

❖ BREAK POINT 15.9 Professionalism on the Rise

The professional conduct of a teacher can be seen and heard in classrooms, with some teachers displaying greater professionalism than others. Keep a list of the professional dos and don'ts of music teachers whom you observe. Which behaviors are critical to all contexts, and which are dependent upon the particular school and system?

CLASSROOM MANAGEMENT

Classroom settings most conducive to learning are those whose teachers understand the importance of classroom (or behavior) management as a key technique. Effective music teachers shape the appropriate academic and social behaviors of their students by acknowledging them, just as they extinguish inappropriate behaviors by applying consequences. They initially ignore the rule-breaking behaviors of students and withdraw praise or rewards from them, or in other ways intervene so as to stop inappropriate activity from continuing or escalating. They give greatest focus to the positive and progressing behaviors of students who are attending to the tasks at hand and who are producing results that demonstrate their development of musical skills and understanding.

Because they are sensitive to individual student needs, teachers can recognize what stimuli may cause disruptive behaviors and thus work to prevent them.

A star system for good behavior and an example of class rules.

They know that verbal noise (constant talking, blurting out, laughing), object noise (tapping desks or stands, slamming books), motor "noise" (arm-waving, foot-tapping), and aggressive behaviors (pinching, hitting, throwing things) tend to happen when students are idle, unmotivated, and disengaged. Student seating next to friends (or foes) is a potential factor in classroom disruption, and thus effective teachers work to mix and match students in chairs, on tiers, and in collaborative groups. They may reinforce and reward students who stay on task, attend to the class and individual activities, and show positive social behaviors befitting good citizenship. These rewards may be in the form of nods, smiles, praise, "star systems" that offer privileges for students who behave appropriately. Still, proactive models are advisable, heading off inappropriate behavior before it happens. They discreetly pull aside students who are struggling and work with them on agreements, contracts, and award systems to shape their behaviors. When necessary, caring teachers invite parents, teachers, and counselors to work together with them so that students may learn more positive and appropriate behaviors that serve them in immediate ways and in the long term.

❖ BREAK POINT 15.10 Motivating and Managing Student Behavior

In your observations of a single teacher's work across several classes, consider the system of classroom management. How is the teacher working with students who struggle to focus, or who willfully go against the grain of the class activity? What system of checks and balances does the teacher employ to reinforce and reward good behavior? How are inappropriate behaviors dealt with? Describe an instance of an appropriate and an inappropriate student behavior and the teacher's response to it.

Music Teachers on Schedule

What do music teachers do all day? They're in early and out late, and active from the moment they step in the door. Depending on the distance from their home to the school, they may be up at dawn and going strong in musical ventures until well after dark. Full-time music teachers in elementary schools may seem to keep the sanest of schedules (when compared to their secondary school colleagues), due to their later start-times and reasonable dismissals. Theirs is often an 8 to 4 work day, starting with thirty minutes to an hour of preparation for a stream of what are typically thirty- to forty-five-minute classes—as many as ten or twelve classes per day. They see children as young as five years and as old as twelve, depending on the school and its age and grade stipulations. Elementary music teachers come up for air about noon, usually for a quick lunch, and then run on through a series of further classes until the dismissal bell rings. There are after-school meetings and lesson planning to follow classes, and in some settings there are after-school lessons and rehearsals. All day long, elementary music teachers are singing, dancing, playing instruments, and speaking to children in approving and disapproving tones. They are modeling appropriate performance and listening behaviors, smiling or showing facial expressions of serious intent and interest, and dispensing reinforcement for jobs well done. They are actively involved in performing on pianos, xylophones, guitars, recorders, djembes, claves, cowbells, didjeridoos, and boomwhackers. Elementary music teachers are nonstop in their interactions with very young children on up to the edge of adolescence.

Consider the lives of high school music teachers. Whether the charge and focus of teaching is band, choir, orchestra, mariachi, steel drum band, AP music, composition studio, or more, their days—and often evenings and weekends—are very full. They start at least a full hour earlier than most elementary music teachers, and while school is technically dismissed an hour earlier, few high school music teachers head out of their complexes before dinnertime. Due to after-school marching band practice, sectional sessions, music theater rehearsals, private lessons, parent booster meetings, and fund-raising projects, high school music teachers may head home on some days closer to bedtime than to dinnertime. Weekends are full, too, during times of festivals, field trips, and all-state performances. On a daily basis, a standard six periods of fifty-five-minute classes can run back-to-back with warm-ups and tunings, and rehearsals of familiar and not-so-familiar music, all wrapped up with the stops and starts to help out singers and players on individual parts or collective phrases that have not yet been fully learned. High school music teachers are on and off their podium, moving center-stage from the conductor's score to the stands of individual students, from the piano to the tiers, and from blackboard to the CD player. They are variously singers, instrumentalists, conductors, and arrangers (sometimes on the spot, as difficult sections are substituted or modified). High school music teachers are physically involved at a pace that is unmatched by most of their other colleagues.

Figure 15.2 presents sample schedules of real-life music teachers in elementary school and high school instrumental settings. Bridget's schedule resembles that of many elementary music teachers, teaching back-to-back classes from the morning bell to the time of dismissal, followed by activity in after-school meetings and rehearsals. Jim, a high school instrumental music teacher, has six periods of teaching divided into three bands, a jazz band, one orchestra, and a composition class. His after-school involvement includes marching band and

Bridget's Schedule (Elementary School Music)*

6:15 AM	Rise and shine
	Run, shower, dress, breakfast
7:45 AM	On the road to school
8:00 AM	Arrival at school
8:05 AM	Check-in with classroom teachers re student/class needs
8:30 AM	(T/Th: grade 5–6 choir; classroom set-up)
9:00 AM	Grade 1, Mrs. Stankowicz (mi-re-do singing games)
9:30 AM	Grade 4, Mrs. Folsom (recorders, two-part song)
10:00 AM	Grade 2, Mrs. Durland (pentatonic singing games)
10:30 AM	Break
10:45 AM	Grade 2, Ms. Aziz (pentatonic singing games)
11:15 AM	Grade 5, Mr. Kemperly (keyboard composition)
11:45 AM	Grade 4, Ms. Green (recorders, two-part song)
12:15 AM	Lunch (W/F: weekly grade 3–4 choir)
12:45 AM	Grade 6, Mr. Monson (Ghana music unit)
1:15 PM	Grade 6, Ms. Can (Ghana music unit)
1:45 PM	Grade 3, Mrs. Bullock (Orff accompaniments)
2:15 PM	Break
2:30 PM	Kindergartens, Ms. Olsen and Ms. Thompson (group-sing)
3:00 PM	Dismissal (T/Th: bus duty)
3:30 PM	Faculty meetings, meetings with parents (W: bell choir)
4:00 PM	Classroom set-up; planning
4:30 PM	On the road again
	Chores
5:00 PM	Dinner
7:00 PM	M: Community chorus rehearsal
	Th: Contra-dancing
9:00 PM	Wind down; include lesson-planning
10:30 PM	Lights out

* Since students are seen twice weekly, the schedule varies

Figure 15.2 • **Sample schedules of real-life music teachers** *(continued)*

Jim's Schedule (High School Instrumental Music)

5:45 AM	Rise and shine
	Exercise, shower, dress, eat
6:30 AM	On the road to school
6:45 AM	Arrival at school
7:00 AM	T/W/Th: "Zero-period" jazz lab (grade 9–10)
7:45 AM	Period 1: Cadet band (grade 9)
8:40 AM	Period 2: Composition studio
9:35 AM	Period 3: Symphonic band (premiere, grades 10–12)
10:30 AM	Period 4: Symphony (all grades)
11:25 AM	Lunch
12:20 PM	Period 5: Concert band (grades 10–12)
1:15 PM	Period 6: Jazz band (grades 10–12)
2:10 PM	Dismissal
2:30 PM	M/W: Marching band practice (autumn)
	Marching band at football game (autumn, afternoon–evening)
	T/W/Th: After-school group/sectional rehearsals (winter/spring)
5:00 PM	On the road again
	Chores
5:30 PM	Dinner
7:00 PM	M (alternate): Band boosters meetings
	Th: Brass group rehearsal
9:00 PM	Wind down; include score preparation and arranging
10:30 PM	Lights out

Figure 15.2 *(continued)*

sectional rehearsals, band booster meetings, and even score study and arrangements to prepare for students in his various ensembles. Long days lead into active evenings, as the dedication of rock-solid music teachers continues through the academic year. It is no wonder that teachers emerge from the school year ready for summer recreation, refreshment, and renewal!

There are many variations on these schedules, and a variety of schedules for choral teachers and teachers in middle school music programs. Moreover, there are many "cross-over teachers" who teach a variety of music classes, such as the high school all-music teacher responsible for band, choir, orchestra, and all the rest of the music, or the middle school music teacher who runs three choirs, a drumming ensemble, and two guitar classes. There are also "itinerant teachers" whose assignment to one school will be supplemented with a day or more at another school, or who are expected to travel daily to teach all music for all grades within a feeder system of elementary, middle, and high schools. At the elementary level, music teachers may be endorsed to teach reading or art as well as music. These are not always ideal situations, particularly when they stretch the resources and energies of a single teacher. With high energy and hard work, however, many teachers find that administrators who hire them for the hodge-podge of classes are eventually convinced that, due to the excitement and continued growth of interest by students in music, an additional music teacher is warranted. This then leaves the music teacher with the flexibility to focus and anchor her course schedule.

Lasting Impressions

Out in the field, music teachers are interacting with students of every size, shape, and hue. They themselves differ from one another in training and specialized interests, and by the perceived mission of music within the curriculum and community of schools in which they work. Yet there are the lasting impressions of effective music teachers that transcend place and the particulars of training—prime characteristics that are observable, even measurable, and able to be adapted into the strategies of those teachers-in-training who are looking to and listening for best practices. The memorable music teachers are without doubt musical, pedagogically astute, and communicators of the first order who have developed the rhythm and flow of facilitating their students' learning. They have learned how to convey ideas, motivate others to embrace them, and reinforce students for work that is well done. For those musicians who will one day enter the teaching profession, continued visits into the climate and culture of school offer opportunities to understand what works and why.

REFERENCES AND RESOURCES

Cruickshank, D. R., D. B. Jenkins, and K. Metcalf. (2004). *The Act of Teaching.* New York: McGraw-Hill. A research-based text intended to guide students in developing the confidence and competence to succeed in the classroom, with recommendations for planning and providing instruction, assessment, and managing and motivating students of diverse learning styles.

Goodlad, J. (1984). *A Place Called School.* New York: McGraw-Hill. An account of the largest on-scene study of schools in the United States; interviews with teachers, students, administrators, and parents led to an analysis of effective education and schooling.

Madsen, C. K., and C. Yarbrough. (1985). *Competency-Based Music Education.* Raleigh, NC: Contemporary Publishing. The classic text on field experiences in music education, offering systematic means of observation and interviews with experienced music teachers. Ideas for the design and management of teaching are presented, along with forms for performance ratings and conducting critiques.

chapter 16

A Teacher's Life in Music

Performance major: It's too bad we don't see you at all the ensemble rehearsals anymore, now that you're a music education major.

Music education major: I still play in the orchestra, plus I'm doing one of the jazz combos. But yeah, I had to drop chamber winds to make room for twice-weekly assignments in the schools.

Performance major: All that running around off campus is going to cut into your performance chops—to say nothing of your social life.

Music education major: I haven't noticed any serious deterioration, actually. In fact, these school visits have their perks.

Performance major: Perks?

Music education major: Well, yeah. I'm actually making music at the middle school: warm-ups in the choir class, coaching a brass ensemble before school, conducting the orchestra—one piece, but it's something. And I'm often sitting in with the students, playing my trumpet (or playing trombone, or French horn, or whatever else they need). All of this early on Tuesday and Thursday mornings, probably before you're even awake.

Performance major: But is this really what you want to do: Teach all day long?

Music education major: It *is* what I really want to do. And teaching does not exclude performance. By the way, what's your long-term plan?

Performance major: Grad school, solo and studio work, teaching privately.

Music education major: Me, too, all of the above. Getting a school job is top of my list for now, but these other things should fill out the rest of my life.

Between Two Worlds

Music majors come from a good many years of accomplishment as performing musicians. They were once the high school students holed up in their bedrooms, shifting between homework and practice, gearing up for public performances in solo and ensemble contests, all-state festivals, community youth ensembles, and in every school music function they could manage. They typically enter universities as music majors on the basis of their audition, which may rest exclusively on their competence on their primary instrument (including voice). It is that drive to make music—lots of it, consistently, and of the highest quality—that is most compelling to those who choose music as their major area of study. They could have studied history, engineering, French, business, or elementary education, but they are drawn instead to music—not as a casual "interest" but as a full-fledged, around-the-clock endeavor. The point of majoring in music, they understand, is to continue to refine their musical craft, and so they seek out and strive for the attainment of the highest level of performance skills they can muster.

For those who major in music education, there is a dual purpose in their course of study: to maximize their performance abilities while developing their teaching skills. They dance between the two worlds of music and education. They balance performance with pedagogy and work toward a broader and more comprehensive musicianship that encompasses all that a soloist requires—and more: sight-reading, sight-singing, error detection, conducting, composing, improvising, arranging, listening/analysis, and a firm grasp of music history and culture. They learn the skills required of all teachers, of all subjects, at all levels, including clear communication skills, motivational and reinforcement strategies, assessment procedures, and sensitivities and techniques for working with young people of all abilities and experiences. They also learn the pedagogical techniques and instructional sequences to employ with students of music, which are particular to the development of the skills and knowledge of children and adolescents.

Because of the dual track in preparation for professional positions as musicians and teachers, the music education program of studies can be time intensive. Students of music education are involved in daily practice on their primary instrument, even as they are also learning the fundamental techniques of other instruments they may one day need to demonstrate and even teach. The extent of their performance in their university ensembles, while genuinely rewarding, can consume considerable chunks of the days, evenings, and weekends. Keyboard harmony is another critical need, and prospective music teachers—from singers to saxophonists—spend many hours at the piano developing skills for harmonizing songs, transposing parts, reducing scores, and accompanying solo and ensemble pieces. They focus their attention on honing their conducting skills, and they eventually work to convert their earlier ear-training into the error-detection skills they will need for classroom lessons and ensemble rehearsals. Improvisation, composition, and arranging may be optional study in some music programs, but for those who will teach, they are often requisite areas of study. Add to these musical matters the supervised practice of the art and science of teaching, and those who pursue training in the music education major are operating at full-tilt throughout the course that leads to their professional certification.

❖ BREAK POINT 16.1 The Comprehensive Musician

Your program of music education studies is designed to support your continuing musical development. Consider the courses and experiences that are close to and not so close to your primary musical interests. Discuss how aural skills, piano proficiency, creative composition, improvisation, and arranging are useful to the craft of music teaching, offering imagined scenarios or actual observed cases of their implementation.

The worlds of music and teaching converge in the lives of music teachers, and music education majors catch glimpses of what lies ahead for them by nature of the areas of emphasis offered to them in their certification studies. Even as they continue to reap the benefits of dedicated attention to their performance competence as soloists and ensemble members, music teachers are also increasingly thoughtful as to how best to bring young people into experiences with their beloved art of musical expression and response. They have toeholds, and then footholds, in performance and education, and with every course and field experience, music education majors come closer to understanding the full life they will live as professional musicians and teachers.

Points of Decision Making

The call to a professional life in music education is heard at various points: in the homes and neighborhoods where, as children, teachers grew up with music; in secondary schools where their own music teachers have served as close, personal role models; on the fast and focused track that some are pursuing in hopes of a performance career; and sometimes even post-college when, in the midst of a performance and private-teaching career, the life of a school music teacher begins to beckon. Heeding the call is both a personal and a social decision that rests on the individual's understanding of self and society. Such an understanding often entails recognizing those music teachers whose work is admirable and who exude confidence in and comfort with their professional lot in life.

Those who pursue a teacher's life in music are often drawn to the altruistic nature of music education work that "gives back" to a society that nurtured them. As is the case of positions in the medical profession, the call to teaching may well be a call to blend particular skill and knowledge sets with the essence of helping others. While the decision-making point varies from one person to the next, it is this decision that defines them for the identity they have constructed—or are willing to construct—for themselves. When music has struck them so deeply that they cannot imagine life without daily musical interplay, music majors know that they have arrived at a decision to teach music. When they have been recognized by music experts and novices for the extent of their musical competence, and when they find themselves drawn to ways of sharing it—modeling music making, guiding and shaping the musical skills of others, and facilitating creative and analytical-listening opportunities for a wide variety of musical expressions—music majors are well on their way to the professional specialization of music education.

MUSIC IN CHILDHOOD

Some music teachers remember "playing teacher" as children even as they were growing in their musical experiences, and as they sang, learned an instrument, and created their own expressions. They may have found themselves at ease in teaching their little friends and siblings how to play "Twinkle" on their violins, or a sequence of chords they had just learned in a piano lesson, or a rendition of "Hot Cross Buns" they had tooted on their recorders in music class at school. They may have grown up in musical families, where dinner table discussion would include comments on the style and gestures of an orchestral conductor or a choral conductor. Perhaps they were raised in families of teachers (of music or another subject), where the natural sense was that what was learned could also be shared with others: it could be taught. They may have known a mother or father, a grandparent, an aunt or an uncle, an older sibling or cousin who taught music in one way or another, so that the idea of making a career of music education was never so very far from their reality. In one way or another, music teachers with these experiences were close to music and teaching in their childhood years and may have taken for granted the fact they might make music and take it to others as well.

MUSIC IN ADOLESCENCE

The plausibility of teaching music may have arisen in secondary school for some. Perhaps their musical achievement was not so evident until their adolescence, when their participation in school music activities became their very identity. It was then that they might have become enamored of music, honing their skills, performing music they could read or learn by ear, developing their identity as musicians, shaping their self-image as singers and players. Still, the idea of teaching was not a long-developing plan, for they might have been drawn to a musical career only in the exhuberance of a senior-level ensemble performance or through the positive reinforcement of a strong social network the ensemble may have offered them. The prospect of teaching music may have bubbled up in an instant (at the musical peak of a high school performance) or may have emerged gradually over several years under the influence of a music teacher with the power to change lives. The thought of becoming a music teacher may have taken on a life of its own as a result of the inspiring way that expert teacher could play or sing; help with tone, technique, and expression; and understand students for who they were and might want to be. The decision to pursue a music degree, and to specialize in music education, is for some traceable to a successful musical ensemble and a first-rate music teacher who served as an important role model.

PERFORMER-TEACHER CROSSROADS

Yet another route taken by some music teachers into the profession began with their experience in preparation for, and sometimes in the midst of, a performance career. From their first musical discoveries onward, they may imagine life as performers with a lively calendar of concerts and club dates, singing and playing for social settings and religious functions, and performing for the pleasure of their listening audiences. They might dream of making a living in musical performance, and a few may fare remarkably well on stage and in transit from one engagement to the next. On arriving at college, these performance-prone musicians may build a life that is almost exclusively applied study, trimmed with academic courses (as required). They may be curious about a teaching career while still a performance major, and may enroll in a pedagogy or music education course. They may even graduate with performance degrees in hand and go on to paid positions in symphony and chamber ensembles, or as conductors of community groups only to return years later for the training that led to teaching. For a few, teaching may develop as a fall-back position when performance careers fizzle or never really take off. Yet for the majority on this route, the turn toward teaching is more a revelation of the value of passing on the knowledge and skills they had themselves developed.

❖ BREAK POINT 16.2 Routes to Life as a Musician-Teacher

Survey some selected teachers for the routes they followed into the music education profession. Seek out information on their family music experiences, their experiences as young musicians in training when they were children and in their secondary school years, and their activity as performing musicians in and beyond college. Share this information with colleagues, and determine whether there are patterns of the professional call.

There is no single way forward in the making of a music teacher, and the individual circumstances of the decision to teach vary from one person to the next. The call does not encompass voices from the unseen, or some shining star in the sky. The decision to teach music is rather a sense that music education is the right and logical choice, based on a combination of experience, observation, discussion, and reflection. The route to music education is circuitous rather than a single straight shot, and yet home and family experiences, positive school music experiences, model music teachers, and personal curiosity and interest to give and facilitate music in others are likely enticements into the profession. Those who follow into a career in music education are thoroughly musical and propelled by a passion to bring others into the realm of musical expression.

The Journey Ahead

With a commitment to music and teaching comes a succession of preparatory steps that lead students of music education to their professional teaching posts. Music education majors become increasingly involved in the essence of their work ahead through coursework, class papers and projects, field experiences, observational reports, and the internship itself. Pedagogical theories are introduced and made meaningful through their practical application to real and simulated classroom situations, and curricular issues from cultural diversity to technology are clarified through a study of schools in which they are operating.

Like musical training, teacher education entails instruction, practice, performance, and critical reflection. Teaching strategies are described and modeled in courses and in the field, and there are expectations that teachers in training will imitate the models. Techniques and methods are typically practiced by music education majors in private, in front of mirrors, for video cameras that allow for follow-up viewing and analysis, and in simulated class settings with peers as students. They are "performed" in classrooms of "real students" when thoughtfully planned lessons are delivered for children and youth in school music classes and ensembles. Critiques follow, including the important process of self-reflection and the evaluative comments that come from university professors of music teacher education, peers and colleagues in the program, the supervising and mentor teachers in the schools, and young students themselves by way of their responses to the teaching they are experiencing. In a sequential unfolding of increasingly real situations, peer-teaching gives way to assist-teaching in which teacher education students assist or even co-teach with the certified teacher, to solo-teaching when teachers in training are charged with the responsibility of wholly developing and presenting lessons. The teacher's role in the instructional process is best understood through this array of experience and study.

METHODS COURSES

Methods courses are tailored to the particular age and grade levels and school contexts in which music learning occurs. Depending on the regional requirements for music teacher certification as well as the philosophy of the music education faculty, methods courses may encompass all areas of music instruction (choral, instrumental, "general music," or classroom music) or selected specializations, and one or more grade levels (elementary, middle, and high schools). There may be several methods courses for each area, too, as in the case of university programs that offer instrumental music methods courses for all levels (elementary, middle, and high school), or required courses in Orff, Kodály, Dalcroze Eurhythmics, and even classroom instruments. Age-appropriate rehearsal strategies and instructional sequences are features of these courses, and material—the music repertoire—hangs in a delicate balance with the components of techniques and method.

The study of methods assumes strong musical skills, so that teaching behaviors can be layered over comprehensive musicianship. Students are encouraged to think deeply about instructional goals and objectives and to gauge the relationship of teaching strategies to student responses. Lesson plans and class activities help prospective teachers develop fundamental skills in sequencing a stepwise progression of events, and bring into focus essential behaviors of eye contact, vocal projection, meaningful gestures, and verbal and nonverbal feedback to student responses. It is not unusual for students in methods courses to teach a rote song, lead a warm-up exercise with peers vocally or on secondary instruments, or run a group through a section of an SATB choral score or an excerpt from a band or orchestral score. These courses are introductory to the complexities of music teaching, setting frameworks for further discovery in the field experiences that are integrated within the program.

Alongside the straight-ahead methods courses are those that build understanding and skills in computer and audio technology, special populations of exceptional childhood, diversity of children and youth of various ethnic-cultural communities, "reading in the subject area" (a regulation in some states that teachers in all subjects require students to do a certain amount of reading), and social issues, including alchohol, drug, and sex abuse. Students of music education frequently join hands with all education majors in these courses within the department, school, or college of education, as well as in those courses that feature child and adolescent development, instructional and learning theory, and historical and philosophical foundations of schools and society. These courses are less methodological in approach than the "instrumental music methods" or "general music methods" courses, but are key to coming to terms with the meta-picture of education and schooling of which music is a part.

THE INTERNSHIP

The student teaching internship or practicum is for many music teachers the single most powerful component of their preparation as teachers. The regional government as well as the university program may determine the length of the internship and whether one or more schools will serve as sites for the practice teaching of individual students. The nature of the state or provincial endorsements—whether they are specific to choral, general, or instrumental music, or intended for "all music" at "all levels" (K–12, rather than elementary or secondary only)—may also determine the configuration of the student teaching experience, affecting the particular schools to which students are assigned.

Following coursework and the more passive nature of field experiences, the internship is intended as a bridge between university studies and the professional life of a teacher. It is a stage for continued exploration, risk-taking, and a thoroughgoing immersion in the on-the-job learning of music education in the schools. Successful internships enable student teachers to think critically, practice effectively, and offer genuine professional support for every student whom they encounter in their classes. Under the supervision of on-site mentor teachers, who cooperate and communicate with the university student teacher supervisor, student teachers learn models of effective music teaching in process as well as professional resources and networks to tap into for use as they take on their own classes.

A typical student teaching internship begins with observation in order to learn student names, class schedules, music, texts, and manuals, and the mentor teacher's philosophy and instructional methods. Interns may begin by assisting with classroom routines (taking attendance, tuning instruments, setting up instructional media, offering suggestions for performance posture and fingering positions). This quickly graduates to work with small groups and teaching small components of classes, including warm-ups. Early on, student teachers are planning lessons and preparing scores with the cooperating teacher, and then independently designing instruction based on the teacher's curricular goals, with submission of detailed plans for review prior to teaching. Within the opening weeks of the internship, students are assuming responsibility for planning and implementing one or two class periods per day. Expectations for class periods and responsibilities increase, so that by midway through the internship, student teachers are assuming full responsibility for all instruction, routines, and classroom management. Meetings with the mentor teacher are constant, so that regular discussions of planned and actual instruction can occur, including assessment of teaching strategies and techniques of classroom management. Meanwhile, the university student teacher supervisor schedules periodic observations, interacts with student interns and mentor teachers, and may in fact hold on-campus seminars and appointments. Closure comes in the final week of the internship, as student teachers gradually relinquish their responsibilities to the mentor teacher, meet for final conferences with their mentor and supervising teachers, and prepare professional portfolios for positions they hope to land.

The internship is essential for discovering "the teacher within," and for orienting oneself to the manner in which all that is natural or has been entrained can be called to use in an instant. Practice teaching solidifies their performance, musicianship, and conducting skills, and their communication and delivery skills, providing a professional awakening in the process of becoming a music teacher. The internship allows them to use a certain number of strategies—even though the number initially may be small—and see these lead to the overall success of a lesson. They thus develop the confidence that all may be very well in their roles as musicians and teachers, particularly over time and with continued practice.

With each lesson plan written, the student teacher becomes more aware of subject matter that is worthy of teaching, and of the broad aims and individual steps and strategies required to develop knowledge and skills in young students. With each lesson delivered, there are opportunities for the student teacher to consider the needs and interests of children and youth in their classes, and to adapt and adjust the delivery of the material so that it can be learned by all students. They may have taught musical segments or partial lessons in their methods classes, but in their internships student teachers are delivering full thirty- and fifty-five-minute lessons in multiple back-to-back sessions across the day. They learn how lessons connect to become units of study as ideas are introduced, practiced, and reviewed over many days so that the skills and repertoire of young students grow as their concepts and values are shaped. In a span of weeks, or one or more academic terms, the music education major is transformed through the internship from student to the beginning professional teacher.

❖ BREAK POINT 16.3 Discovering the "Teacher Within"

How does the "teacher within" emerge? Make time to talk with a student teacher intern about the professional and academic expectations of an internship: the daily work in preparation of scores and lessons, the importance of looking and listening to the mentor teacher for models, the careful weaving of university course material and method with the mentor's manner, and the manner in which rapport may build with students as a result of rock-solid teaching and lessons/sessions with musical integrity. Each internship is different from the next and is dependent on the individuals involved: student teacher, mentor teacher, students, and district policy makers. Still, by the close of the term, students begin to feel more like teachers than at the start of the experience. Discuss when and how this occurs.

THE FIVE-YEAR PLAN

A successful internship is the springboard to the first music teaching position. Left to their own devices, operating independently and out from under the mantle of protection afforded them by the university and the "real" teachers who supervised their internships, first-year teachers fashion programs that honor the tradition and vision of the school, district, and community while also reflecting their own training and experience. The teaching certificate, along with the degree certifying that a course in music teacher education has been successfully completed, is a learner's permit that paves the way for applying principles that were earlier introduced, modeled, practiced, and critiqued in the music education program. Day by day, the musical and teaching skills of music teachers are further refined.

As the years run on, some teachers achieve mastery of the art and science of teaching music. They professionalize, learning from their daily experiences, observing and talking with experienced teachers, attending clinics, workshops, master classes, and conferences. They gradually take on the qualities of master music teachers, committing themselves to their musical and teaching crafts, and to their students' learning. They strive for a rapid pace of instructional give-and-take between themselves and their students, and yet they move their students along in the small and discrete steps it takes to acquire knowledge and skills. They provide ample time for their students to learn, and they persevere in applying a variety of ways to ensure that learning occurs. They model skills and concepts and provide specific feedback to their students. They are generally positive in demeanor, enthusiastic, and genuinely interested in their students. They join professional societies of music education as outlets to learn more and to share what they know with those less experienced than themselves.

In the corporate world, where CEOs and boards of directors create five-year (and ten-year) plans, long-term goals and the means for achieving them are laid out in advance and periodic checkpoints are set up along the way. A five-year plan for successful teachers may include the introduction of a new pedagogical method and sequence; broad programmatic changes through the addition, deletion, or change of courses; the acquisition of new or higher-quality instruments and equipment; and personal goals that include the teacher's own retraining and further refinement of professional skills. Teachers may seek specialized training with a successful conductor or learn the techniques and sequence of Orff-Schulwerk in a graduating series of "levels courses." They may study a reed instrument if they have not had sufficient training on clarinet, saxophone, oboe, or bassoon, or learn more about the changing voices of middle school boys and girls through specially arranged observations of a successful middle school choir director. Because

The "object" of a musician-teacher: the development of independent musicianship.

they may have focused on the Western art music styles of concert band, choir, and orchestra, they may need to develop skills and repertoire in other musical cultures so they can develop a samba band, a world vocal ensemble, or a Latin-based jazz ensemble. They may appeal to administrators and parents to begin fund-raising and grant-writing to purchase new instruments, uniforms, and a piano (if these are not in the music budget), and to initiate or continue a tradition of touring student performance groups.

Occasionally, the question of a five-year plan emerges in an interview for a teaching position. With questions of philosophy ("How do you justify music within a curriculum dedicated to basic skills?"), repertoire ("What music would you program for a spring PTA meeting?" "What pieces would you want your most advanced ensemble to be able to perform well?"), and behavior management ("What classroom rules would you present?" "How would you enforce these rules?") candidates may be asked: "What would your ideal music program look like five years from now?" and "What professionally do you wish to have happen for yourself in five years?" It is important to do the homework on the school and district in advance of the interview to know the school program in which one might be working. As a result, it is then possible to determine the long-standing music curricular traditions that appeal to the community, and to speak to facets that can be maintained, strengthened, reconfigured, or newly developed to fit the needs and interests of students. The most intriguing projections for the future are those that give good weight to continuing the past successes of the program while also offering an idea or two for the design and delivery of innovative instruction. An impressive response to the question of the long-term plan, then, includes the balance of *what is* with *what could be*. Those who respond with realistic goals for the school music program, while also considering their own continuing education and training (including prospects for study in a graduate program relevant to music and education), are on the pathway to success.

Parting Shot

An orientation to a professional practice is meant to open doors to the knowledge base in order to allow entry into the field. A general sense of the territory is possible in an orientation, and key principles of the practice can be revealed, given reflection, questioned, and even retained for future reference. Still, the details must necessarily come later, as music majors move into the thick of music education in theory and practice. Only then will the complete puzzle picture of music education be understood, as the pieces of continued experience and study of music and teaching fit together to make the whole. The varied themes and schemes for teaching music to children and youth are not just another chapter in the evolution of a musician-teacher; they are in fact another book, multiple books, and certainly information that can be had in the additional courses found in the education of music teachers. Nonetheless, the scene is set, and many of the items and issues, and the philosophy and practice, of teaching and learning music are introduced and clarified.

A musician's life in the teaching profession is a rewarding one, particularly when the teaching musician remains thoroughly involved in music. There is always the danger that the music teacher can fall into the black hole of dull and dry pedanticism, and become swallowed by the *curricular-ese*, that string of curricular standards, goals and objectives, and assessments, and by the administrative work of lesson plans, curricular reports, communiqués, and other paperwork. Such is the nature of holding a responsible position in the public or private sector, where teachers are held accountable for their work and there are procedures in place and paperwork to be done. Yet there is no need to plod woodenly through these professional tasks, not when there is the music ahead to be made by children and youth, awaiting the teacher's able hand in guiding it. It is this presence of music in the lives of teachers that serves to revitalize them and remind them every day of reasons they chose the professional pathway of music education.

The road taken to the career of a professional music teacher winds this way and that, from music to pedagogy, with challenging twists and turns all along the way. This pathway ultimately leads to a life of wrapping oneself into the deep joy of making music even while drawing others into that expressive process. As one of life's noble callings, music teaching requires that special blend of musical and personal qualities that allow select individuals to give music to others even as they gain from the giving. "Musicians who can, teach," and in this way they may more fully realize their human potential.

REFERENCES AND RESOURCES

Bruner, J. S. (1996). *The Culture of Education*. Cambridge, MA: Harvard University Press. This classic work by the notable Harvard scholar of educational psychology is in fact nine stimulating essays on the subject of how individuals make sense of the world and engage in the values and symbols of the culture at large.

Evans, A. (1994). *The Secrets of Musical Confidence*. London: Thorsons. A handbook for musicians that discusses ways of maximizing performance potential, "the zone" of peak performance, creativity, and performance anxiety.

Raessler, K. R. (2001). *Aspiring to Excel*. Chicago: GIA Publications. A reflective commentary on the quest for excellence by music teachers in elementary and secondary choral and instrumental school settings, with considerations of curriculum development, use of technology and the media, and relationship-building among students, teaching colleagues, administrators, and the public.

Credits

Chapter-opening icon: © Martin Barraud/Getty Images.

Chapter 1
p. 3 (clockwise from top left): Photograph by Sean Ichiro Manes. Used with permission; Jerry Gay; Photograph by Sean Ichiro Manes. Used with permission; Jerry Gay; Jerry Gay; Photograph by Sean Ichiro Manes. Used with permission.
p. 10 (clockwise from top left): Photograph by Sean Ichiro Manes. Used with permission; Jerry Gay; Jerry Gay.

Chapter 2
p. 18: Photo by Patricia Shehan Campbell. **p. 26:** Jerry Gay. **p. 27:** Jerry Gay.
p. 32: Photograph by Sean Ichiro Manes. Used with permission.
p. 33: © Westend61/Alamy.

Chapter 3
p. 44: Based on an illustration from the book *Lessons from the World* by Patricia Shehan Campbell (Macmillan, 1991). Drawing revised by La Neu. **p. 45:** Based on an illustration from the book *Lessons From the World* by Patricia Shehan Campbell (Macmillan, 1991). Milan, Bibliotecca Ambrosiana, MS D.75.INF. Drawing revised by La Neu. **p. 47:** Reproduced from the book *Lessons from the World* by Patricia Shehan Campbell (Macmillan, 1991). **p. 49:** Based on an illustration from *Music Educators Journal*, March 2003, p. 27. © Copyright by MENC: The National Association for Music Education. Used with permission. Drawing revised by La Neu. **p. 51:** Jerry Gay.
p. 53: Jerry Gay. **p. 55:** Photograph by Sean Ichiro Manes. Used with permission.

Chapter 4
p. 61: Jerry Gay. **p. 72:** Jerry Gay. **p. 81:** Photograph by Sean Ichiro Manes. Used with permission.

Chapter 5
p. 91: Photograph by Sean Ichiro Manes. Used with permission. **p. 101:** © Martin Poole/The Image Bank/Getty Images.

Chapter 6
p. 109: Illustration by La Neu. **p. 110:** © age fotostock/Superstock. **p. 120:** © Meeke/zefa/Corbis. **p. 121:** Illustration by La Neu.

Chapter 7
p. 126: © Michael Newman/PhotoEdit, Inc. **p. 132:** Photograph by Sean Ichiro Manes. Used with permission. **p. 134:** Illustration by La Neu. **p. 135:** Photograph by Sean Ichiro Manes. Used with permission. **p. 141:** © Charlotte Nation/Getty Images.

Chapter 8
p. 147: Photo by Ailisa Newhall. **p. 150:** Photo by Ailisa Newhall. **p. 156:** © Odile Noel/Lebrecht Music and Arts Photo Library/Alamy.

Chapter 9
p. 172 (from left): Photo by Claire Waistell; Photo by Steven J. Morrison. **p. 177** (from top): TigerSwingBand.org; Photo by Della Martin. **p. 179:** Photo by Steven J. Morrison.

Chapter 10
p. 189: Jerry Gay. **p. 193:** Jerry Gay. **p. 196:** Photograph by Sean Ichiro Manes. Used with permission. **p. 198:** Photograph by Sean Ichiro Manes. Used with permission. **p. 201:** © Digital Vision. **p. 204:** Photograph by Sean Ichiro Manes. Used with permission.

Chapter 11
p. 217: © Bubbles Photolibrary/Alamy. **p. 222:** Photograph by Sean Ichiro Manes. Used with permission.

Chapter 14
p. 269: Used by permission of M. Subotnick. **p. 270:** Used by permission of PG Music Inc. **p. 271:** Used by permission of Ars Nova Software, LLC.

Chapter 15
p. 281: Photos by Steven M. Demorest. **p. 291:** Jerry Gay. **p. 292** (both images): Jerry Gay.

Chapter 16
p. 309 (from top): Jerry Gay; Photo by Steven M. Demorest.

Index

Note: An *f* following a page number denotes a figure.